Advance Praise

Authentic native of the Bible Belt, fully conversant with mainstream biblical scholarship, and experienced archaeologist, John Laughlin offers a new translation and refreshing no-nonsense commentary on one of the most troubling books of the Bible. He pulls no punches. For starters, he conveys and confirms the thinking of both mainstream biblical scholars and Palestinian archaeologists that the Joshua story of how the Israelites conquered Canaan and purged the land of its native population never really happened. And the really troubling thing for him is that the writers of Joshua "have their god not only approving such actions but also ordering them in the first place."

—*J. Maxwell Miller*
Professor Emeritus, Emory University

Laughlin has produced an unflinching critical commentary on the book of Joshua, basing his analysis on extensive research into the latest and best archaeological evidence. By adding a touch of "moderate" postmodernism, he provides an analysis that places this book into its own historical and ideological context—without preconceived religious notions of what Joshua is "supposed to say." Laughlin gives us not only a critical commentary on the text, but also a critical commentary on the ideology that created the text.

—*Jeffrey A. Fager*
Professor of Religion and Philosophy (ret.)

In a book dedicated to the memory of Joseph A. Callaway, John Laughlin has distilled his long-term fascination with Joshua into a study that follows a decidedly unconventional approach. In *Reading Joshua*, Laughlin blends conclusions reached during a long teaching career with his extensive archaeological fieldwork. The result is an eclectic approach guaranteed to motivate readers to dig into many of the author's interpretations and figure out where they stand on critical issues. From readers who still speak Albright's name with reverence to the biblical minimalists, nobody will agree with everything here, since John has interacted with the biblical text and secondary literature in a creative, provocative, and (occasionally) infuriating manner.

—*Gerald L. Mattingly*
Johnson University

For a variety of reasons, one of which is its violence, the book of Joshua has been quietly "swept under the rug" by the church and is virtually ignored in contemporary Christian preaching. The ecumenical lectionary used in many denominations only includes three passages from Joshua, all of them safe and inoffensive. John Laughlin's *Reading Joshua* breaks the silence and unflinchingly asks the questions that many commentators and preachers may shy away from, but which many, both in and out of the church, are asking. While some readers may disagree, even strongly, with some of his conclusions, *Reading Joshua* will excite every reader to both *read* and *engage* with this controversial biblical book, both of which would be worthy accomplishments indeed.

—*Ralph K. Hawkins*
Chair of the Department of Religious Studies
Averett University
Author of The Iron Age I Structure on Mt. Ebal: Excavation *and* Interpretation and How Israel Became a People

READING JOSHUA

Smyth & Helwys Publishing, Inc.
6316 Peake Road
Macon, Georgia 31210-3960
1-800-747-3016

Library of Congress Cataloging-in-Publication Data

Laughlin, John C. H., 1942-
Reading Joshua : a historical-critical/archaeological commentary / by John C. H. Laughlin.
pages cm
ISBN 978-1-57312-836-0 (pbk. : alk. paper)
1. Bible. Joshua--Commentaries. I. Title.
BS1295.53.L38 2015
222'.207--dc23

2015028100

Reading Joshua

A Historical-Critical/Archaeological Commentary

John C. H. Laughlin

Also by John C. H. Laughlin

Archaeology and the Bible

Fifty Major Cities in the Bible

In memory of Joseph A. Callaway
1920–1988

Contents

Editor's Foreword

The *Reading the Old Testament series* shares many of the aims and objectives of its counterpart, *Reading the New Testament.* Contributors to the current series, like those to its predecessor, write with the intention of presenting "cutting-edge research in [a form] accessible" to a wide audience ranging from specialists in the field to educated laypeople. The approach taken here, as there, focuses not on the minutiae of word-by-word, verse-by-verse exegesis but on larger literary and thought units, especially as they function in the overall conception of the book under analysis. From the standpoint of method, volumes in this series will employ an eclectic variety of reading strategies and critical approaches as contributors deem appropriate for explicating the force of the text before them. Nonetheless, as in RNT, "the focus [will be] on a close reading of the final form of the text." The overarching goal is to provide readers of the commentary series with an aid to help them become more competent, more engaged, and more enthusiastic readers of the Bible as authoritative Scripture.

The title of the series prompts several comments. For the editor, at least, the term "Old Testament" is a convenient convention, since any alternative seems either awkward or provocative. The Hebrew Bible is the shared heritage of Judaism and Christianity, the body of believers whom Paul once described as branches from a wild olive tree who have been "grafted contrary to nature into a cultivated olive tree" (Rom 11:24). Since the beginnings of Christianity, questions concerning how and in what sense the Hebrew Bible/Old Testament functions as Christian Scripture have perpetually confronted the church. Nonetheless, throughout its history, in the spirit of Paul, the church has insisted that the God of Abraham, Isaac, and Jacob is the God of the New Testament. Rather than impose a detailed doctrine of the unity of the two Testaments or specify a particular hermeneutical approach, the editor and the publisher have chosen to invite contributions to the series from scholars selected because of their learning and insight, again in the spirit of Paul, we hope, without regard to faith tradition or denominational identity.

The books of the Hebrew Bible were the fountainhead for the faith of both Paul and Aqiba. May it be that, through the scholarship presented in the pages of this series, the books of the "Old Testament" water the faith of another generation.

—Mark E. Biddle, General Editor
Richmond, Virginia

Author's Preface

I doubt if anyone knows how many trees have lost their lives to produce the paper on which are written all the words now contained in publications, short and long, on the biblical book of Joshua. So why write another one? One reason is that critical scholarship does not stand still in any discipline. Each generation of critical students of the Bible needs to reexamine what previous generations concluded and decide for itself what is worth keeping, what is not, and what, if anything, needs to be added to the ongoing conversation. Beginning over thirty years ago, major paradigm shifts have occurred in the scholarly understanding of the book of Joshua. The main models developed throughout the twentieth century (see below for specifics) attempting to explain and understand the so-called "conquest of Canaan" as described in the Bible have been found wanting and often either radically revised or totally rejected by the majority of mainstream biblical historians and archaeologists. This is especially true of the "military" model found in Joshua itself. The situation today was adequately summarized in a 1992 article by Neil Asher Silberman:

> . . . a new generation of archaeologists working in Israel has come to challenge the scriptural account in a manner that might seem heretical to some. Their survey, excavation, and analysis of finds from hundreds of Early Iron Age settlements in the rugged hill country of the West Bank and Galilee have led them to conclude that the ancient Israelite confederacy did not rise in a divinely directed military conquest from the desert but through a remarkable socio-economic change in the lives of a few thousand herders, farmers, and villages in Canaan itself. (22)

It is probably a safe bet that most people in the United States, including those who claim to be practicing Christians and Jews, have never heard of this new theorizing concerning the book of Joshua and, by necessary extension, other parts of the Bible as well—in particular the story of the Exodus. So much has been published on the questions of the origin of "Israel" and its relationship, if any, to the biblical version of the story that it can be overwhelming to anyone who is beginning to become aware of the problems. The following publications are highly recommended as essential background reading and will be referenced throughout this study: Faust, 2007; Finkelstein 1988a, 1991, 1995, 1999; Finkelstein and Na'aman; Mazar, 2003; Finkelstein and Mazar; Dever 1990, 1992, 2001a, b; 2003a, b; 2005, 2012; Levy, 1995, 2010. There are many other studies, of course, but those listed here are good places to start. All of these publications deal with the major controversies and suggested solutions now surrounding the study of the so-called "conquest" as presented in the book of Joshua.

One of the truly sobering facts about writing a book such as this one is the knowledge that no matter how up to date I may think my own understanding and conclusions are, in a relatively short period this effort will also be passé. All one has to do to justify this pessimism is to go back a few years and see what passed for a "scholarly consensus." One will discover that the "assured results" of scholarly research and writing often turn out not to have been so "assured" after all and represent, at best, only current consensus among specialists (which, simply stated, is what a majority of scholars seem to agree on at any one time, but always subject to revision if not outright rejection!). Thus, most if not all conclusions of a study like this are tentative, and anyone attempting to engage in such an undertaking, writer and reader alike, needs to be comfortable with uncertainty, ambiguity, and incompleteness. This is not to deny that progress in the understanding and interpretation of the Bible, in this case the book of Joshua, has been made. It has, and the clock cannot be turned back no matter how badly a few dissenting voices may wish (see below on the discussion of biblical literalists and decoders). Anyone engaging in a critical study of the Jewish Scriptures should take seriously J. J. Collins's recent observation: "Scholarship is an ongoing process; its results are always provisional and never final. . . . Today's results may be overturned by tomorrow's excavation" (2005, 6). Why bother, then, to invest an enormous amount of time in research and writing when the results may be dated by the time the results are published?

To quote the historical Jesus scholar, John Dominic Crossan,

> Historical reconstruction is always interactive of present and past. Even our *best* theories and methods are still *our* best ones. They are all dated and doomed not just when they are wrong but even (and especially) when they are right. They need, when anything important is involved, to be done over

> and over again. That does not make history worthless. We ourselves are dated and doomed, but that does not make life worthless. It just makes death inevitable. (Crossan 1998, 43, emphasis original)

An even more pessimistic appraisal of the human endeavor of writing books comes from an editorial note added to the ending of the most skeptical book found in the Bible: "Of making many books there is no end, and much study is a weariness of the flesh" (Eccl 12:12).

Nevertheless, despite being "dated and doomed" and causing much "weariness of the flesh," the writing of books is a unique human activity. Twentieth-century philosopher/mathematician Jacob Bronowski (1906–1984), reacting to the analogies made between animals and humans by behavioral psychologists such as B. F. Skinner, voiced this witticism: "[such papers] tell us something about man. But they cannot tell us everything. There must be something unique about man because otherwise, evidently . . . rats would be writing papers about B. F. Skinner" (412). And, I suppose, rats would also be writing books about Joshua!

Even so, writing a commentary on any biblical book is a challenging if not frightening task. It is challenging and frightening because there is already a wide assortment of published commentaries on the book of Joshua, representing a wide range of approaches and interpretations. The publications referenced in this brief volume could easily be expanded many fold. Even translations of biblical texts are often little more than the interpretations of the translator. Compare Isaiah 7:14 in the King James Version with the same passage in the New Revised Standard Version. Readers of the Bible who are not trained to check original sources are at the mercy of the translator unless, of course, they have a critically written commentary to go along with their biblical text. With so many commentaries already available on the book of Joshua why, indeed, write another one? Is there anything new to say that has not already been said, and in many cases, said well (e.g., Soggin 1972; Miller and Tucker; Coogan 1990b; Coote 2005; Nelson 1997; Hartmut)? For a brief history of interpretations of Joshua up through the mid-1990s, see Auld 1998, 129–49, and 1999.

The task of writing a commentary is also daunting for any number of reasons. In this "postmodern" world where millions (billions?) of people appear to get most, if not all, their information from the Internet, Facebook, Twitter, etc., who actually buys and reads biblical commentaries? Is there such a thing as the "general public" who will invest not only the money but also, more important, the time to read a biblical commentary? Perhaps an even more important question is, how many people in today's world actually read the whole Bible closely? When was the last time you read any part of the book of Joshua? Studies have shown that even self-described evangelical Christians who make exceptional claims about the Bible (e.g., "it is the literal word of God"; "it is infallible"; and so forth) rarely read it; and when they do, they mostly "cherry pick" (Altemeyer, 136–39). What are "readers" supposed to take away from such an encounter that is relevant to their own lives in the twenty-first-century world in which they live? Furthermore, is not one person's interpretation of the Bible as good as another's? In America it seems that anybody who wishes to do so can claim to be an "expert" on the Bible, especially politicians! It will be seen in what follows that even genuine "experts" often come away from reading the same biblical texts with very different interpretations. This is especially true when these experts engage in different methodologies while doing their research and writing. (The 1993 publication edited by Hayes and McKenzie lists thirteen different methods of biblical criticism. See also the work edited by Exum and Clines, 11–25.)

In an essay published in 2003, F. N. Gorman, Jr., identified two operating assumptions, rarely made explicit, underlying the writing of most commentaries: "First, the biblical text needs clarification, explanation and interpretation by a professional who is technically trained and professionally competent, as well as institutionally recognized. Second, the reader reads [Joshua], and presumably the commentary, for concrete reasons and with specified interests" (100). From his own study, Gorman concluded that the goal of commentary writing is

> to provide information, analysis and discussion that illuminates and "opens up" biblical texts. Does the genre have a future? . . . For whom is the commentary written? Why would someone want to write one? Why would someone want to read one? Who would want to read one? What is a commentary to do? What is it that we are trying to understand when we read a biblical text and why do we want to understand that? What is the relationship of our discussions of the past and our discussions of the present? What is the future of the genre? (118, 119)

Each of these critically informed questions is important for both the writer and the imagined reader of commentaries. In the case of the book of Joshua, why would anyone in today's world want to read and study a book that seems to portray the God of ancient Israel as a xenophobic and genocidal mass killer (see Josh 10:40; 11:16-20)? Moreover, while I am well aware of the role the Bible has played in American social, economic, and political as well as religious life, and still does for millions of people, in no case will it be assumed in this work that Joshua is the "word" of the god, Yahweh, the local tribal deity of the people who would eventually become "Israel." I have no way of knowing whether there is a transcendent reality that deserves to be called a "god" who is worthy of being worshiped, and neither does anyone else, despite dogmatic claims to the contrary. The number of people who actually believe there is such a reality does not constitute evidence. (Over a billion Hindus believe in the monkey god, Hanuman. Does that mean that Hanuman is a real god in the same sense that Christians believe their god is "real"?) My purpose in what follows is to try to make some sense out of the complexity that characterizes the book of Joshua, not convince a reader there really is a "god," an English word that now carries a lot of baggage. Whether or not one accepts the theological/ideological purpose(s) of the final author(s)/editor(s) of Joshua, commonly known as the Deuteronomic Historian (Dtr) (see below), is up to the individual reader.

Moreover, who, besides other critically informed scholars, really cares one way or the other? Are there those in the "general public" who still value knowledge for its own sake? At what point, if ever, can the worldview assumed by the writer(s) of Joshua intersect with the worldview held by twenty-first-century inhabitants? A contemporary critically informed worldview must deal with the real possibility of nuclear annihilation, global warming, and the concomitant destruction of rain forests and other natural habitats, as well as the exponential explosion of our own species, *Homo sapiens.* And perhaps most disturbing of all, there is the fact that the more we humans understand about the universe, its age and inconceivable vastness, and the incalculable amount of suffering to every form of life on this small plant since life first arose some three and a half billion years ago, the more pointless it all seems. (If you have never done so, I invite you to get on YouTube, type in the name "Carl Sagan," and listen to a three-minute clip titled "a pale blue dot.") Does a book written some twenty-five centuries ago still have anything valuable to say to the modern world? Ultimately, the readers of Joshua will have to answer this question for themselves.

If I were honest, and I hope to be, I have always accepted requests to write articles/books/book reviews and so forth not because I think many people will read them but because it forces me to do research/writing I would otherwise never have undertaken. I have learned a lot about the book of Joshua during the preparation of this volume, and I am sure there is still much more to learn. If one person reads this small commentary and comes away with new perspectives and questions on this biblical book, I will be gratified.

As is always the case, without the support of my wife, Janet, who tolerates the messiest reading/writing habits imaginable, I would not, and could not, have finished this manuscript (at least not during the past six-plus years since I first signed the contract). Finally, to my many students who, over nearly a forty-year teaching career, forced me to rethink over and over again what I thought I already knew about the Hebrew Bible, including the book of Joshua, I would like to express publically my deepest gratitude.

John Laughlin
Danville, Virginia
February 2014

Abbreviations: Journals and Series

BI: Biblical Illustrator
DBI: Dictionary of Biblical Interpretation
JE: The Jewish Encyclopedia (This encyclopedia can now be accessed for free on the Internet.)
MDB: Mercer Dictionary of the Bible
NEA: Near Eastern Archaeology
NEAEHL: The New Encyclopedia of Archaeological Excavations in the Holy Land
NIDB: The New Interpreter's Dictionary of the Bible
Rev & Exp: Review & Expositor
SJOT: Scandinavian Journal of the Old Testament

Preparing for a Critical Journey through the Book of Joshua

Introduction

"The initial mystery that attends any journey is how did the traveler reach his starting point in the first place." (Bogan, 2)

Before looking directly at the book of Joshua, assumptions governing this study need to be clearly stated. All thinking rests on assumptions held by the thinker, whether consciously or unconsciously and whether openly expressed or not. A simple example comes from comments on the book of Joshua by the late G. Ernest Wright (d. 1974). In an unpublished manuscript he wrote the following: "the gap between a popular understanding of the book of Joshua and a biblical understanding is so wide that one may well wonder whether it can ever be eliminated or even narrowed" (Wright, n.d., 1). The phrase "biblical understanding" in this quote is vague, ambiguous, and raises other questions. However, if one changes it to read "critical understanding," Wright's observation seems valid. For, indeed, there is no evidence of which I am aware to suggest that the gap between a popular, versus a critical, understanding of the book of Joshua has narrowed over the intervening years. In fact, if anything, the gap seems to have widened. However, while Wright was right (no pun intended) in his observation about the "gap," he was wrong in his suggested solution, which was to embrace a restrictive theology that interprets the exodus-conquest cycle as "God's gracious gift to those who had been outcast" (10). It never seems to have occurred to Wright that among these "outcasts" would soon be the Canaanites who, according to the "biblical understanding," were slaughtered or enslaved by the "Israelites" because their own God, Yahweh, commanded it! Moreover, his sermonizing, "There is in the world a mysterious creative power that is expressed on the human scene in both positive and negative, redemptive and judgmental ways" (11; how did he know all of this?), is hardly compelling, especially if you are a Canaanite or some other "ite" (Deut 7:1 lists six other "ites":

Hittites, Girgashites, Amorites, Perizzites, Hivites, Jebusites, all supposedly killed off by the other "ites," the Israelites).

Nevertheless, the "gap" of which Wright spoke is there for a number of reasons. One is surely the scientific revolution that began with the discoveries and publications of Copernicus (d. 1543) and Galileo (d. 1642). This revolution has had more impact on biblical studies than any other in history. We now know that the universe is billions of years old (13.7 as of 2003 astronomical calculations), is populated by hundreds of billions of galaxies, and that we humans are a product of random mutations and natural selection called evolution. For people who believed, and still do, that the Bible is the inerrant word of Yahweh, this scientific model or paradigm that now reigns supreme in the free world is a major challenge to their faith. But unless one wishes to come to the Bible with blinders on, what contemporary scientists now know about our universe, particularly planet Earth, must be taken seriously.

A second major reason for this gap is that despite a legacy of critically informed biblical studies that stretches back into the seventeenth through nineteenth centuries (Jean Astruc, French, 1684–1766; Johann Gottfried Eichhorn, German, 1752–1827; W. M. Lebrecht de Wette, German, 1780–1849; and especially Julius Welhausen, German, 1844–1918), much of what is now known about the Bible has remained in the academy. Most of the critically informed studies of the Bible, including Joshua, have been written by scholars for scholars. This is not necessarily bad, but it explains in part the widespread ignorance of the Bible by the majority of laypeople. This is particularly true in America, where there is no established public venue for the dissemination of the results of scholarly work done by both biblical historians and archaeologists working in the Levant (which includes modern-day Syria, Lebanon, Jordan, Israel, and the Palestinian territories). In fact, there seems to be a suspicion on the part of the American public regarding critically informed biblical scholarship in all its forms. Non-academic publications such as *Biblical Archaeology Review* attract far more subscribers than academic ones such as the *Bulletin of the American Schools of Oriental Research* and its sister publication, *Near Eastern Archaeology* (which tellingly was called *The Biblical Archaeologist* until its name was changed in December 1997).

Thomas E. Levy, a Chalcolithic specialist, suggested recently that "Levantine archaeologists may have lost the ability to communicate outside the academy" (2010, 10). The same observation could also apply to critical biblical scholars. Archaeological discoveries that may have relevancy on how one interprets certain biblical stories (such as the "conquest" story in Joshua) seem rarely, if ever, presented in a medium that reaches a wide public audience. One rare exception may be a 2008 NOVA presentation on PBS titled *The Bible's Buried Secrets: Beyond Fact or Fiction.* Despite the somewhat wordy title, some of the "talking heads" in this program are among the most recognized experts, both biblical and archaeological, in the field (only the beginning of the program deals with issues with which this commentary is primarily concerned). While a relatively large audience may have viewed this program, one such program does not a paradigm shift make. One is reminded of an observation made by the late Moshe Weinfeld (d. 2009): "The Bible is an exotic book about which modern people understand very little."

The problem can be approached from another direction. In two relatively recent polls, the Pew Forum (2007) and the Gallup Poll (2009), some 60 percent of adult Americans do not accept evolution as a proven scientific theory, and a third of the population believes that "the Bible" (the polls did not reveal which particular version was meant) is the "literal word of God." More specifically, among evangelical Christians, the largest Protestant group in America, 59 percent believe the Bible is the "word of God, literally true word for word." It is as if the "Age of Enlightenment" (a.k.a., "The Age of Reason") that occurred during the seventeenth and eighteenth centuries never happened. The oldest scientific society in the English-speaking world, The Royal Society of Great Britain, was founded in 1660. Its motto is "*nullius in verba,*" "nothing in words." That is, "take nobody's word for it." We are warned not to accept claims to truth without being able to verify such claims by appeal to facts determined by experiment. One is reminded of a witticism by the late Christopher Hitchens (d. 2011): "What can be asserted without evidence can also be dismissed without evidence" (150). When the discussion turns to all things biblical, such unsubstantiated claims abound. (For an informed and frightening analysis of how and why many right-wing evangelical Christians will believe almost anything they are told that affirms their religious/political ideologies whether true or not, see Altemeyer.)

It is difficult for most of us to listen carefully to those who raise relevant, critically informed questions about the beliefs we hold sincerely, especially when those beliefs are religiously held (see below on "comfortable theories"). The late Carl Sagan (d. 1996) said it much more gracefully than I can in his book, *Varieties of Scientific Experience*:

> Many religions lay out a set of precepts—things people have to do—and claims that these instructions were given by a god or gods. For example,

> the first code of law by Hammurabi of Babylon, in the second millennium B.C., was handed to him by the god, Marduk, or at least so he said. Since there are very few Mardukians today, perhaps no one will be offended if I suggest that this as a bamboozle, that it's a pious hoax. That if Hammurabi had merely said "Here's what I think everybody ought to do," he would have been much less successful, although he was king of Babylon.
>
> I recognize that the next step, saying that other law givers who are better known today are in the same situation, might produce some degree of outrage at the impiety, but I ask you to nevertheless think it through. (2006, 186; The relevant Babylonian texts can be found in the *ANET*, 164, 165. I will leave it up to the reader to think of "law givers who are better known today" who made similar claims as Hammurabi.)

Where the book of Joshua is concerned, I too would ask readers "to think it through." All religious people believe their religion is the true one; otherwise they would profess the one they do think is true. This is an obvious truism, but its implications are sometimes overlooked. One major implication is how the followers of one religion think about the beliefs of followers of a different religion. This was expressed on a bumper sticker I once saw that read, "Everybody else's GOD is IMAGINARY but not YOURS." Thus it is not my purpose to persuade any interested readers of this commentary to look at the issues and questions involved from any particular religious point of view, but from a historical-critical, archeological point of view. On the other hand, neither is it my desire to alienate readers who have cherished religious beliefs that differ greatly from mine. None of us particularly enjoy having our most strongly held beliefs challenged by those who ask critically informed questions and expose us to information we did not know. Such questions and new knowledge can make us feel more threatened than enlightened, especially when they seem to undermine our starting assumption we have taken for granted. Thus my hope is that anyone who seriously reads this volume will come to appreciate more fully both the many critical issues raised in studying Joshua and the value of the use of critical tools for this study that scholars have long used in our own academic pilgrimage. Above all, I hope no readers will be afraid to change their minds when the evidence warrants it. None of us come to this task fully equipped. Changing one's mind is one of the greatest pleasures of intellectual pursuits. If I am wrong, I want to find out as quickly as possible. I want to get it as right as I can for the few short decades I have to live. I wish the same for everyone else.

Any critical study of Joshua must deal with two major questions regarding the book: (1) What are the relevant sources for understanding this book, and (2) how are those sources to be critically assessed? The sources, of course, are written materials both biblical and extra-biblical, along with a wide assortment of archaeological discoveries. Without the constant use of critical thinking, brainwashing and indoctrination are the inevitable results. It has recently been suggested that in America there has been "an erosion of interest in the Bible and its centrality in the history, philosophy, law, and other dimensions of western culture to the point that it is not taught in the majority of K-12 public schools in the United States today" (Levy 2010, 10). Assuming the accuracy of Levy's observation, one might think that the solution to such biblical ignorance is simple: teach the Bible from a non-sectarian, critical perspective in our public schools. Unfortunately this is easier said than done. For example, the state of Texas has mandated the teaching of the Bible in its public schools. But apparently what is being taught to these young, impressionable minds is anything but a critical, non-sectarian viewpoint. It has recently been reported that in some Texas public high schools, students are being taught that all races literally came from Noah's sons (there is, of course, only one human race alive on planet Earth today, *Homo sapiens*) and that the earth is a mere six thousand years old (reported by the *Texas Freedom Network*, 17 January 2013).

To put the matter bluntly, Americans are among the most scientifically ignorant people among the world's democracies, second only to Turkey. Turkey's claim to last place is due to a large influx of Muslims in recent years whose belief that every word in the Koran, given to Mohammed by the angel Gabriel, is inerrant and as rigid, if not more so, than that among the most conservative Christians towards the Bible. It never seems to occur to members of either group that they might be wrong. Furthermore, Muslims seem even more stridently opposed, if that is possible, to the scientific theory of evolution. Ironically, the day (20 January 2013) I was working on this part of the manuscript, it was reported in the *Turkish Hurriyet Daily News* that the Turkish government has suspended the publication and sale of any book that promotes the theory of evolution! Ignorance and anti-intellectualism know no geographic, linguistic, religious, or any other cultural boundaries. The only solution to such blatant ignorance is knowledge gained through the development and trust in one's own critical reasoning abilities and in abandoning such rigid and unsupported religious dogmas. It is to be hoped that what follows in this commentary will be justified by critical reasoning and not faith claims. To quote the great twentieth-century theologian, Archie Bunker, "Faith is something that you believe that nobody in his right mind would believe" (*YouTube,* "Archie Bunker on faith"). This commentary is written with the optimism that it will narrow the gap between the academy and the public, at least a little, for the biblical book of Joshua.

But first a word of caution: while critical scholars of the Bible (and I suppose scholars in other disciplines as well) like to think that we can be objective and even-handed in our critiques of the Bible, we probably all suffer from what the late Samuel Sandmel (1911–1979) called the "comfortable theory" syndrome. That is, we like to believe that we can do unbiased, objective studies and be willing to change our minds when the evidence warrants it. And, of course, we should always strive to do this. It is one of the cardinal principles underlying all critical thinking. Nevertheless, Sandmel warned us,

> A comfortable theory is one that satisfies the needs of the interpreter, whether theological or personal, when the evidence can seem to point in one of two opposite directions. All of us gravitate to comfortable theories. . . . A comfortable theory need not be an acquiescence in some traditional views; modernists and iconoclasts alike have their comfortable theories; untraditionalism breeds just as many comfortable theories as does traditionalism. (139; compare Dever 2003a, 41; another expression for this tendency is "confirmation bias," that is, we like to read and hear things that "confirm" the biases we already hold.)

To recognize and critically appraise one's own "comfortable theory" can in itself be uncomfortable because it forces us to consider seriously the possibility that we are the ones who need to change our minds. It should at least force us to give up a notoriously rigid dogmatic approach to the issues reflected in the all too familiar colloquialism, "My mind is made up. Don't confuse me with a bunch of facts I know nothing about." Perhaps a good way to start is to learn to ask certain critical questions concerning the nature of the subject one is studying, which in this case is Joshua. G. W. Ahlström (d. 1992), in his book, *The History of Ancient Palestine,* suggested four points that should underlie attempts to reconstruct the past. Here these points will be paraphrased as questions: (1) To what extent can we recover what actually happened? (2) How were these presumed events understood by the writers whose literary products we now possess? (3) What did the writers hope to gain by their writings? What were their aims? (4) What audience were the authors writing for? (Ahlström, 19) These questions reflect the concerns of what is usually referred to as the traditional historical-critical methodology, a method that has come under extreme critical review during the last thirty years or so but still has managed (in my opinion) to stand the test of time (Exum and Clines; Carter and Levy, 205–40).

While it may be correct to argue that there is no such thing as a single "true reality" of the past, without some corrective methodology in hand to begin with there is no control over any of the discussion. Postmodernists may, and have, raised serious questions concerning the issue of how one's own biases affect the interpretations and meaning(s) given to texts (see below). They have also argued that no claim to truth is absolute (unless, of course, this last observation is "true," in which case there is at least one absolute claim to truth! Carter and Levy, 214–17). Moreover, to abandon the question of the historicity of biblical stories as many postmodernist and anthropologists have suggested seems counter-productive. On the other hand, accepting uncritically the historicity of the Bible is not just an academic issue. It stands behind much abusive use of the Bible in both ancient and modern times. The "cultural wars" now occurring in the United States over such issues as gay rights, "intelligent design," abortion, and homosexual marriages are waged by many based exclusively on the assumption that the Bible is a source of divinely revealed truths. Consequently, I see no reason to give up the historical-critical method that provides a basic approach to biblical studies while employing newer methodological approaches where they might be useful (see below). Concerning the historical-critical method itself, Ronald Hendel recently concluded,

> To put it simply, the critique of knowledge about texts and history is itself a part of the historical-critical method. The "critical" aspect of the method goes all the way down, including the conditions and limitations of the method itself and the ways it is practiced in the lived world. The task of critique never ends, and is not immune to itself. In my view this is a good thing, and not at all a sign of the death-knell of critical inquiry. (252; Miller, 1999; see also below and Collins 2005; Miller 1999)

False dilemmas (either/or fallacies) are neither necessary nor appropriate to such studies. As will be argued below, while historical-critical analysis of biblical texts is not the only way to study an ancient text, and indeed may not be the best way, to this author it still seems a necessary method if disciplined control over what is concluded is desired. Final conclusive answers to these critical questions may always remain tentative. None of us can go back into the past and observe for ourselves what actually went on. Uncertainty and ambiguity must always be our traveling companions. They should make us commit ourselves to intellectual honesty and realize that whatever conclusions we reach must be tentatively held. How most people lived, believed, and behaved in the past is lost forever except for what can be learned about them primarily through archaeological discoveries (Dever 2012) and the biased epigraphic remains at our disposal. This is so because most people living in the past were illiterate and wrote nothing. Furthermore, how many of these illiterate people ever heard of the stories collected in the Bible (they could not have read them), much less what they would have thought about them if they had heard them, is anybody's guess. Only a small minority of elite scribes wrote what is often referred to so glibly as "the Bible." To quote one well-known authority in the field, "The urban elites who wrote and edited the Hebrew Bible *cannot possibly* have constituted more than a tiny fraction of one percent, isolated from and largely alienated from the vast majority. How '*representative*' were they when they spoke of religion?" (Dever 2005, 276, emphasis original; compare Collins 2005, 39–43)

The Bible was written for a small minority of people who were alive at the time of its composition. It certainly was not written with us in mind! Moreover, none of us started our "journey" uncommitted; we all have our "comfortable theories." Perhaps admitting that and being consciously aware of them can at least give us a chance to engage in critical and rational discussion. However, while admitting that all scholars work with personal agendas ("comfortable theories"), this does not force the conclusion that all agendas are equally valid. In his critique of the influence of postmodernism on biblical studies, J. J. Collins argued that despite the fact that "assured results" are simply what most scholars agree upon at any given time, "Scholarship is a conversation, in which the participants try to persuade each other by appeal to evidence and criteria that are in principle acceptable to other participants. This model of conversation has served the academy well and is not something that should be lightly abandoned" (2005, 11). Furthermore, in reaction to postmodernism's absurd claim that we cannot know anything objectively about the past, Collins asserted that traditional historical criticism "Sets limits to the conversation, by saying what a given text could or could not mean in the ancient context. A text may have more than one possible meaning, but it *cannot mean just anything at all*" (2005, 10, my emphasis). Unfortunately, not all approaches to the study of the book of Joshua (as well as the other biblical books) follow Collins's insight. In this "conversation," all points of view should be welcome; and no point of view is exempt from severe critical appraisal.

Two Very Wrong Approaches to Understanding Joshua

It is simply impossible here to give even a cursory review of the history of interpretations of Joshua (for one such attempt, see Auld 1998; see also the discussion in Rowlett). While recognizing the ever-present danger of over-simplifying complex issues, among evangelical Christians at least, there appear to be two popular approaches to the Bible in general and Joshua in particular. For lack of better terms, I will call them "literalists" and "decoders."

The Literalists

It is probably safe to conclude that the most commonly held assumption regarding the Bible, including Joshua, at least in America, is that it contains historically and scientifically true accounts of things as they "actually happened" in Israel's history (see survey results above). That is, the Bible contains the history of ancient Israel in the same way a modern, trained historian would write a history of the American Civil War, the French Revolution, and so forth. People who start with this assumption are usually called "biblical literalists" and/or "fundamentalists." Relevant to this study, the literalists claim that the book of Joshua describes an actual historical event that occurred around 1400 BCE. This date is derived from a passage in 1 Kings 6:1, which reports that Solomon began to build the temple 480 years after the exodus out of Egypt (the number "480," by the way, is a multiple of 12, the traditional number of Israelite tribes, times "40," a very stereotyped number in the Hebrew Bible: Gen 7:4; 25:20; 26:34; 50:3; Exod 16:36; 24:18; 34:28; Num 23:25; 14:34; Deut 9:18; Josh 14:7; Judg 3:11, and 105 more times). A commonly assumed date for the beginning of Solomon's building project is 960 BCE. This figure plus 480 is 1440 BCE. Subtract the "40" years of wilderness wandering and you arrive at 1400 BCE as the beginning of the conquest. This is not the date mainline biblical historians and archaeologists accept, assuming there was any kind of an "exodus" of biblical proportions at all, which many scholars, including this one, deny (see below for details). In any case, we are told that hordes of "Israelites" swarmed across the River Jordan and in a space of five years or so (Josh 14:6-10, see below; compare Deut 2:14) slaughtered all the inhabitants of the land of Canaan. In order to defend this literal interpretation of the story, claims are made that should offend the ethical sensibilities of most modern people. For example, William Lang Craig, a well-known and articulate Christian apologist, has argued the following on his website, "Reasonable Faith":

> God had morally sufficient reasons for his judgment upon Canaan and Israel was merely the instrument of His justice. . . . But why take the lives of innocent children? The terrible totality of the destruction was undoubtedly related to the prohibition of assimilation to pagan nations on Israel's part. In commanding complete destruction of the Canaanites, the Lord says, "You shall not intermarry with them, giving your daughters to their sons, or taking their daughters for your sons, for they would turn away your sons from following me, to serve other gods" (Deut 20:18). This command is part and parcel of the whole fabric of complex Jewish ritual law distinguishing clean and unclean practices.

Craig does not stop with this very naïve, if not self-righteous, and simplistic use of what has been called "The Divine Command Theory," which raises the question, "Is an action morally good because a god commands it, or does a god command it because it is morally good?" Plato addressed this moral dilemma more than twenty-four centuries ago in his dialogue, *The Euthyphro*, and through the voice of Socrates demolished it. This philosophical argument can get a little complex, but the gist of it goes like this: if everything a god commands is moral, and thus he cannot command what is immoral, then we humans, in order to recognize whether or not a god's command is moral or immoral, would already have to know *in advance* what is moral and immoral. This conclusion clearly implies that morality must then be independent of any god's commands, thus the DCT is false. Craig, however, embraced the first option and used DCT to justify the slaughter of Canaanite children. In so doing he resorted to a disturbing, dark, and depraved rationalization:

> Moreover, *if we believe, as I do*, that God's grace extended to those who die in infancy or as small children, the death of these children was actually their salvation. We are so wedded to an earthly, naturalistic perspective that

> we forget that those who die are happy to quit this earth for heaven's incomparable joy. Therefore, *God does these children no wrong in taking their lives.* (my emphasis)

This justification for the slaughter of children based simply on Craig's naïve usage of a story embedded in an ancient "sacred text" may say a lot about Craig's personal theological beliefs, but it says little about any critical understanding of the book of Joshua. Craig's banality and superficiality are not finished yet, however; according to him, the real people who were traumatized by the slaughter were the *Israeli* (sic) *soldiers* (my emphasis):

> So whom does God wrong in commanding the destruction of the Canaanites? Not the Canaanite adults, for they were corrupt and deserving of judgment. Not the children, for they inherit eternal life. So who is wronged? Ironically, I think the most difficult part of this whole debate is the apparent wrong done to the Israeli [sic] soldiers. Can you imagine what it would be like to have to break into some house and kill a terrified woman and her children? The brutalizing effect on these Israeli [sic] soldiers is disturbing.

Well, no, I cannot imagine what it would be like to kill a mother, terrified or not, and her children. Craig's analysis of this story is morally reprehensible as well as inexcusable, and rests solely on the unproven theological assumptions with which he began. Before one can argue whether or not a god's command is moral, one would have to prove that there is a god who commands anything. Craig assumes his god's existence and, despite his theological sophistication, comes across as little more than a biblical literalist who defends a killer god: a celestial despot. It is such theological nonsense as Craig's that led the late Christopher Hitchens to conclude, "religion poisons everything" (13). It is as if the purpose of Craig's god is to make the lives of non-Israelites as miserable as he possibly could. Craig's religious beliefs, or theological posturing, may supply answers to questions about the book of Joshua, but they are bad answers (see L. Krauss 2011 for a critique of Craig).

Moreover, to appeal to biblical authority to justify genocide is not only dangerous (see below) but also unethical (Collins 2004, 193–95; 2005, 69). For modern examples, one only has to think of right-wing Christian attitudes towards gay marriage and of global warming deniers, all based, for the most part, on their appeal to biblical authority. How far are biblical literalists willing to go? Leviticus 20:13 clearly condemns to death men having sex with one another. Yahweh gives this command verbatim to Moses (Lev 20:1;

compare 1:1; 5:14; 6:1 and many more). Why does someone with Craig's method of biblical interpretation not call for the execution of homosexuals since it is his god's will and thus morally right (for other irrational and inconsistent beliefs of this group, see especially Altemeyer 2006)? Hopefully, there are far more satisfying ways of dealing with the moral, ethical, and other issues raised by a literal reading of Joshua.

Anyone attempting to read and interpret the book of Joshua should take seriously the advice given by David Clines in an essay titled "The Postmodern Adventure": "At the very least, the critic in the postmodern age will need to be asking, What does this text do to me if I read it? What ethical *responsibility* do I carry if I go on helping this text to stay alive" (1998, 286, my emphasis)? It seems to me that this question must be taken seriously, especially when dealing with texts such as those found in the opening chapters of Joshua that theologically justify the extermination of entire populations—men, women, and children as well as all of their possessions, including animals.

Less disturbing, perhaps, but just as facile and naïve are those who seem to take the details of the stories in Joshua at face value when discussing other, non-biblical issues. A website, under the name of "STRATFOR," describes itself as "a subscription-based provider of geopolitical analysis." A recent profile of Israel titled "The Geopolitics of Israel: Biblical and Modern" stated, "For convenience, we will use the term 'Israel' to connote all of the Hebrew and Jewish entities that have existed in the Levant *since the invasion of the region as chronicled in the Book of Joshua*" (my emphasis). The article goes on to explain that geopolitics involves three dimensions (I will have to take their word for it). In Israel's case, the first dimension began "*with the invasion led by Joshua* [my emphasis] and lasted through . . . the Babylonian conquest . . . ." It will be argued below that there was "no invasion" led by Joshua or anyone else that we know of as described in the Bible. The person(s) who wrote this article is/are simply assuming, without providing any evidence, that the narrative of Joshua's "conquest" is a historical record accurately describing what happened in Israel's history rather than an ideological/theological story created centuries later by the biblical authors long after the event supposedly occurred. What this means for the "geopolitics of biblical and modern Israel," I will have to leave to others to decide. The point here is that the academic study of the book of Joshua (and the rest of the Bible as well) has stayed for the most part in the academy. If it were otherwise, perhaps only a minority of people would applaud such a literalist and depraved interpretation as offered by Craig. Websites such as

STRATFOR would be more intelligently written, and high school students in Texas, as well as elsewhere, would be taught to think critically for themselves about all issues, the Bible included, instead of being brainwashed by biblical dogmatists.

But even a previous generation of supposedly non-fundamentalist, critically informed biblical scholars often expressed views that today would be (or should be) considered by a majority of scholars as unethical and simplistic. This is true of one of the most influential biblical scholars of the twentieth century, W. F. Albright (d. 1971). In his famous publication, *From the Stone Age to Christianity*, Albright wrote,

> From the impartial standpoint of a philosophy of history, it often seems necessary that a people of markedly inferior type should vanish before a people of superior potentialities, since there is a point beyond which racial mixing cannot go without disaster. . . . It was fortunate for the future of monotheism that the Israelites of the Conquest were a wild folk, endorsed with primitive energy and ruthless will to exist, since the resulting decimation of the Canaanites prevented the complete fusion of the two kindred folk which would almost inevitably have depressed Yahwistic standards to a point whose recovery was impossible. Thus the Canaanites, with their orgiastic nature worship, their cult of fertility in the form of serpent symbols, and sensuous nudity, and their gross mythology, were replaced by Israel, with its pastoral simplicity and purity of life, its lofty monotheism, and its severe code of ethics. (Albright 1957, 280–81; compare Feinman, who traced Albright's misguided abhorrence of all things "Canaanite" to Albright's youthful environment of rigid Methodism and his revulsion of all things Roman Catholic)

That one of America's leading biblical/archaeological scholars could publish this in 1957 without his views being attacked (until the 1990s, see Whitelam 1996, 88) for his racist and totally unsupported assumptions concerning the "historicity" of the biblical conquest story, the corrupting influence of mixing "races," and his use of biblical fiction to support the extermination of an entire culture, speaks volumes on how the biblical book of Joshua needs to be viewed as critically as possible. Albright's analysis can also serve as an example of how an interpretation of Joshua that was commonly accepted in academic circles more than fifty years ago is now rejected by the majority of contemporary biblical scholars and archaeologists.

The Decoders

Because of the serious historical and theological/ethical issues raised by a literalist reading of Joshua, there have been attempts by other scholars to "Christianize" the book by treating the stories as "myths," "metaphors," "allegories," and/or "symbols" while looking for theological nuggets (Earl 2010a, 2010b; Creach 2003; Hess, 1996a). This approach begins with the unsupported theological assumption that the Bible is "the inspired self-revelation of God to humanity" (Earl 2010a, 2; 2010b, xi). How those who believe this dogma actually "know" this we are not told (here is a good example where Hitchens's observation concerning unsupported claims fits perfectly; see above). While this method of interpretation does avoid the horrible consequences envisioned by the literalist approach, it is as dogmatic and as unconvincing as that of the literalist. In order to escape the horrible portrayal of the god of Joshua as a xenophobic and genocidal deity, the supporters of this approach "decode" what would seem to be the clear meaning of the Joshua stories into Christian theological concepts (for examples, the crossing of the Jordan is interpreted as "Christian baptism"; Rahab, the prostitute, as a "Christian convert"; and so forth (Earl 2010a, inter alia). ". . . Joshua should be read as theological literature, not as history in the modern sense" (Creach, 5; see also his discussion of Rahab from a Christian perspective, 31–43). While the nature of the literary forms present in the book of Joshua is a necessary critical question to ask, answering it in terms of evangelical Christian unsupported theological absolutes is theologically simplistic as well as misleading. Attempts to do this can result in little more than moralizing "Christian" nuggets (a good example of this attempt can be seen in Hess, 2006). Moreover, rejecting a literal interpretation of the stories in Joshua (as I certainly do) does not justify the mental/theological gymnastics engaged in by those in this camp who seek to find meanings that obviously were never intended by the original authors. Most important, such machinations do not justify trying to "Christianize" the book of Joshua. Attempting to do so results in such obtuse claims as the following:

> Thus one may say that Joshua is revelatory today as Christian Scripture *if* it is generative of contemporary Christian life and experience by providing a faith fitting witness to God by developing the existential significance of foundational "inspiration events" into the present. The interpreter's task is to consider whether, and if so, how, it is, which is something of a dialectical process . . . concerned with exploring the plenitude–or surplus of meaning–and fittingness of the text with respect to its tradition of reception when viewed from the interpreter's contemporary context. Whilst one

> might like to "stand outside" the tradition to seek to discern an objective view of its truth, in doing so one cuts oneself off from the very manifestations which make such discernment possible. But one must recognize the provisionality of the traditions itself that is oriented towards an eschatological telos. (Earl 2010a, 61, my emphasis)

The above Christian confession, as it were, is very unconvincing. Moreover, while a reader may be impressed with the tortuous words of its author, it is an example of ghastly writing. Furthermore, how does Earl, or anyone else for that matter, know that readers of Joshua cannot "discern an objective view of [Joshua's] truth" unless they begin with Earl's biased assumptions? Can one "discern" the "truth" of Marxism only by becoming a Marxist? While it may be true that a non-Marxist scholar may not get the same emotional satisfaction from a non-partisan study of Marxist philosophy and practice, it is nothing more than a biased and unsubstantiated opinion to say that a non-Marxist cannot come to rational, critically informed opinions about Marxism. In fact, taken to its extreme, Earl's methodology would mean that only a Jewish scholar could rightly understand the Hebrew Bible, which, after all, was written in its entirety by Jewish scribes (at least in its final, edited form known today) for other Jews! Not a single word in it was written by Christians for Christians. When Christians use the Hebrew Bible for their own purposes, they are "reading someone else's mail" (I can no longer find the source for this witticism, but I thoroughly agree with its sentiment).

Furthermore, according to Earl, without accepting his starting dogmas, one is cut off from "manifestations." Manifestations of what? Divine self-revelations from "Yahweh"? One gets the clear impression that those advocating such views recognize that the book of Joshua cannot be taken at face value, which is true as far as it goes. But in order to save some dogma of "divine revelation" they have to resort to the obfuscation witnessed in the above quote. Moreover, this approach assumes that it does not really matter what the authors of the Bible intended originally (for example, the command by Israel's god to destroy all living things in Canaan, Josh 10; 11 and so forth). All that matters is what the text is said to mean after it is decoded into some kind of "Christian mythology/theology." Such claims sound hollow and unconvincing unless one allows the starting assumptions of those who argue this way, and I know of no good reason(s) to grant those assumptions. One has to wonder if those in this camp would also argue for the same interpretive method concerning the stories of Jesus in the New Testament. Who gets to decide which stories "really happened" and which are "metaphors" or "myths"? And how does one decide which is which? Actually this last question is easy to answer. Those who approach the Bible in this fashion are simply "cherry picking." Such theological posturing as Earl's makes one's head spin. This is too much assumed and unproven religious dogma to grant before the discussion even begins. Such efforts at interpretation are little more than attempts to make the biblical text say something totally different than what the original authors thought they were saying.

Earl was right in abandoning any notion of the literal historicity of the conquest story, as all but the most conservative evangelical scholars have. But this does not save Joshua from the nightmare of its ethical implications. As the late James Barr (1924–2006) put it, "the problem is not whether the [Joshua] narratives are fact or fiction, the problem is that, whether fact or fiction, the ritual destruction is *commended*" (1993, 209, emphasis original). And, I might add, commended by none other than Yahweh! One of the most famous stories of "ritual destruction" in Joshua is that of the account of the fall of Jericho (see below). Speaking of this story, John J. Collins observed, "The story of the capture of Jericho is almost certainly fictitious, but this does not lessen the savagery of the story. We are not dealing in Joshua with a factual report of the ways of ancient warfare. Rather, the slaughter of the Canaanites, here and elsewhere, is presented as a *theologically correct ideal*" (2004, 193, my emphasis).

Moreover, why would anyone who believes the Bible is the revealed word of a god have to use such convoluting, confusing language as in the above quote from Earl to decode its true message? Why would a god, who actually desired to communicate with the recipients of his "disclosures," not have made it clear in the first place? (I am reminded of an anecdotal story about a response once given by the atheistic British philosopher, Bertrand Russell [d. 1974], to the question, "Lord Russell, what will you say when you die and are brought face to face with your maker?" Russell, without hesitation, responded, "I should say, 'God, why did you make the evidence for your existence so insufficient?'" [A. J. Ayer, 131].) One would think that this god would have wanted to communicate with everyone who was mentally competent to understand plain language. Moreover, interpreting Joshua as a "Christian" book does not follow from Earl's arguments, but it is the a priori assumption on which they are based.

This theological dogma characterizes much of evangelical writing. On the "Editorial Preface" page of T. C. Butler's 1983 commentary on Joshua (which, by the way, does contain many helpful textual clarifications), one reads, "The broad stance of our contributors can rightly be called *evangelical*, and this term is to be understood in its positive, historic sense of a commitment to *scripture as divine revelation* and to the truth and power of the Christian gospel" (my emphasis). Assuming such theological propositions before the discussion begins is not only counterproductive but also undermines any attempt to have an open discussion dictated by the principles of critical thinking—not by a traditional religious dogma, however old it may be, or by how many people may believe it. Moreover, notably, the people advocating this view usually never get around to informing you as to exactly how they know that the Bible is a product of "divine revelation." All theology is a product of human thinking and is predicated on the unsubstantiated belief that its truth comes from an unseen divine authority. The word itself derives from two Greek words, θεος = god and λογος = word, and literally means "a word (or study) of god." As a product of the human mind, no one's theology should be taken at face value. Anyone can make such claims; all theological claims should be subjected to the most rigid scrutiny. One should listen to typical Sunday TV preachers (even some politicians, Sunday or not) and ask oneself a simple question: "How does this person know this?"

Furthermore, as will be argued in more detail below, the fact that the story of the "conquest" is fictitious and no "Canaanites" were actually slaughtered (at least not to the extent the Bible claims) does not relieve the story of its major point. According to the story's authors, this slaughter was commanded by Yahweh. The divine command served the interests of the biblical writers (Collins 2005, 62–63). This should serve as a warning to anyone seriously trying to make sense of this story that the Bible served the interests of its authors, just as it does today for those who still believe it contains some sort of divine truth "once delivered to the saints." Such is always the consequence of theological speculations based on the claims of "revelation" that escape any hope of empirical confirmation and thus seem hollow and unconvincing, except, of course, to those making the claims in the first place. In a short piece titled "The Emptiness of Theology," Richard Dawkins (2006a) offered the following critical critique of theology in general:

> What has theology ever said that is of the smallest use to anybody? When has theology ever said anything that is demonstrably true and is not obvious? I have listened to theologians, read them, debated against them. I have never heard any of them ever say anything of the smallest use, anything that was not either platitudinously obvious or downright false. If all the achievements of scientists were wiped out tomorrow, there would be no doctors but witch doctors, no transport faster than horses, no computers, no printed books, no agriculture beyond peasant farming. If all the achievements of theologians were wiped out tomorrow, would anyone

> notice the smallest difference? Even the bad achievements of scientists, the bombs, and sonar-guided whaling vessels work! The achievements of theologians don't do anything, don't affect anything, don't mean anything. What makes anyone think that "theology" is a subject at all?

This is not to deny, of course, that fictional literature can and often does speak to the human condition (think of powerful novels that articulate our common humanity such as *The Brothers Karamazov* or the existential novels of Jean Paul Sartre and Albert Camus, just to name three). Our lives would be much poorer without the myriad productions of the human imagination. But the only reason fictional works of whatever order speak to our condition is because we already know, from purely humanistic endeavors such as the hard sciences and philosophy, what that human condition is. We did not learn this condition through "revealed metaphors" or "myths." If we did, whose "revealed" metaphors and myths are we going to choose? Hindus? Muslims? Jews? Christians? Greeks? Romans? *Homo sapiens* who lived 100,000 years ago? Consequently, what exactly are we modern readers to make of not only the condoning but also the commanding of the ethnic cleansing so vividly described in the book of Joshua that reflects the ideology/theology of its final authors/editors? Faith assertions are not adequate responses to serious literary, historical, and archaeological questions (compare Prior 1997, 226, n.5). To quote an apropos observation by Collins, "When we are told that the conquest of Canaan was justified by divine command or that God gave his unconditional support to the king, we may suspect that we are dealing with *ideological rhetoric rather than theological truth*, however tentative" (1990, 13; my emphasis).

In his 2005 commentary on Joshua, Robert B. Coote made the following observation:

> The purpose of a careful study of the book of Joshua is not in the first place to redeem it but to understand it better; and through it to understand ourselves better. In order to understand the book of Joshua better, along with other helps we need to use the imperfect knowledge of it that is available—with all its mere likelihoods and probabilities, its uncertainties, puzzles, gaps, and voids. When looked at in terms of its historical context, the values represented in the book of Joshua, whether ostensibly bad or good, are not pure, like offhand abstractions, but multifaceted, mixed, and ambiguous . . . . Such ambiguities cannot finally be resolved but must be grappled with if the Word of God is to be discovered in the book of Joshua. (2005, 104)

Here Coote assumed that the "Word of God" could still be discovered in the book of Joshua. Whether or not there is any word of a god to be discovered in this book is a question that individuals who read the book will need to decide for themselves. It is not my intention in what follows to try to redeem or save the book of Joshua from itself and make it somehow applicable and palatable to the interests and tastes of modern people. It is not clear to me that just because a book finally made it into the Jewish canon, it automatically has contemporary importance, much less "religious" usefulness. These are claims that need to be supported by carefully, critically crafted arguments, not simply assumed as true before the discussion even begins. Whether such a convincing argument can be made remains to be seen. Interested readers will have to decide for themselves.

For all of this convoluted, confusing language, attempting to "decode" the language of Joshua seems to ignore the real point of the story found in Joshua 1–11: Yahweh, a tribal deity, is a killer god on Israel's behalf. This is at least what the author(s) of the book as we have it would have its readers to believe. The fact that it never happened is not the point (well, not perhaps from the point of view of the authors who wrote the story; but it is an important issue for anyone who wishes to understand the story today). The point is that the writers of the Bible have their god not only approving of such actions but also ordering them in the first place. As one well-known archaeologist put it, "The biblical writers are not telling it the way it was, but the way it would have been had they been in charge" (Dever 1992, 28; there is a "revised" version of this witticism in Dever 2012, 287). What follows will be an attempt to approach the book of Joshua from the perspective of contemporary mainstream critical biblical scholarship. Speaking of the Hebrew Bible in its entirety, Collins concluded,

> The idea that the Old Testament be viewed through the lens of the New or that the two be construed as a unity . . . requires a peculiarly narrow and dogmatic view of Christianity. Many Christians find these books meaningful quite apart from any consideration of the New Testament . . . . And theological interpretations of these books, construed as the discussion of what they have to say to the modern world, is of interest to others besides Christians. My interest lies in examining the problems raised by any theological interpretations of biblical texts rather than in conforming the Old Testament or Hebrew Bible to Christian dogma, (2005, 134)

The following observation by Coote should also be carefully considered by anyone trying to deal with the stories found in Joshua: "Now it is clear that the Bible describes not the origin of Israel, but what some *later court writers thought* was the origin of Israel, on the bases of ideas and experiences belonging to their own time and place" (1990, 71, my emphasis).

Packing One's Intellectual Suitcase for a Critical Journey through the Book of Joshua

Given the twenty-five centuries or so since the book of Joshua was composed as we now have it, is there a satisfying way, considering the critical issues the book raises, to understand it that makes any sense to a twenty-first-century CE reader? The two approaches already discussed, the literal approach and the attempt to "decode" the original text to make it conform to evangelical Christian dogma, are simply inadequate and theologically naïve. There are, however, two intellectual disciplines that, when used critically and in conjunction with each other, may provide helpful "maps" for our journey. One is in the field of literary-critical studies known as "postmodernism," and the other is in the field of archaeology.

Postmodernism

Reference has already been made to the postmodernist movement, and interested readers may wish to consult the sources listed here: Collins 2005; Adam 1999, 2009; Clines 1998; Davies 1991. Postmodernists reject traditional historical criticism of the Bible and insist that there is no such thing as "objective" reality. This approach is also heavily politicized and is often subjective in its interpretation of literature. According to postmodernists, there is no one "right" way to read texts, including biblical texts. This latter point may be conceded without concluding that all interpretations are of equal value. They are not (see Collins comment quoted above). At the outset, it should be noted that if the claims above are true, the postmodernists invite an inherent contradiction in their methods (Collins 2005, 12). In the words of W. G. Dever, postmodernism "is essentially a theory of knowledge according to which *there is no knowledge*" (2012, 26, emphasis original; compare his remarks in 2001a, 23–52). Dever has characterized postmodernism as a "failed value-system, filled with arrogance, cynicism, moral relativism and nihilism, as well as being passé in real intellectual circles" (2012, 29; and footnote 48). This negative critique should be balanced with the more positive assessments by such scholars as Collins (2005), Adam (1999, 2009), Clines (1998), and Davies (2008). At the present it would seem that most biblical scholars have not adopted postmodernists' methods (Adam 1999, 307; Clines 1998, 289–91) and perhaps will not in the foreseeable future. But Collins has suggested that postmodernism has pushed traditional historical criticism to its logical conclusion (2005, 25).

Perhaps of more significance is Collins's insistence that the greatest challenge of postmodernists to biblical students is their claim that the biblical character, "Yahweh," the Israelite god, does not refer to some supernatural entity but to a literary construct created by the biblical authors. For those who read the Bible from a historical-critical perspective, this conclusion should not pose a problem. To quote Collins, "The whole drift of historical criticism has been away from the view that the Bible is a timeless revelation of God, and an insistence that its writings are time-conditioned products of human authors, and that its wisdom, to adapt a phrase of Stanley Fish, is 'of an age and not for all time . . .' (2005, 23; note that after quoting Fish's remarks, Collins added his own observation: "at least not in most cases," but does not cite any biblical examples in which Fish's view does not hold. Neither can I. If there are such "cases" where Fish's conclusion does not hold, what are they, and who gets to decide which ones? This would seem to be another instance of "cherry picking."The reference is to Fish's book, *The Trouble with Principle* [Cambridge MA: Harvard, 1988] 46; compare Miscall, 85–86).

Despite the vigorously negative attack on postmodernism by some of its critics (Dever, for example), important issues/questions have been raised by representatives of this movement whether or not one embraces their methodology in whole or part. One such postmodernist spokesperson is David A. J. Clines. In a seminal article published in 1998, Clines concluded that he did not believe that scholars who understand postmodernism would "turn their backs on it . . . and carry on the traditional biblical scholarship that they produced in another, earlier world. But of course I know that that will never happen . . . . But if we all do that, or even most of us do it, we are doomed—we, our subject, our jobs . . . . The postmodernism is an adventure it will be more perilous to refuse than to embark upon" (291). He also warned that those who dismiss postmodernism as a "fetish," a "fashion," or an "aberration" are dooming biblical studies to extinction (1998, 290). Whether or not such dire predictions will occur if most biblical scholars ignore postmodernism, which seems to be the case at the moment (Adam 1999, 305–309), dismissing postmodernism out of hand may be a mistake for anyone wishing to engage in serious biblical studies. Perhaps the best approach is to avoid at all cost an either/or fallacy, or false dilemma, and look at postmodernism in relationship to traditional historical-critical scholarship from a both/and perspective (Collins 2005; Carter and Levy, 205–40). Postmodernism does not necessarily supplant traditional historical criticism of the Bible nor does it make traditional studies obsolete (Miller, 1999, among others). Apparently for Clines, it creates instead a paradox: "I have been saying that modernism and postmodernism are not to be set up as an oppositional pair—or, if they are, only as part of a wider argument in which they are also shown to interpenetrate one another, implying one another at the same time as they exclude one another" (1998, 290).

Collins, commenting on Clines's observation, righty pointed out that postmodernism

> can be construed as pushing historical criticism to its logical conclusion, in a way that historical critics have traditionally failed to do. . . . Because of its canonical status, the Bible has often enjoyed a presumption of transcendent value, even if that value is not distributed equally in all its parts. Clines is surely right that such a presumption *has no place in critical scholarship*. (2005, 25, my emphasis)

Unfortunately, as long as some scholars begin their study of the Bible with the dogma that the Bible is a divine revelation (for examples, Butler, xi; Earl, above), the insights of postmodernist study will most likely fall on deaf ears. Nevertheless, the following observations, some of which may not be original or unique to postmodernism, seem to this author to be crucial intellectual, critical tools that should be in the bag of anyone who is contemplating a "journey" through the Bible—in this case the book of Joshua.

1. "Yahweh" is not a reference to a supernatural deity but a literary construct created by the biblical storytellers/writers. In his essay, "God in the Pentateuch: Reading Against the Grain," David Clines described the character, God, thusly:

> We need to realize that when the narrative says, "The LORD proclaimed," "The LORD, the LORD, a God merciful and gracious . . ." (Exod 34.6), this self-description does not consist of the words of God himself (what language does *he* [original emphasis] speak?) but the words of the narrator (in Hebrew). These are no more than words put in the mouth of the Character God by the narrator, and, behind the narrator, by the author. (1995, 187)

Again, "Let us recognize that the God of the Pentateuch is a character in a novel. God in the Pentateuch is not a 'person'; he is a character in a book. And there are no people in books, no real people, only fictions; for books are made, not procreated" (1995, 190).

To unpack Clines's observations, he is asking readers of the Bible to make necessary distinctions between three types of biblical characters. The first person to recognize is the actual author(s)/editor(s) of a text who were real historical individuals who lived and died on this planet. In the particular case of Joshua, the final author(s) is/are dated by most contemporary critical scholars to the fifth-sixth centuries BCE. When they give their own opinions of what is taking place, these opinions will be called "reporting speeches" (Josh 9:14-18 is a good example; 2 Kings 17:7-41 is a classic example; see below on these "speeches"). The second person to recognize is the narrator in the story itself who is a literary construct of the "real" first person(s). Examples abound: Moses, who "narrates" most of Deuteronomy, and Joshua, who "narrates" much in the book bearing his name (see especially his "farewell speeches" in chapters 23 and 24). These "story narrators" are those in whose mouths are placed "first-person speeches" called "reported speeches" in this commentary (see below). The third type of persons encountered in the text are all the characters in the stories, both named (for examples, Abraham, Jacob, Moses, Joshua, Samuel, Saul, David, and so forth) and unnamed (the pharaoh in Gen 12 and Exod 1; the Levite's concubine who was raped all night in Judg 19:1-30; the spies sent to Jericho, and many others) who act or are acted upon. Sometimes, of course, the same character can also be the narrator of a "reported speech." Since it is the real anonymous human author who is omniscient, the characters do and say, go and come, believe and disbelieve, as the actual author wishes (compare the comments of Miscall).

2. The Bible is not a "revealed" book but a document that speaks with many often, contradictory voices. "Why not suppose that the Old Testament is *not* [emphasis original] a unity, that each writing in the Old Testament speaks in its own voice, whether explicitly or implicitly in dissent from or contradiction to the other writings" (Clines 1998, 280)? Examples are legion. One has to go no further than comparing the creation and flood myths in Genesis 1 and 2 and 6 and 7, respectively.

3. It might be possible to read the Bible as an important "cultural-literary" text, but not a book of absolute historical truth (Collins 2005, 83–84). This raises the all-important question concerning the extent to which biblical texts reflect the actual reality of the past. Given the ideological/theological nature of the texts, can we ever really know the past (Carter and Levy)? This does not mean that the biblical writers were not intending to write a "history" of their past, but given the circumstances of their own lives, the centuries separating them from the "events" they wrote about, and, most important, the nature of the "sources" at their disposal, were they successful (Kofoed, 221–26)? This question is more complex than it may seem on the surface and has to be answered on an individual basis relevant to what part of the "story" is being studied and what sources are available to evaluate such claims.

4. The goal of biblical scholarship is not recapitulating the meaning of the text.

> You do not find scholars of a "modern" persuasion saying, This is what my text means, and personally, I do not believe a word of it. Mostly they think their job is done when they have said again in their own words, what the text has already said. . . . At the very least, the critic in a postmodern age will need to be asking, What does this text do to me if I read it? *What ethical responsibility do I carry if I go helping this text stay alive* (Clines 1998, 286, my emphasis)?

This raises an important question in my mind: What part, if any, of the Bible is relevant to the twenty-first century? This is especially important apropos the book of Joshua, which, in context, dehumanizes the indigenous populations of Canaan (Deut 7:1; Josh 10:40-42; 11:16-20) and justifies their extermination by the hand of the "Israelites," on command from their god, Yahweh.

5. Should the Bible be used as a source for the ethical behavior of modern-day humans? If there is any relevant value in the Bible for the contemporary world, it would seem to lie in the realm of ethics. This is problematic because much in the Bible does not commend itself in terms of how one human should treat another. This can clearly be seen in the biblical portrayal of male-female relationships. (The Ten Commandments, for example, are not addressed to females, only to males. Thus, there is no commandment prohibiting a wife from being envious of her neighbor's husband!) Without cherry picking texts that do not offend modern sensibilities, many biblical texts are simply demonic when taken at face value, including texts in Joshua. (For shocking examples, read Num 15:32-36 and

Deut 18:18-21; 22:13-30, note esp. vv. 28-29 that justifies forcing a woman to marry a man who has raped her! There are many more such texts. For examples, Deut 25:11; Lev 15:1-33; 18:1-30; 20:10-21; compare Collins 2005, 131–61.) What all of this means for any attempt to understand the character of the god of the Bible is today a much-discussed subject. Miscall has summarized the problem this way:

> Narrative critics are willing to look at the dark side of human characters like Absalom and David, and of human society in general. The latter is evidenced in the mistreatment of women and in the prevalence of violence as the chief way to deal with problems. The focus on the human side is matched by a concern with understanding and evaluating God, who is not only involved with this human scene but is often also the initiator, the one who sets violent events in motion. The flood, the conquest, the seemingly unending wars of Samuel–Kings, and the destruction of Judah and Jerusalem are prime examples. Humans, whether individuals or the whole people are flawed or worse; and God is the one who chooses them to play a role in the divine. Critics have begun raising the question of how all of this reflects on God. (85–86)

Not particularly well at all, I should think, unless one believes in the Divine Command Theory, as does William Lane Craig (and many others, of course), discussed above. It would appear that the people who wrote the horrible tales found in the book of Joshua believed that their god hated and wanted destroyed the same people as they did. I do not know the original source of the following witticism but it is worth quoting (or paraphrasing) here: "When you think your god hates the same people you do, you can rest assured that you have created your god in your own image." Carl Sagan, in his book, *The Demon-Haunted World* (if you read only one book in the coming year, I highly recommend this one), has described how morally ambiguous human behavior is:

> . . . consider the mainstream religions. We are enjoined in Micah to do justly and love mercy; in Exodus we are forbidden to commit murder; in Leviticus we are commanded to love our neighbor as ourselves; and in the Gospels we are urged to love our enemies. Yet think of the rivers of blood spilled by fervent followers of the books in which these well-meaning exhortations are embedded. (290)

Think especially of all the violent deaths, and those who killed in the name of their god, recorded in the book of Joshua.

Archaeology and the Book of Joshua

See the following references: Faust 2007; Finkelstein 1988a, 1988b, 1991, 1994, 1995, 2010; Dever 2003a, 2012; Levy 1995; Finkelstein and Silberman; Finkelstein and Mazar; Finkelstein and Na'aman.

The Emerging Archaeological Picture

Between the 1920s and 1970s, many biblical scholars and historians were optimistic that archaeological discoveries in Israel, and the Ancient Near East in general, corroborated if not proved the historicity of the conquest stories told in the books of Numbers and Joshua (Dever 1990, 39–84; Davis). Although there are exceptions, this optimism is reflected in many publications on the Hebrew Bible dating to this period (Albright 1957, 276–89; Anderson, 122–4; Harrelson 1964, 109–10; Wright 1957, 69–84; and many others). Beginning in the 1970s, however, new archaeological methods and discoveries have completely undermined the so-called "military" model reflected in Joshua and supported by a former generation of scholars (for a sampling of critiques of this model see esp. Miller 1977; Finkelstein 1988a, b; Soggin 1989, 187–97; Silberman 1992; Laughlin 1995; Dever 2003a, 37–74; Collins 2004, 183–202; Finkelstein and Mazar, 53–55; 61–65; Coogan 2014, 196–214). There are many more publications on this issue. My main purpose for listing even this many is that there is simply no excuse among intelligent, serious students of the Bible to continue to advocate totally outdated views concerning the "conquest" of Canaan by some group of people later to be known as "Israelites." Most mainstream scholars would agree with the conclusion of L. L. Grabbe: "The 'conquest' model is now only of historical interest, but it should alert scholars to the fact that vociferous adherence by large numbers of academics is no guarantee that a particular theory will stand the test of time" (101). Richard Nelson, in his 1997 commentary on Joshua also offered a cogent observation:

> The overall narrative structure of invasion and total conquest is the contribution of the authorial and redaction process and not something dictated by the earliest forms of the constituent tales. . . . It should come as no surprise, therefore, that Joshua's account of a large-scale invasion of Canaan cannot be supported by the archaeological evidence. (1997, 3)

There are several major problems that need to be clarified carefully and understood by anyone who seeks to read the book of Joshua intelligently. The biblical and archaeological data available for students interested in this thorny issue are extremely varied and complex. Thus any attempt to evaluate these sources with the goal of reconstructing the actual process by which "Israel" came to occupy the land of Canaan involves a significant amount of tentative conclusions based on the literary critical and archaeological evidence currently available. Standard works on Joshua all suggest various "models" for interpreting the "conquest" theme. (For summaries and critiques of most of these models see Collins 2004, 186–91; Ray, 79–93; Dever, 1990, 37–84; Gottwald, 1985, 261–88).

The Nature of the Late Bronze Age—Iron I Cultural Collapse (1250–1150 BCE): The "Conquest" Story in the Larger Context of Ancient Near Eastern History

It has been my experience as a teacher of the Hebrew Bible for over forty years that many, if not most, people who claim to "believe the Bible" have little or no appreciation for the broader cultural/historical context in which Israel and Judah existed and out of which the Bible came. The stories told in the Bible, for all intents and purposes, might as well have taken place in Kansas. Ask yourself the following question: "While Joshua was presumably slaughtering all of the inhabitants of Canaan, what was occurring elsewhere in the Ancient Near East?" For example, what was going on in Egypt southwest of Canaan and Anatolia (modern-day Turkey) to the north/northwest? What was taking place in the Mycenaean world of Greece and the rest of the eastern Mediterranean? At the beginning of the Late Bronze Age (c. 1550/1500 BCE), all of these empires flourished and international trade thrived. By 1150 BCE they had all collapsed (Van de Mieroop, 127–206). Consequently, one of the major critical reasons that most scholars (who still argue for a "conquest" at all) now accept this LBA date is that during the transition period from the end of the Late Bronze Age to Iron Age I, there was a long, general collapse of LBA culture lasting a hundred years or more throughout the region, stretching from Anatolia in the west to the kingdom of Elam in the east (in addition to Van de Mieroop's thorough discussion, see also Miller and Hayes, 55; Finkelstein 1988, 1994, 1995; and esp. Na'aman 2004, 222–30, who summarizes many discrepancies between the biblical versions of "conquest" and the archaeological evidence dating to this period). Different causes for this collapse have been suggested. Among the more important causes is the arrival of the "Sea Peoples," who appear in the coastal regions of Canaan by the late thirteenth century BCE. Among these peoples were the famous Philistines well known in the Bible. Other suggested causes are environmental disasters including earthquakes and deforestation. Recently it has been suggested that the major culprit in this cultural collapse was widespread drought. According to a report published in the *New York*

Times (22 October 2013), a recent study of pollen grains extracted from the sediment in the center of the Sea of Galilee and the western margins of the Dead Sea have confirmed that the major cause of the collapse of the Late Bronze Age culture in the ancient southern Levant was indeed drought. For a recent discussion of the causes of the collapse of the Bronze Age, see Eric H. Cline's *1177 B.C.: The Year Civilization Collapsed* (Princeton University Press, 2014). Unfortunately, this book reached me too late to incorporate Cline's conclusions in the discussion here.

Politically, this collapse led to the decline of Egyptian influence in Canaan (Killebrew 2005, 37–42, 81–83; Leonard, 349–56), which removed a major obstacle that would have stood in the way of migrating groups of peoples who settled in the central-hill country of Canaan during Iron Age I. The central (and controversial) question raised by these migrations is from where did these migrants come? The archaeological remains of hundreds of small settlements discovered here are now associated by some scholars with the rise of the ancient Israelites. This debate is not settled to everyone's satisfaction and may never be, at least in the foreseeable future. (The ethnogenesis of ancient Israel is now one of the most debated topics among biblical historians and archaeologists. The following literature will orient a careful reader to the major questions involved and the range of positions offered by their authors: Block-Smith and Nakhai; Dever, 2003a; Finkelstein, 1996, 2007c; Faust 2007b, 2010; Rainy 2008a, b; van der Steen; Killebrew 2005.) But what does seem clear is that the appearance of these small villages, farmsteads, and hovels was not a unique occurrence but the third stage in a long process of "urbanization" of this area discussed above (see in particular Finkelstein 1994, 1995, 2007b). The rise of ancient "Israel" must now be placed in the wider context of what took place at the end of the Late Bronze Age/Iron Age I and not seen as an isolated, unique event as has been traditionally interpreted (see below; for a recent publication containing several essays on the question of the emergence of ancient Israel from a very conservative perspective, see Hess et al.). Yet Joshua 14:7 and 10 imply that Joshua conquered all of Canaan within a span of just five years or so. Furthermore, even in cases where some Canaanite sites show destruction from this period, the cause of the destruction is often unknown, at least archaeologically speaking.

Thus, in recent years, many biblical historians and archaeologists have assumed that if there were a "conquest" of Palestine by the "Israelites" led by Joshua, it would have some connection with this international cultural collapse and the hundreds of new Iron Age I villages and hamlets that suddenly appeared in the central-hill country of Canaan between

1250–1150 BCE. (The current relevant publications on these issues are vast. The following analysis of the archaeological picture that has emerged over the past thirty years or so needs to be appreciated thoroughly as critical background knowledge for the "starting point" of anyone interested in making a critically informed "journey" through Joshua.)

This might be a good time to briefly summarize the biblical story, pointing out contradictions and inconsistencies often skipped over in popular "sermonizing" of this tale. We are informed that following the death of Moses and under the leadership of Joshua, the "Israelites" invaded the land of Canaan, organizing their attack into three phases: the central-hill country, including Jericho and Ha'ai (Josh 6–10; for an explanation of this name see below); a southern campaign, defeating Libnah, Eglon, Hebron, and Debir (Josh 10:29-43); and finally a northern assault that resulted in the total destruction of Hazor (Josh 11:1-15) and other towns located on tels (Josh 11:13). Thus we are told that within a space of five years (compare Josh 14:7, 10), "Joshua defeated the whole land, the hill country and the Negev and the lowland and the slopes and all their kings; he left none remaining, but utterly destroyed (חרם) *all* that breathed, as Yahweh the god of Israel commanded" (Josh 10:40).

The impression one gets from the above readings is that the "conquest" of Canaan by Israel was sudden, swift, and complete. However, it is obvious that something is very wrong with this picture, not only from the point of view of archaeology but even from within the Bible itself. Judges 1, for example, opens with the announcement of Joshua's death, with the Israelites having taken none of the Land of Canaan! Furthermore, what is described here is neither a unified effort by "*all*" (for a critical discussion of this word that occurs 137 times in Joshua, see below) Israel, nor is the land taken solely by military action. What is reported instead are scattered military battles by individual tribes or groups of people, and in at least one instance the peaceful migration of one faction (Judg 1:16). In fact, this version of the story ends with a long list of some twenty cities whose inhabitants we are told the Israelites could not drive out. Some of these turn out to be among the most important cities in the land such as Megiddo (1:27), Gezer (1:29), and Jerusalem (1:21).

To make matters worse, the literary discrepancies in the Bible are not just between the traditions in Numbers–Joshua and those in Judges 1. A careful reading of Numbers–Joshua also reveals tensions within the text that are hard to reconcile with one another. After the sweeping claims of Joshua 10:40 and 11:16-20, we are told in 13:1 that Joshua "is old" and much land still remains "to be possessed." This note about Joshua is followed

by a long list of unconquered territories. Moreover, Joshuah 10:29-43 claims

that Joshua destroyed all the cities of the hill country, including Hebron and Debir. What, then, are we to make of the claim in Judges 15:13-19 that Hebron was destroyed by Caleb and Debir by Othniel, not Joshua? Many other examples of the inconsistencies in these traditions could be cited, but enough has been said, hopefully, to enable a critical reader to realize that the stories of the taking of the Land of Canaan by the Israelites are highly idealized and overly simplified. To this long list of critical issues, we can add the following.

1. Archaeological evidence of sites actually destroyed in Palestine, but not mentioned in the Bible. During the period of around 1250–1150 BCE, several sites located in Palestine have yielded archaeological evidence of LBA destruction. The problem, however, is that some of these sites are not even mentioned in the biblical story (Dever 1990, 60, table 3). Such sites include Ashdod, Aphek, and Tell abu-Havvam, among others. On the other hand, other destroyed sites have not yet even been identified. Most archaeologists are agreed that some of these towns/cities were no doubt destroyed by the "Sea Peoples," among whom were the famous "Philistines" of the Bible (Bietak, 1990; Stager 1995; Dothan and Dothan 2004; Killebrew 2005, 197–246; 2010; Ortiz, 191–204).

2. Sites claimed destroyed or captured by Joshua. The physical remains of sites said to have been destroyed or taken by the Israelites but spared destruction either did not exist (archaeologically, at least) during this time, or the LBA remains that have been found are archaeologically ambiguous. Sites that are claimed to have been destroyed but were nonexistent during the LBA include Jericho (Josh 6:1-21), Ha'ai (et-Tell; Josh 8:24), Arad, and Heshbon (Num 21:25-30). Sites that are claimed to have been conquered by Joshua but not necessarily destroyed include Gibeon (Josh 9:16), Gezer (Josh 10:33), Ashkelon, and Ekron (Judg 1:18; for more listings see Dever 1990, tables 1 and 2, 57–59).

L. Stager, in a 1998 article, has identified thirty-one such sites (98–99) and suggested archaeological problems related to each site. It cannot be emphasized enough that although this book is called a "commentary," a minimal understanding of the archaeological picture that has been and still is emerging is essential in understanding the book of Joshua. Every archaeological site that has been identified and excavated almost always has a different history of occupation, the discussion of which can only be minimally included here. There are some relatively easily accessible sources available for those who are willing to take the time to search for themselves. (For general orientation see specific site entries in the *NEAEHL*, *NIDB*, and the older but still very useful *ABD*.) The broader point here is that the authors of the book of Joshua made explicit claims about "what happened" at certain sites. If what is claimed is false, as it appears to be in many cases (see below), this should have a significant impact on how a reader goes about trying to decide of what value, if any, such a story can have. To illustrate here, all but the most conservative/evangelical scholars now agree that the stories of the destruction of Jericho (Josh 6) and Ha'ai (et-Tell; Josh 7–8) by the "Israelites" are ideological/theological fictions (compare Miller's observations, especially on et-Tell/ Ha'ai, 1977). This does not make these texts worthless, of course, but their literary nature must be taken seriously in any attempt to reconstruct the past. The issue revolves around the difficult question concerning at what point the ancient texts and the archaeological record intersect, if ever (Levy 2010, inter alia).

Since the 1970s there have been recovered from excavations and surveys (on surveys see below) in modern-day Israel and Jordan, as well as elsewhere, enormous amounts of archaeological data that were not available to earlier archaeologists and biblical historians interested in the question of Israel's origins (Killebrew 2005, 155–71). It should be emphasized, however, that not all archaeologists are agreed on what this new evidence means, and a lot of contentious arguments have been the result (consult the references below). However, while these differences of opinion can be disconcerting to those who are just beginning a serious study of these questions, it should be noted that such discussions among the experts are quite common and are no cause for unnecessary alarm. Moreover, while there may be just one totally correct interpretation or meaning of archaeological remains, we can never be absolutely sure that we have it. But while archaeological data do not interpret themselves, they become meaningful only when they

> . . . are fitted into some larger story. But some data cannot be fitted into some stories. The archaeological evidence for the land west of the Jordan in the Late Bronze and Early Iron Ages can be contrived so as to support more than one historical reconstruction. But it *cannot*, on the basis of the evidence now available, be made to support the account of the conquest presented in the book of Joshua. (Collins 2005, 38, my emphasis)

One is reminded of the tongue-in-cheek definition of archaeology proposed by the late Anson Rainey (d. 2011): "archaeology is the science of digging a square hole and the art of spinning a yarn from it" (140). There may be a kernel of truth in Rainey's witticism, but he forgot to observe that not all "yarns" are equal. This is especially true when the "yarn" is based on material remains recovered from a "square hole" using the best excavating techniques now available. Nevertheless, it is this uncertainty and disagreement that drives research forward and, it is to be hoped, moves us closer to the truth. Regardless of this caveat, anyone the least bit interested in the "conquest" stories in Joshua must be cognizant of the archaeological picture that has now emerged relevant to the LBA-Iron Age I transition in the Ancient Near East in general, and modern day Israel-Jordan in particular, if they wish to be taken seriously.

Furthermore, it needs to be carefully understood that, archaeologically speaking, we have practically no evidence for the origins of Israelite religion, particularly the worship of the Israelite god, Yahweh (Miller and Hayes, 102–106; Smith 2001, 2002, inter alia, and see below). The Late Bronze Age/Iron Age I inhabitants of the central highlands of Canaan may indeed have engaged in some kind or form of cultic practices, but at the moment there is little unambiguous archaeological evidence of the nature of such activity. This includes the celebrated so-called "Mount Ebal Altar" that Zertal claimed to have discovered in 1980–1981 (Josh 8:30-35; see below).

When all of the above archaeological evidence is taken into account, the most unbiased assessment seems to be that the process by which the Iron Age I central-hill country was occupied, and by whom, during the Late Bronze-Iron I periods was a complicated and multifaceted affair (Na'aman 1994; Finkelstein 1995; Block-Smith and Nakhai; Killebrew 2005; Rainy and Notley 2006, 112–30; Finkelstein and Mazar; compare Killebrew 2005, 184: "The mixed multitude theory interprets the biblical and archaeological evidence as reflecting a heterogeneous, multifaceted, and complex process of Israelite ethnogenesis").

Moreover, Finkelstein has repeatedly argued that the emergence of the small Iron Age I villages traditionally associated with the arrival of "Israel" from the Transjordanian region was not a "unique event," but the third re-urbanization of the region in a cycle of urbanization and collapse that had occurred over a two-thousand-year period (Finkelstein 1995, 362; Finkelstein 2007c, 73–83; compare Na'aman 1994, 231–35). Thus, whatever happened in the Iron I central highlands and to whomever it happened was but the third and last cycle in a long process in the social-political and demographic development in the region stretching back to the Chalcolithic-Early Bronze Age I (c. 3300–2000 BCE). In Finkelstein's own words,

> The literary depiction of early Israel as a singular event in the annals of the region appeared only centuries after the Iron I. It was shaped by the history

> of the Judahite state in the late-Iron II period. The biblical description of the rise of early Israel was cast by the Deuteronomistic Historian in such a way as to serve the southern, Judahite-centered ideology and historical-national aspirations, and to convey its theological message. That narrative has prevailed until recently, when archaeology came to the center stage of historical research on Canaan-Israel. (Finkelstein, 2007c, 83)

And again: "The genuine exceptional event in the highlands of the southern Levant in the late second to early first millennium BCE was not the 'Israelite Settlement,' but the emergence of the United Monarchy—the unification of the entire region and most of the lowlands under one rule" (Finkelstein 1995, 362). It should be noted here that when Finkelstein wrote of a "United Monarchy," he was not referring to the traditional United Monarchy of a David and Solomon popularized in the Bible, but a united monarchy established by Omri (886–875 BCE), the ninth century BCE king of Israel (Finkelstein and Silberman 2006, 103; Finkelstein 2007d, 115). For Finkelstein, two critical questions remain:

> . . . the first is related to the formation of the early Israelite ethnicity: can we identify a new ethnic entity in the archaeological record of the highlands in the Iron I? The second: what can we learn from the archaeological record about the origin of the people who settled hundreds of new Iron I Villages in the hill country? (Finkelstein 1996, 198; compare Dever 1992, 54; Faust 2007)

Beginning in the 1920s and 1930s, two totally opposed scholarly theories were suggested to explain Israel's settlement in the land of Canaan. The most popular and most influential, in America at least, was the view advocated by the late William Foxwell Albright, who for many years taught at The Johns Hopkins University. Using the archaeological discoveries that were being made at such great LBA Canaanite tels as Tell Beit Mirshim (which Albright identified, probably erroneously, with Debir), Lachish, and Bethel, he accepted the basic historical reliability of the opening chapters of Joshua and championed the so-called "military" model presented in the Bible as the literal way in which Israel acquired the land of Canaan (1949, 104; 1957, 278–79). Of the three basic theories discussed here, Albright's is the least satisfactory and is simply no longer viable in light of advancements made in contemporary literary, historical, and archaeological studies.

While Albright and his students were supporting the military model in America, A. Alt in Germany was approaching the problem from a different perspective altogether. Using the tools of form and traditio-historical criticisms, he and his students concluded that the conquest stories were, for the most part, etiological legends with little or no historical value (Alt, 173–221). These scholars concluded that "Israel" emerged on the land of Canaan through the "peaceful infiltration" of pastoral groups over a long period. One of the major strengths of this theory is its recognition that the "Israelite" settlement was a long, complicated, and multifaceted process. But Alt's insistence on the "nomadic" origin of these peoples has brought the theory a great deal of criticism, especially from the advocates of the third model or theory.

In 1962, George Mendenhall argued that the origin of Israel was due neither to a pan-Israelite invasion under Joshua nor to a peaceful migration of pastoral nomads, but to an internal revolt of indigenous Canaanites against their overlords (66–87). This theory has been expanded by N. Gottwald (1979, 210–27; 1983, 5–24; 1992, 70–75) into what he called the "peasant revolt" model, and has gained some acceptance, in part at least, by others. (For a caustic critique of Gottwald's views, see Rainey 2008a, where he sneeringly referred to Gottwald's theory as the "*revolting* peasant theory" (47; emphasis original; for a more positive evaluation of Gottwald's theory see Faust 2006, 96–97; 172–74; Dever, 1990, 55–56; 2003, 52–54). Based on sophisticated social theories, this "sociological" model has raised many pertinent issues relevant to ancient Israel's emergence. However, it too has been severely criticized both for its perceived methodological flaws and its failure to explain adequately the material culture now known to have existed in Canaan during the period under investigation (for brief descriptions and critiques of all the above theories, see Dever 1990, 37–56; 1992, 27–85; 2003a, 41–74; Finkelstein 1988a, 295–314; Gottwald, 189–227; Halpern 1983, 47–63; Collins 2004, 183–96; Coogan 1990a; 2014, 196–203; Laughlin 1995). Perhaps of most importance is that all of these "models" assume that however "Israel" emerged, it was a unique event.

The point at issue here is the most adequate explanation for the material culture dating to Iron Age I (roughly 1250–1150 BCE) that has recently come to light in the central-hill country of Palestine (for the most up-to-date synthesis of the archaeological data see Block-Smith and Nakhai). This data includes pottery forms, architectural remains (especially the so-called "pillared buildings" and "four-room" houses; on four-room houses see now Yasur-Landau and Younker), layout of sites, silos, and water cisterns, as well as hundreds of Iron I sites now known through surveys to have existed during this period but that have not yet been excavated (Finkelstein 1988a, 15–234).

Archaeologists are not all agreed on where the people came from who built and lived in these towns and villages. Some believe they were displaced Canaanites who settled in the sparsely inhabited regions of the central hills during and following the breakup of the Late Bronze Age (Dever 1990, 37–84; 1992, 27–56; Fritz, 84–100), while others have argued that the newcomers were pastoralists who were in the process of being "resedentarized" (Finkelstein 1988a, 336–51). In some ways, the disagreements among such "experts" are disconcerting. If they cannot arrive at some semblance of agreement on major issues, there would seem to be little hope for interested non-specialists. However, they do agree on some very basic issues. One is that the real evidence for the origin of "Israel" is not the biblical stories, which for all intentions are of very limited or of no historical value (Fritz, 98; Finkelstein 1995, 351; Block-Smith and Nakhai, 63; Dever 2012, 105). They also agree that the most important questions relevant to the entire "conquest" discussion revolve around the origin(s) and ethnicity of the Iron I settlers of the central-hill country villages and camps (Dever 2003a, 121; Finkelstein 1996, 198; Faust 2007). But the differences highlight the often-ambiguous nature of the evidence and the subjective interpretations given it. Perhaps as more archaeological data become available there will be something of a consensus, at least among those qualified to make an informed judgment. Many questions still remain, and all conclusions are tentative and mostly likely will need modification, if not total revision, as more information is forthcoming. Nevertheless, taking into consideration all of the evidence that is currently available, especially the archaeological data, the following conclusions by Dever seem reasonable: "The literal biblical story of an Exodus from Egypt, and a subsequent pan-Israelite conquest of Canaan, can no longer be salvaged, for all the wishful thinking in the world" (1992, 84; see also Fritz, 98). And, the inescapable conclusion ". . . is that the Israelite settlement in Canaan was part of the larger transition from the Late Bronze to the Iron Age. It was a gradual, exceedingly complex process, involving social, economic, and political-—as well as religious—change, with many regional variations" (1990, 79).

At the moment, this much can be said with some confidence: the older models for reconstructing Israel's origins are now seen to be seriously flawed and passé. This is especially true of the military model made famous by Albright. In fact, all of the three popular models—"Military Conquest," "Peaceful Infiltration," and "Social/Peasant Revolution"—that dominated the discussion throughout much of the twentieth century are now considered obsolete (Killebrew 2005, 181–85). Moreover, all of these reconstructions assumed that the appearance of "Israel" in Canaan was a unique event in the occupational history of the area. They have now all been seriously questioned by the "ugly facts" of archaeology (Dever 2003a, 41–54). That the biblical writers seem to know little or none of the views now advanced by scholars, especially archaeologists, need not surprise or upset us. How much the biblical writers actually knew of Israel's true historical origins is uncertain and questionable (Dever 2001a). From their perspective, "Israel" existed only because of the activity of Yahweh. Neither archaeologists, biblical historians, nor anyone else for that matter can prove or disprove such theological claims. In the end, all interested readers must decide for themselves whether or not such claims have enough warrants to merit acceptance.

Since Dever has published prolifically on this subject, two more quotes from him on the implications of archaeology for understanding the so-called "conquest" are worthy of repeating:

> . . . it may be stated confidently that the archaeological evidence today is overwhelmingly against the classic conquest model of Israelite origins, as envisioned in the book of Joshua and in much biblical scholarship until recently. Many Late Bronze–Iron I sites were not destroyed at all; of those that were, more must be attributed to the Philistines or to unknown causes than to any groups to be identified as Israelite. (1990, 61)

Finally, in a later publication Dever was, if anything, even more emphatic in his conclusions:

> We must confront the fact that the external material evidence supports *almost nothing* (emphasis original) of the biblical account of a large-scale, concerted Israelite military invasion of Canaan, either that of Numbers east of the Jordan, or of Joshua west of the Jordan. Of the more than forty sites that the biblical texts claim were conquered, no more than two or three of those that have been archaeologically investigated are even potential candidates for such an Israelite destruction in the entire period from ca. 1250–1150 BCE. (2003a, 71)

While it may be true that the stories in the conquest traditions preserve in some instances old collective memories passed down basically through oral tradition (Mazar 2003, 85–89, for some suggestions), all such suggestions are only guesses. We have no "oral tradition" today, only texts: the books known to us that were written centuries after the events supposedly took place, and then from an ideological/theological perspective. What seems to be certain is that the stories in Joshua (as well as Numbers and Judges) cannot be taken at face value.

In 1999, Block-Smith and Nakhai published a thorough study of Iron Age I (c. 1200–1000 BCE; also called the Early Iron Age). Their conclusions vis-à-vis the dramatic changes seen in the archaeological record of sites dating to this period also deserve to be quoted in full:

> There is no easy reconstruction of the Israelite conquest and settlement based on *combined* [emphasis original] archaeological and biblical evidence. *Were it not for the Bible* [my emphasis], no late thirteenth-early twelfth century Israelite invasion would be suspected. For the most part, languages, dress, pottery, architecture, and cultural features demonstrate continuity from LBA into the Iron Age. Early "Israelite" access to perennial water sources necessitated a working relationship with the autochthonous populations. While towns and cities were destroyed in the appropriate period, they do not necessarily correspond to the cities allegedly destroyed by the "Israelites." In addition, no one can prove that the "Israelites" were the agents of destruction. Cities prominently mentioned in the biblical account, such as Jericho and 'Ai, were not even settled in the period preceding the new Iron I settlements. Neither of those sites has produced an appropriate destruction level. The conquest of Canaan by a unified "Israel" as described in Joshua 2–12 *is unsubstantiated* [my emphasis]. The bulk of the archaeological evidence points to small-scale, peaceful settlement both in the vicinity of LBA Canaanite sites and in more remote regions. The biblical authors of Iron II may have chosen to emphasize conflict in order to legitimate monarchial territorial acquisition. Similarly, they may have co-opted past and contemporary destructions, attributing them to early Israelites as means of creating a national history. (118–19)

3. Archaeological surveys. Perhaps the most important advance in archaeological methodology and interpretation of "Israel's" origins emerged during the 1970s after the Six-Day War of 1967. Briefly mentioned above, this advance was due to systematic surveys of Palestine that began in the 1970s and were conducted over a period of several years. While such surveys must be used with caution and can lead to questionable conclusions, they have proven to be of immense value in the attempt to understand what "actually happened" in Canaan during the period under discussion (Miller 1992; Dever 2003a, 91–100; Banning 2003, 164–67). Particularly important for this study are the surveys conducted by Israeli archeologists such as Finkelstein (1988a) and Adam Zertal (1980–81; *NEAEHL* 375–77). The surveys, conducted in Galilee in the north and southward to the northern

Negev, as well as parts of central and northern Transjordan, clearly revealed that during the Late Bronze Age–Iron Age I period (1250–1150 BCE), hundreds of new small sites were established in the central-hill regions (Finkelstein 1988a; Finkelstein 2007c, 67–98, part 3; Stager 1998; Dever 2003a, 91–100; Finkelstein and Na'aman). What was learned from these surveys "totally revolutionized our understanding of the origins of ancient Israel" (Dever 2003a, 92). Most of these new sites were small, unwalled villages of no more than one or two acres in size. While it is sophisticated guesswork at best, one of the most significant consequences of these surveys is the population estimate for these newly established sites. In all, nine areas were surveyed: upper and lower Galilee, the central hills of Samaria and Ephraim, in Benjamin and Judah, the northern Negev, and parts of central and northern Transjordan (Mazar 2007a, 85). It was discovered that in the preceding Late Bronze Age, 88 settlements occupied around 500 acres with a total population estimate of around 50,000. In the same areas (particularly the central hills and plateaus) during Iron I, 678 sites were discovered, 633 (93 percent) of which were built on virgin soil. These occupied around 1,500 acres of built-up area with an estimated population of 150,000 (Stager 1998, 94–102). Finkelstein has drawn, perhaps, the most radical conclusion from these surveys relevant to the question of the origins of ancient "Israel":

> These surveys provide us with invaluable information on the number of sites, their size, the number of inhabitants, and their location, including the economic factors that dictated their distribution . . . . As far as I can judge, the rise of early Israel was not a unique event in the history of Canaan. Rather, it was another repeated phase in a long-term cyclic, socio-economic, and demographic process that started in the fourth millennium BCE. The wave of settlement that took place in the highlands in the late-second millennium BCE was merely another chapter in alternating shifts along the typical Near Eastern socio-economic continuum between sedentary and pastoral modes of subsistence. (Finkelstein 2007, 75–76)

And again:

> In the [biblical] text you have the story of Israelites coming from outside, and then besieging the Canaanite cities, destroying them and then becoming a nation in the land of Canaan, whereas archaeology tells something which is the opposite. According to archaeology *the rise of early Israel is an outcome of the collapse of Canaanite society, not the reason for that collapse.* (2008, my emphasis)

If Finkelstein's as well as other scholars' similar conclusions are valid and reliable, all claims of a pan-Israelite invasion from the Transjordan regions by Joshua should now be abandoned. Prior has clearly and succinctly stated the critical conclusions drawn from such studies as Finkelstein's:

> A historiography of Israelite origins based solely, or primarily, on the biblical narratives *is an artificial construct* determined by certain religious motivations obtaining at a time long post-dating any verifiable evidence of the events. The way forward is to write a comprehensive independent history of the Near East into which the Israelite history of origins should be fitted. While there is nothing like a scholarly consensus in the array of recent studies on Israel's origins, there is virtual unanimity that the model of a tribal conquest as narrated in Joshua 1–12 is untenable. Leaving aside the witness of the Bible, *we have no evidence that there was a Hebrew conquest.* Moreover, there is a virtual scholarly consensus that the biblical narratives which describe the conquest settlement period come from authors writing many centuries later than the "events" described (whether in the exilic or postexilic periods) who had no reliable information about the distant past. (1999, 250–51, my emphasis; compare Na'aman 1994, 246–47)

In addition, both Dever and Finkelstein have also argued for the non-historical character not only of the "Conquest" but also of the "Exodus" story. It should be obvious that if there were no "exodus" of biblical proportions, there was certainly no "conquest" as described in the Bible (compare Grabbe 2007, 84–88 for similar conclusions regarding an "exodus"). In his latest book (as of mid 2012), Dever concluded,

> All histories of Israelite religion have been little more than histories of the literature *about* that religion. *The Hebrew Bible, written by elitists (and propagandists)*, is an ideal portrait, not of what most people actually believed and practiced—and would have, had these theologians, these nationalist orthodox parties, been in charge. The Hebrew Bible is thus best considered as a "minority report." The real report—the more accurate portrait—is the one that we can and must now derive from information supplied by modern archaeology. (2012, 287, emphasis original)

How much of this current archaeological theorizing will influence the general public's understanding and use of the book of Joshua (as well as the Hebrew Bible in its totality) is questionable. The "gap" between the academic study of these issues and what passes for biblical study in the general public seems wider than ever (see above). None of this, of course, will dissuade those who approach the Bible with the unquestioned assumption that the biblical stories are literally true. But barring the possible, but unlikely, event of new epigraphic discoveries from the Late Bronze Age dealing specifically with events mentioned in the biblical stories, the only sources of new information that can further clarify our understanding of the so-called "Conquest" of Palestine by the "Israelites" is archaeological (Laughlin 2006; Dever 2012, inter alia). No doubt new archaeological discoveries will impact future studies just as they have already altered radically, in some instances, past conclusions. This is an open-ended search requiring the drawing of tentative conclusions. This realization indicates that all research/writing, no matter how up to date it may seem at the moment, is doomed to becoming dated. This is why every generation needs to rethink, and in most cases revise, if not throw out, the conclusions of previous generations (see Preface above).

Many questions still remain: How did the cult of Yahweh originate? When can such terms as "Israelite" and "Canaanite" actually be used to describe real ethnic entities rather than being used anachronistically by the biblical editors (Dever 1992, 54; Killebrew 2005, inter alia; Faust 2007, inter alia)? Why did the "Canaanites" move from the lowlands into the highlands of Palestine during the Iron Age I?

Extra-Biblical Textual Witnesses

Another critical tool that needs to be in anyone's intellectual travel bag for a journey through Joshua is an awareness of, and appreciation for, what is known and not known about biblical Israel from non-biblical texts (translations of significant non-biblical texts can be found in the *ANET*; Thomas; and Chavalas). One way of asking the question regarding these extra-biblical texts is this: If there were no Bible, only ancient inscriptions from Israel's neighbors such as Egypt and Assyria, what could be said historically about "Israel"? We begin with the earliest claimed non-biblical inscription containing the word "Israel": The Merneptah Stele. (Recently Manfred Görg, an Egyptologist, reported finding in the British Museum a fourteenth century BCE hieroglyphic inscription on a broken granite piece of a statue's pedestal that contained the name "Israel." A controversy has already arisen, not so much about the date of the inscription, but about the hieroglyphic translated as "Israel." If the claim is upheld by other scholars, this would become the oldest known non-biblical reference to "Israel"; Shanks.)

1. The Merneptah Stele. The earliest non-biblical reference to "Israel" is on the now famous Merneptah Stele that is dated to the last decade of the thirteenth century BCE. Sir Flinders Petrie discovered it in 1896 in Egypt in Merneptah's temple located in Thebes, and it is now housed in the Cairo museum. The inscription is a long hymn celebrating Merneptah's military victories over a variety of enemies. Toward the end of the inscription, it reads, "Plundered is the Canaan with every evil; carried off is Ashkelon; seized upon is Gezer; Yanoam is made as that which does not exist; Israel is laid waste, his seed is not" (*ANET*, 378).

While scholars have long sought a possible connection of the "Israel" mention on the stele with the "Israel" of the Bible, most of the discussion of any such connection is little more than unproven conjecture (for a full discussion of issues and scholarly suggestions see Hasel 1994; 2008, 47–59; Dever 2003a, 201–208; Faust 2007, 159–66). Without assuming the historicity of the biblical story of the "exodus" out of Egypt and the "conquest" of Canaan by the "Israelites" in advance, there is nothing on the stela to suggest that the *biblical stories* ever took place. This is not to deny the importance of this inscription, and the following cautionary note by McNutt should be taken seriously:

> The Merneptah stela . . . provides us with evidence that some entity called Israel existed in the latter part of the thirteenth century B.C.E., but at present it provides no clear answer of what that entity was, what its size or internal organization was, what the sources and socioeconomic status of its members were, or how, or even if, this "Israel" is related to the Israel depicted in the stories in the Pentateuch or the books of Joshua and Judges. (McNutt, 44–45; but see Faust, 2006, 159–66)

Arguments supporting the identification of Merneptah's "Israel" with biblical "Israel" are circular at best. A footnote in the *ANET* (378, n. 18) following the part of the inscription quoted above reads,

> Much has been made of the fact that the word Israel is the only one of the names in this context that is written with the determinative of people other than land. Thus we should seem to have *the children of Israel* in or near Palestine, but not yet as settled people. This would have important bearing on the date of the Conquest. *This is a valid argument.* (my emphasis)

Well, not exactly. This quote is a perfect example of a circular argument that has been defined as ". . . generating a cultural and historical 'reality' from a text and then turning around and trying to understand the same text in relation to the background that was reconstructed from it" (McNutt, 3). Thus the above argument begins with the uncritical assumption that the reference to the "children of Israel" mentioned in the "conquest story" in the Bible is the same "Israel" supposedly found on the Merneptah stele. Then this generated "cultural and historical reality" given to the stele's "Israel" based solely on the story of the "biblical Israel" is used as evidence for the biblical conquest by this same "children of Israel"! In point of fact, neither "Israel" implies or proves the other.

Miller (1991, 94) has voiced similar skepticism as McNutt's. Such skepticism seems justified when one appreciates the fact that after the ambiguous reference to "Israel" on Merneptah's stele, it is a good 350 years later before the name "Israel" is found on any other non-biblical inscriptions. In fact, this 350-year gap between 1200 to around 850 BCE has been called a "Dark Age" (Van de Mieroop, 201–206; compare Redford, 257–80). The next mentions of "Israel" on extra-biblical inscriptions all date to the last half of the ninth century BCE: the Mesha Inscription (a.k.a "The Moabite Stone"), two Assyrian inscriptions, and the Tel Dan Stele.

2. The Mesha Stele (Moabite Stone). The "Mesha Stele," also known as the "Moabite Stone," was found in Moab in 1868 and is dated between 855–830 BCE (Schmidt, 2006a). It celebrates King Mesha's victory over the Israelites and mentions by name "Omri, king of Israel": "As for Omri, king of Israel, he humbled Moab many years, for Chemosh was angry at his hand. And his son followed him and he also said, 'I will humble Moab.' In my time he spoke (thus) but I have triumphed over him and over his house, while Israel hath perished forever!" (*ANET*, 320).

Omri is dated from around 886–875 and his son, Ahab, to 875–853 BCE. This is the oldest non-biblical reference to any king associated with "biblical Israel," and it dates over 350 years after Merneptah's stela and well over a hundred years after David supposedly lived. Omri was the most important king Israel had, attested to by the fact that for over a hundred years after his death the Assyrians still referred to Israel as "Omri's land" (*ANET*, 283, 284, 285). It should also be noted in passing that the Mesha inscription also contains the first non-biblical mention of "Yahweh," the god of Israel (line 18).

The Bible gives Omri all of thirteen verses, just enough for the Dtr to condemn him in classic Deuteronomistic theology: "Omri did what was evil in the sight of Yahweh; he did more evil than *all* who were before him. For he walked in *all* the way of Jeroboam son of Nebat, and in the sins that he caused Israel to commit, provoking Yahweh, the god of Israel, to anger by their idols" (1 Kgs 16:25-26). This is classic Deuteronomistic "theology" speaking, not "history."

3. The Tel Dan Stele. In July 1993, a fragment of an Aramaic inscription, called now the "Tel Dan Stele," was found at Tel Dan, a large mound located in northern Israel on the Syrian-Lebanese borders. Its excavator, A. Biran (1909–2008), dated it to the last half of the ninth century BCE (Biran and Naveh 1993; other scholars date it to the early eighth century BCE; see also Finkelstein and Silberman 2006, 261–66; Schmidt, 2006b). The inscription celebrates a victory over Dan by the king of Damascus. According to the story recorded in 1 Kings 15:20, Ben-hadad captured Dan during his reign as king. Consequently, Biran concluded that the conquering king mentioned on the stele was, in fact, Ben-hadad. Others have suggested later kings, particularly Hazael, Ben-hadad's son (Schniedewind, 1996; Finkelstein and Silberman 2006, 261–66), or Bar Hadad II, Hazael's successor (Athas 2005). Regardless of the precise date or which king was intended, the stele is of upmost importance because of one word in line 9 from the top. It is the word *bytdvd*, translated by most scholars who have studied the stele as the "house of David," that is, the dynasty of David (see for example, Isa 7:1, 13; note also that Athas suggested that the word should be translated as the "city of David"). But also of much importance is the stele's reference to the "*king of Israel*" in line 8 of Fragment A. Which king of Israel is a matter of dispute and depends on when the inscription is actually dated. Thus the Israelite king could be anyone from Jehoram (c. 852–841 BCE) to Jehoahaz (c. 814–805 BCE). The Judahite king could be anyone from J(eh)oram II (c. 849–841 BCE) to Joash I (c. 841[835]–796 BCE). According to the biblical story, Joash's mother, Athaliah, who may have been the daughter of Jezebel (1 Kgs 8:26), usurped the Judean throne around 841 BCE. Six years later she was assassinated, and Joash was restored to his rightful place and reigned, so we are told, for nearly forty more years (1 Kgs 11:1-16). If the name of the Judean king could be known for sure, it would be the first clearly named king known from Judah in a non-biblical text.

The Tel Dan Stele may contain the only mention of the name "David" in any source other than the Bible. However, based on this inscription, some scholars have suggested that a broken line (12) in the Mesha inscription also makes reference to the "House of David" (Chavalas, 312–15). If so, then the phrase "House of David" is twice mentioned outside the Bible, and both date to the same century. Neither of these inscriptions, of course, confirms in any way what the Bible claims "David" did or said, nor do they offer any new information about him. But they do imply that a hundred and forty years or so after David, Judean kings belonged to a dynastic line traced back to him (Finkelstein and Silberman 2006, 265–66). Regardless of how these arguments pan out, the point here is that after the mention of "Israel" in the Merneptah Stela, it is over 350 years later before any other non-biblical inscription mentioning "Israel" appears.

4. The Assyrian Inscriptions of the Late Ninth Century BCE. Important inscriptions date to the reign of the Assyrian king, Shalmanezer III (858–824 BCE). One is called the "Kurkh Monolith" found in Turkey that dates to c. 853 BCE. This Inscription mentions the "house of Omri" (*mat Huum-ri*; *ANET*, 281). Another inscription, the Black Obelisk, found at Nimrud in modern-day Iraq, mentions a certain *Ia-u'-a Hu-umri*, translated as "Jehu, son of Omri" (*ANET*, 281). While neither of these texts specifically mentions "Israel," it is probably a valid deduction that the "Omri" mention here is the same "Omri" on the Mesha inscription. But without the biblical story, not much else could be said of this king or of Israel. Miller has pointed out for some time that without assuming the biblical stories in advance, it is unlikely that such obscure references in these ninth-century Assyrian texts would receive the attention they have by biblical scholars (1977, 1991, 1991, and 2003). His conclusion in his 1991 essay deserves repeating:

> While it is theoretically possible to write a history of early Israel without relying on the Hebrew Bible, the result would be a very thin volume indeed and would have little in common with the current discussion. Anytime historians, archaeologists, sociologists, or whoever speak of Israelite tribes settling the central Palestinian hill country during Iron I or any sort of Israelite monarchy before the 9th century BCE, they are assuming information derived from the Hebrew Bible. (101)

Later important Assyrian texts that date to the last half of the eighth century BCE refer to both Israel and Judah, and Babylonian texts that date to the exilic period contain references to Judah, but they need not be detailed here. (Information on all of these non-biblical, as well as biblical, texts can be found in Kitchen 2003, esp. 32–51, and in Chavalas 2006, inter alia.)

All of the above caveats are not meant to imply that nothing of historical value can be gleaned from a critical analysis of the biblical texts. But until, and unless, older non-biblical inscriptions containing undisputed references to "Israel" are discovered, the question still remains: if "Israel" was such a major political force as stories in the Pentateuch (such as the exodus), Joshua, and Judges clearly imply, why are there no extra-biblical references to it known for over 350 years after Merneptah? One could counter-argue that this is an argument "from silence." And technically it is. But it is not unreasonable to expect something over such a long time span if Israel, as portrayed in the biblical stories, actually existed as described. On the other hand, it is not an axiomatic truth that biblical texts can be taken at face value either. For the conquest story, the question then becomes how historically reliable is the Hebrew Bible, especially for such books as Joshua? Can the Bible be used constructively when dealing with such stories as the "exodus" and the "conquest?" Using the biblical stories to identify the ethnicity of the Iron Age I people who settled in the central-hill country as "Israelites," then turning around and using this created "cultural and historical reality" assigned to the material remains as evidence of the "conquest of the central-hill country by Joshua and the Israelites," is totally circular. Maybe any argument put forth to locate and identify the ethnicity of the Iron Age I inhabitants of the central-hill country involves some circularity (for a recent example of the same kind of circular argument despite all attempts to avoid it, see Bunimovitz and Faust 2010). The issue is not whether the Bible is going to be used in any attempt to understand the archaeological data coming from excavations or surveys that seem relevant to the questions. But how is it going to be used? W. G. Dever contends,

> The critical issue for biblical archaeology, properly conceived as a dialogue, has always been (and is even more so now) its understanding and use of archaeology on the one hand, its understanding of the issues in the biblical stories that are fitting subjects for archaeological illumination on the other hand and the proper *relationship* between the two. (2010, 355; repeated from 1985, 61, emphasis original; however, in the 1985 version, the word "between" was emphasized by Dever, not "relationship")

How does one explain such a long period of silence if "Israel" was a major ethnic group already well established by Iron I in the central-hill country of Canaan? What is the relationship, if any, between the "Israel" in these extra-biblical texts, including the ambiguous "Israel" on the Merneptah Stela, and the Iron I settlers in the central highlands of Canaan (Mazar 2007, 93–94; Na'aman 1994, 247–49; Rainy and Notley, 118–22; Faust 2006, 2007)? From the above discussion, it should be obvious that the scholarly debate over the ethnogenesis of Israel is far from over. A perusal of the sources listed above will at least acquaint one with the many important questions and issues that have been raised by those participating in this conversation while at the same time highlighting the differences that still exist among scholars. Nevertheless, on one issue, all or at least most of the above specialists do agree: the military model presented in the pages of Joshua has lost all credibility.

The Literary Nature of Joshua

As alluded to above, the question of the authorship of Joshua is complex and involves other books of the Bible. Moreover, most critical scholars of the Bible have concluded that the book of Joshua belongs to what scholars since the seminal work of M. Noth (in the early 1940s) have called "The Deuteronomistic History of Israel," hereafter DH (Weinfeld; Mayes, 1999; McKenzie 1992, 2007; Rowlett, 30–48; Knoppers and McConville 2000; Coote 2005, 94–103; Kofoed; Na'aman 2006, and many more could be added to this list). This "history" comprises Joshua, Judges, 1 and 2 Samuel, and 1 and 2 Kings. G. N. Knoppers has succinctly described the DH as ". . . a modern theoretical construct which holds that the books of Deuteronomy, Joshua, Judges, Samuel, and Kings constitute a single work, unified by a basic homogeneity in language, style, and content" (1). Thus theoretically the DH covers over six hundred years in scope: circa 1250–587 BCE. While some scholars have argued for a first edition of DH dating to the time of King Josiah (c. 640–609 BCE; for example, Nelson 1981a, 1981b; see also a brief history of the discussion in Rowlett), it is now generally accepted among critical scholars that the DH reached its final form sometime during the Babylonian Exile (586–539 BCE) or shortly thereafter, perhaps as late as the fifth century BCE. However, it has been well argued that an earlier edition or redaction of Joshua was produced during the time of Josiah (see references to Nelson and Rowlett above; both with extensive bibliographies). On this take, Joshua was an "ideological document" (Rowlett, 44) written to support Josiah's violent reforms recorded in 2 Kings 23:1-25. Here Josiah is portrayed as being in a power struggle with religious leaders throughout the land reaching from "Geba to Beer-sheba" (2 Kgs 23:8). In order to gain control of Judah and rid his empire of those who were accused of abandoning Yahweh and his covenant, Josiah engaged in a violent crusade. According to R. Coote, "Joshua is molded on Josiah and his conquest on Josiah's murderous rampage through the highland in the attempt to recover the glory of David's kingdom" (1990, 164).

For those scholars who believe that the book of Joshua was produced at this time by the Deuteronomic Historian or Redactor (Dtr), Joshua was invented as a kind of "stand-in" (Rowlett, 174) for Josiah, who, as Yahweh's earthly representative, violently destroyed the "outsiders," just as Joshua did centuries earlier. To quote Rowlett, the Dtr "seems to believe in a hierarchical society with the king, or someone standing in his place, as the leader, as the chosen by Yahweh (Moses, Joshua, Deborah, Samuel, and so forth) functioning as a necessary hinge in the divine-human relationship" (54).

Moreover, it has been shown that the image of a divine warrior fighting for his people was not unique to Israel but was widespread throughout the ancient Near East. This is especially so in the texts of the neo-Assyrian Empire (c. 934–609 BCE; Rowlett, 71–120; for Assyria, 100–19). In 627 BCE, the empire began to disintegrate due to civil wars, and by 612 Nineveh, its capital city, had been destroyed. In the meantime Josiah had become king in Judah around 640 BCE at the ripe old age of nine and ruled until his death in 609 BCE. Thus the turmoil going on in the Assyrian Empire created an ideal time for Josiah's reformation. It will be assumed in what follows that even though the final form of the DH derived from the time of the Babylonian Exile or later, the book of Joshua best fits with the time of Josiah. In any case, it is important to keep in mind that the DH, regardless of how many redactions there may have been, reflects not the viewpoints and beliefs of the people who supposedly existed during the periods in which the stories have been placed but rather the ideology/theology of the author(s) who wrote the books centuries later. These Deuteronomistic author(s)/editor(s) of the DH will be referred to in this commentary by the symbol Dtr, regardless of how many there might have been. At the moment, the DH is the best literary theory we have to explain the material in Joshua through 2 Kings. It is thus incumbent upon those wishing to understand Joshua to the fullest extent possible to be informed concerning Deuteronomic methodology (see references above, esp. Knoppers and McConville, for a collection of essays that present various views on the DH).

An important methodological motif found in DH, as mentioned above, is the use of "speeches" to express the ideology/theology of the Dtr. These "speeches" are of two kinds: "reported speeches" that are put into the mouths of the characters in the story such as the "speech" given by Yahweh in the opening chapter of Joshua (1:2-9, compare the "reported speech" of Moses in Deut 1 with the "reported speech" of Joshua in Josh 1:10-15). Such "speeches" are easily recognized in English translations because they are always enclosed in quotation marks. Thus the moniker "reported speech" because the Dtr is claiming that these speeches are the exact words spoken by the characters in whose mouth they are placed. The other type of "speeches" used by the Dtr are called "reporting speeches." Today these might well be called "editorial" speeches, for through these "speeches" the Dtr gave voice to his own interpretation of why events happened as they did. Almost always these speeches deal with the themes of "obedience" versus "disobedience," "covenant," and "law of Moses." These are basic theological motifs found throughout Joshua through Kings (see especially Deut 27–30). The entire DH is made up of one example after another where obedience leads to success (as in the "conquest" story), and where disobedience leads to disaster (examples abound: Judg 2:11-23, a classic "reporting speech" by the Dtr; compare the Dtr's "theological" reason why Saul failed: 1 Sam 15:10-31; finally, see the "reporting speech" about why both Israel and Judah were ultimately destroyed: 2 Kgs 17:7-23).

While this hypothesis of the DH seems to be universally accepted by critical scholars of the Bible, other, more conservative scholars reject most of it (Kitchen 2003, 234, where he flippantly dismissed the idea of a Deuteronomistic History as a "disease"), primarily because of the fact that if the hypothesis is correct, it means that the form of the books as we now have them is the creation of scribes who lived centuries after the events described in the books supposedly took place. One of the obvious questions then raised is how historically reliable can such stories, including that of the "conquest," be if they were composed centuries after such "events" supposedly occurred? This question is especially relevant to the discussion when it is remembered that the scribes who wrote it did so from a biased theological/ideological agenda. Scholars differ widely on what parts of this "history" may contain older, popular traditions that may have been passed on orally for a long time. But trying to decide which parts may belong to this earlier period has often created as much heat as light. Trying to recover earlier, older pericopes from the stories as we now have them has been compared to trying to unscramble an omelet (Leach, 24)! The DH attempts to come to terms with the situation that existed during the time of Josiah and the Babylonian Exile (end of the 7th century, beginning of the 6th century BCE) or perhaps later for its final redaction. Towards the end of the eighth century BCE, the Assyrians destroyed the kingdom of Israel, and 135 years later the same fate awaited the kingdom of Judah at the hands of the Babylonians. Ultimately, the DH should be understood as a theological attempt to explain the destructions of these two petty states as the result of the constant disobedience of the peoples of Yahweh throughout their long history (1 Kgs 17:7-41). The story ends with a note clearly implying the death of King Jehoiakin, Judah's last Davidic monarch (2 Kgs 25:27-30). Whatever hopes the Dtr had for a restoration of the Davidic empire presumably died with Jehoiakin.

While it may be true as a starting assumption that the Bible should play an important role in any attempt to reconstruct the "history of Israel," this role is not equally important for all periods. It would seem to be the case that the further one goes back in time, the less reliable, historically speaking, the Bible becomes. In fact, the results of many years of archaeological discoveries in the southern Levant have shown that there is almost no archaeological data that can support the historicity of the so-called Patriarchal period (as well as the exodus/conquest stories). Most mainstream scholars today interpret these stories as legendary folktales. The "exodus" story is seen as mostly fictional as is the story of a pan-Israelite "conquest" that resulted in the slaughter of all the "Canaanites" in a military invasion originating in the Transjordan (on the issue of migrants entering Cisjordan from the area east of the Jordan River see Van der Steen, 1996). The critical question now becomes not one of historical reliability but one of ideological intent. Why was this "history" written in the manner that we now know it? For whom was it written and with what expectations? The intent here is to examine the book of Joshua as critically as our tools will allow and let any interested readers make up their own minds regarding the book's theological value, if any. M. Z. Brettler has summarized the difficulty and ambiguity that accompanies any attempt to reconstruct Israelite history from biblical texts:

> . . . biblical exegetes and historians should be more sensitive to the problems of recreating the history of ancient Israel. They should develop more tentative, open-ended readings to biblical texts which take into account various possible historical situations which stand behind the text. This is difficult to accomplish . . . . Though modern historians cannot always know whether the biblical historical texts are even attempting to describe the actual past, they must not give up, and must continue to apply the general criteria used by historians to decide which of the alternative reconstructions of the Israelite past best fits the evidence. This evidence is not always univocal; this explains, for example, why the current debate concerning competing reconstructions of such fundamental past events as the sojourn of the Israelites in Egypt or the settlement/conquest of Canaan will continue . . . . To repeat the opening words of the chapter, "let us learn to live with ambiguity." (144; the quote is from Redford, 311)

If Joshua stands at the beginning of a "theological history" that ends with the last king of Judah in captivity (2 Kgs 25:29-30), the situation that ultimately called forth the final redaction of this long "history" was the Babylonian Exile (598–539 BCE). What sources, oral or written, the editor(s) had are unknown. Scholars have speculated that the editor(s) had at his (their) disposal older traditions, folktales, etiologies, and so forth. However this discussion turns out or whatever might have been the original intent of such supposed older traditions, our focus is on the use the Dtr put to them. This especially concerns any theological interpretation given the stories by the final editor(s). In fact, it is questionable whether or not these traditions had any theological meaning before their adaptation by the final author(s).

It will be assumed throughout this brief commentary that the original audience for whom Joshua was first written was the literate elite during the time of King Josiah, and that a short time later it was redacted for the remnants of the Judean community who were taken into exile in the early part of the sixth century BCE, or (possibly) their survivors from the time of Ezra-Nehemiah (the exact date for Ezra-Nehemiah is a matter of critical discussion, but scholars widely accept sometime during the fifth century BCE; for example, Butler, xxiii–xxvii). However, who would have actually ever heard of, much less "read," the book of Joshua is impossible to answer. It has been suggested that the DH may have been read in the context of public gatherings, but its length suggests otherwise (Rowlett, 47). Rowlett's own suggestion that the DH was "aimed at an audience who would have been among the leadership in diverse areas of life" (48) is extremely vague and is only a suggestion for which there is no supporting evidence as of yet. How would the literate of the day have even been aware of such a document, and how would they have obtained a copy? While it would seem common sense to suggest that the DH was written with some audience in mind, who exactly would have read it centuries ago is simply unknown.

Furthermore, the literary forms comprising the book of Joshua are complex and varied. They include speeches, etiologies, historicized cultic celebrations or liturgical stories, tribal boundary descriptions and city lists, and "miracle" stories (for example, Jericho). The first twelve chapters of the book have also been identified as "campaign reports" known from Assyrian texts, particularly those dating from the time of Esarhaddon (681–669 BCE) and his son, Ashurbanipal (668–627 BCE; Van Seters; Rowlett, 70–120). Here it will be assumed that Joshua is the first book in the long DH.

Ultimately the book of Joshua appears to be a kind of "novella," and a very violent one at that, written to impress upon its intended readers or listeners that Joshua was the legitimate successor of Moses, Yahweh's representative on earth, and that whatever they might have believed up to their present moment, Israel's existence in the land of Canaan had always been ambiguous and tenuous—made possible only by their god's undeserved acts of grace and a creative and dynamic application of the laws of Moses. How much "real history" can be gleaned from this story is another issue altogether.

It is customary to divide the book into three major but unequal sections: chapters 1–12, which treat the theme of conquest; chapters 13–19, which describe the division of the land among the tribes; and chapters 20–24, which include several stories, including two "farewell speeches" by Joshua, that close the book.

The Hebrew Text of Joshua

Textual criticism of the Bible is a technical discipline that stretches back at least as early as the second century CE (for a general introduction to the discipline see Tov; both Nelson 1997 and Butler contain helpful textual notes in their commentaries on Joshua; Greenspoon offers a technical analysis of the text of Joshua). Max L. Margolis produced the standard critical work on the book of Joshua in Greek (hereafter, LXX), titled *The Book of Joshua in Greek.* There are many textual difficulties in Joshua that raise numerous questions concerning the history and validity of the different textual traditions. A comparison of the Hebrew (the Masoretic Text: MT) with the Greek text (the Septuagint: LXX) highlights these differences. The LXX was translated in Egypt during the third–second centuries BCE from a Hebrew text quite different from the standard MT that was produced by the Tiberian scribal families of ben Asher and ben Naphtali (sixth–eleventh centuries CE). In the twelfth century CE, the Jewish philosopher Maimonides declared the textual products of the ben Asher family normative for Judaism. A critical edition of this textual tradition lies behind all English translations of the Bible, the latest edition of which is called *Biblical Hebraica Stuttgartensia* and was published in Stuttgart by the Deutsche Bibelgesellschaft in 1983. In addition to the publications listed above, for those who have a working knowledge of Hebrew, Auld (1998) has also published a collection of technical but insightful essays on textual issues found in the book of Joshua.

While the original manuscripts of the Hebrew Bible, the oldest of which are among the Dead Sea Scrolls that date to the third–second centuries BCE, were divided into books from earliest times, the chapter and verse numbers used in modern translations did not appear before the late Middle Ages (1300–1500 CE). People in biblical times did not speak in numbered chapters and verses any more than you and I do. The translations of the Hebrew text cited in this commentary, including the entire MT of Joshua, are the author's own unless otherwise noted. The traditional numbering of verses used in most English translations of the Bible, such as the NRSV, will be used here in order to facilitate easy references to particular parts of the biblical text.

Yahweh and ’^{e}*lohim*

Translating from one language into another language is not as easy as it might sound to someone who has never had to do it. Oftentimes it is only by context and familiarity with the word being translated that an appropriate corresponding word can be found in the other language. While there are many problems in translating the Hebrew text of Joshua into English, two Hebrew words in particular call for clarification. First, I will refrain from using the traditional English word “LORD” (all uppercase) to translate a frequent Hebrew expression that literally reads in English, “Yahweh (יהוה : *yhwh*) the god of Israel” or some variant thereof (unless I am making a direct quote in which the word “God” [upper case “G”] occurs). In most English translations of the Bible (one exception is the NJB) where the MT reads “Yahweh,” the personal name for the deity of Israel, the English word “LORD” is substituted and all four letters are in uppercase. Jewish scribes introduced this substitution of “LORD” for “Yahweh” sometime after the Babylonian Exile (586–539 BCE) in part to avoid violating the commandment, “you will not take the name of *Yahweh*, your god in vain.” One way of trying to keep this commandment is by not saying the name at all. The word “lord” is not part of the original MT. One more text-critical note: these substitute readings are called the *qere* (Heb., ירק), which means “to say,” and were written by the scribes in the margins of the manuscripts. The word that is actually in the MT for which the *qere* is being substituted is called the *k*^{e}*thib* (Heb., כְתב, what is “written”). In this instance, if the *qere* (Heb., אדני : *adonay*) were literally translated, it would read “My Lord.” Since such a translation would be a little clumsy in English, just “LORD” is used.

Particular attention needs to be paid to the English word, “God” (uppercase “G”), that occurs in English translations of the MT when referring to the god of Israel. The Hebrew word, more than any other, translated as “God” (uppercase “G”) into English is ’^{e}*lohim* (אלהים). This word occurs over 2,600 times in the MT (Ringgren; Seow) and is a masculine plural Hebrew noun that literally means “gods,” or “deities.” The names used in the Hebrew Bible for the Israelite god have long been a topic of scholarly discussion (Seow; for the most up-to-date publications on this topic see now Smith 2001, 2002). The word ’^{e}*lohim* is first encountered in the Bible in Genesis 1:1: “In the beginning ’^{e}*lohim* . . . .” It is used throughout the Hebrew Bible to describe Yahweh as well as the “gods” of Israel’s neighbors. In point of fact, there are three different “**el**” words used to speak of the Israelite god in the MT: אל *’el*; אֱלוֹהַ *’eloah*, and אלהים ’^{e}*lohim*. *Eloah* occurs only 57 times in the MT, 41 of which are in the book of Job. ***El*** is the name of the chief or senior god of the Canaanite pantheon of which Yahweh, the personal name of

Israel's tribal deity, was a subordinate warrior god (Smith 2002, 32–43; Deut 32:8-9). *El* was also the first god of *Isra-el* (this name means "*El* strives" or "contends"; for an in-depth discussion of "el" see Cross). At what point Yahweh and *El* merged is unclear, but Smith suggested it may have occurred during the Iron Age I and perhaps at different rates in different places (2001, 147; already in Num 23:8 *El* and Yahweh are the same god; compare the Hebrew text in 2 Sam 22:32 and Ps 82).

Because the Hebrew Bible is often translated by those motivated more by Christian apologetics than they are by grammatical/ textual/historical issues, such distinctions as discussed here are frequently ignored and, where the Israelite deity is concerned, hidden behind one English word, God, with an uppercase "G." I am not a Christian apologist, so that will not be the path followed here. When one of these *el* names appears in the text describing Yahweh, it will simply be translated into English as "god" (lowercase "g") except in rare instances where *el* is the proper name of the Canaanite god, El. The most common appellative used with Yahweh in Joshua is, in fact, *'elohim.* This noun is usually translated in English Bibles with its correct plural meaning, *gods* (lowercase "g"), only when referring to the "*gods*" of Israel's foes or neighbors (see below). However, when this word refers to Yahweh it is translated in the singular, "*god*," with upper case "G." Israel was originally a polytheistic society (Smith 2001, esp., 135–94), and perhaps that had something to do with using the masculine plural form when full-blown monotheism emerged during the exilic period. Nonetheless, why the final authors/editors of the Hebrew Scriptures continued using a plural form when there were other options is still not clear. It has been suggested by some scholars that this plural noun when used as an appellative for Yahweh represents a "plural of majesty." But this suggestion brings up other theological questions and ignores the ambiguity created by using this noun to describe the god of Israel. Perhaps a better explanation is that these common Hebrew words ultimately achieved the force of proper names (Seow, 589). Whatever the case may be, my intent here is to encourage English readers to *slow down* and read the text closely instead of assuming that the ancient Hebrews were already talking about what normally passes for our own contemporary understanding of our English word "God" (always with uppercase "G"). When someone living in ancient Judah and/or Israel during the Iron Age II (c. 900–586 BCE, archaeologically the main period of the Hebrew Bible) heard the word *'elohim* (most people could not have *read* it), it is most unlikely that they would have given it the same connotations that people today do when they hear the word "god" (if you only "hear" it, is it *capitalized*, as in such expressions as "god bless America"?). English translations of the Bible often make the situation worse by translating *'elohim* as "God" (singular, uppercase "G") when the text is referring to the god of Israel, but "gods" (plural, lowercase "g,") when referring to non-Israelite deities. Compare, for example, the translation of Deuteronomy 4:28 in the NRSV: "There you will serve other gods (*'elohim*, lowercase g, plural) made by human hands . . . ," with how it is translated in the very next verse: "From there you will seek the LORD your God" (the same *'elohim*, but now uppercase G and in the singular)! But the word is the exact same *'elohim* as in the preceding verse. Many more examples could be given of how translators vacillate between the ways they translate this identical noun. The main point here is that this is a theological move more than a grammatical one (for other examples of *'elohim* translated as "gods," see 1 Kgs 14:9; 2 Kgs 17:7, 35, 37, 38). Especially relevant to this discussion is 2 Kings 1:16 where Baal-zebub is called the "god (singular, lowercase g, same *'elohim*) of Ekron." Consequently, in the translations that follow, when Yahweh is identified as the "god of Israel" (lowercase "g"), it may be assumed unless otherwise noted that it is the word *'elohim* that occurs in the MT.

My intention here is not to offend anyone who believes that Yahweh really is God—or a god (whether they actually know that this is his name in the MT or not), but to try to achieve some sort of neutral objectivity in writing about the theological purpose(s) implicit in the book of Joshua without assuming a transcendent source for these claims before the discussion even begins. I suspect that the ancient folks who believed that Baal-zebub was a "real" god would have wanted the appellative *'elohim* also translated into English with an uppercase "G." Perhaps complete objectivity is never possible, but hopefully it will cause both writer and reader to become ever more critically aware of, and sensitive to, our own assumptions and biases and to stop dead in its tracks the all-too-common approach to the Bible in the United States, as well as elsewhere, where unexamined and uncriticized assumptions seem to determine the approach and conclusions drawn from much biblical study and use (for an enlightening as well as a frightening examination of the use of the Bible by fundamentalist and many evangelical Christians in this country [a.k.a. "right wing authoritarians"], the book by Altemeyer is highly recommended, and it is free!).

Kol (כּל)

A second major translation consideration has to do with the monosyllabic Hebrew word *kol. Kol* is a non-declinable masculine noun, singular (it never occurs in the Hebrew Bible in the plural), that literally means "whole" or "all." To avoid awkward English grammatical construction, this word is commonly translated into English with such words as "all," "every(one)," "entire," "each," "whole," or "any(one)." Thus, the same word is often translated in English versions in ways that a non-Hebrew reader would not easily understand that it is the same Hebrew word being translated. The importance of this monosyllabic noun in the DH can hardly be overstated as can be readily seen in the first verse of Deuteronomy: "These (are) the words that Moses spoke to *all* Israel beyond the Jordan in the Arabah . . . ." *Kol* occurs well over one hundred times in the book of Joshua. My translation of it into English will be put in italic font, such as *all, each, every(one), whole.*

Consequently, one of the most important motifs in the DH is that of the inclusiveness of the foundation story of Israel. Such claims delineate the national entity, "Israel," from "*all*" other ethnic groups. This noun is used throughout Joshua to differentiate between "insiders" and "outsiders." Heard during the time of Josiah's reforms and/or the time of the exile, such Dtr ideology would have been a clear reminder that those who subjected themselves to Yahweh's commands mediated through Yahweh's chosen leader (Joshua; King Josiah) could once more identify with the national foundational myth of Israel. Everyone is included. An imperfect, but not totally irrelevant, analogy is the July 4th celebration by Americans. "*All*" Americans are expected to participate in the celebration of the Revolutionary War and the founding of our nation. Yet we know that we had nothing to do with that war and that there were no fifty "states" fighting it, only thirteen colonies. But, as "Americans," we still find our identity in that foundation story. So too did the DH seek to convince those for whom it was written that they belonged to the "Israel" of the past. Thus the editor/author of this chapter used the exaggerated *all* not only for Joshua and Israel but also for their enemies, *all* of whom were to be slaughtered (8:25-28). As the story unfolds, it will be noted that sometimes this *all* includes those who were originally "outsiders" (Rahab and her family; the Gibeonites). It has been suggested (Rowlett, 157–58) that while the Dtr used this inclusive term to emphasize "unequivocal identity . . . the exact opposite may be the case. Otherwise, why would it require reinforcement with constant repetition" (158)? (Compare modern politicians who regularly say such things as "the American people are fed up with this and demand whatever," as if *all* Americans are demanding and fed up over the same issues at the exact same time! A close reading of the text of Joshua should convince the reader of the importance given to this one monosyllabic word by the Dtr. However, the portrait painted here of a monolithic group of people, *all* of whom gathered to hear the instructions of Joshua and *all* of whom followed him or other leaders without hesitation into battle, seems artificial. This conclusion is further supported by the biblical stories found in Judges 1, 5, and 20. Compare Creach, 9.) The modern word for a group of people who claim that they have the absolute truth about religion, politics, or what-have-you and that everyone else outside their group has the wrong religion, wrong language, and so forth is "ethnocentrism," defined by Altemeyer as "dividing the world up into in-groups, and out-groups" (87). There is no book in the Bible that is any more ethnocentric than Joshua. And according to the story line, the consequences of such ethnocentricity were absolutely horrible, just as they are today (Shiites killing Sunnis; Sunnis killing Shiites; Catholics killing Protestants; Protestants killing Catholics; and the list could go on and on).

Each section of the commentary will begin with my own translation of the MT of Joshua. In many places the English may sound somewhat unnatural and unfamiliar to anyone who has been exposed only to popular English translations such as the KJV or the NRSV. This is a deliberate move on my part. It has been my experience as a teacher of the Hebrew Bible spanning four decades that it is often the case that people who have never actually read the biblical text closely still think they know what is in it. In my translations, I try to make coherent sense of the original Hebrew while at the same time sticking as closely as possible to literal meanings of Hebrew idioms often lost in standard translations. My goal is to provide non-specialists an opportunity to get a sense of how the Hebrew language reads literally, often with poetic, beautiful images sometimes lost in translations.

Joshua the Person

Apart from the story of the tumbling walls of Jericho recorded in chapter 6, it is doubtful that much else is known about this book or its main character, Joshua, outside the academy. The name Joshua is a compound of *yhw*, the first three letters of the so-called "Tetragrammaton" (*YHWH*) + *shua*, which means "salvation" or "help." Thus the name means something such as "Yah is my help or salvation." Despite familiarity at a superficial level, there are serious historical issues that suggest that the Joshua character as portrayed in the Bible does not reflect historical reality (Ramsey 1992; Na'aman, 259). In fact, he is something of a "cardboard," one-dimensional character (Coogan 2014, 203). The name "Joshua" abruptly appears in Exodus 17:9 for the first time, where he is described as a warrior who, with "some men," is told to go fight the Amalekites, a frequent enemy of Israel (Num 24:20; Deut 25:17-19; 1 Sam 15:2, 7-8, 32-33; 27:8; 30:1-3).

The name appears over two hundred times in the Bible, and over eighty percent of those occurrences are in the book of Joshua itself. In fact, the total occurrences of the name in Exodus, Numbers, and Deuteronomy combined are a mere twenty-eight. All three books call Joshua the "assistant of Moses" (Exod 24:13; 33:11; Num 11:28; Deut 1:38). He is also mentioned a few times in the opening chapters of Judges that contain a very different account of the "conquest" than the one recorded in Joshua (compare Judg 2:23 with Josh 1–11). Following the last mention of his name in Judges (2:23), Joshua's name occurs only once more in the entire DH: 1 Kings 16:34. He is never mentioned in any of the Latter Prophets (Isaiah, Jeremiah, Ezekiel, the Book of the Twelve) or in any of the Psalms. Moreover, whereas the New Testament mentions Moses some eighty times, it refers to Joshua only twice: Acts 7:45 and Hebrews 4:8. The Chronicler links Joshua's genealogy to the tribe of Ephraim (1 Chr 7:27) as does Numbers 13:8. In this latter case, however, the name of the person is "Hoshea" not "Joshua." What is believed to be a priestly addition to this story is found in Numbers 13:16, where we are told that Moses changed the name "of Hosea son of Nun to Joshua" (for entertaining rabbinical folktales explaining the name change, see Hirsch).

There is also a chronological problem here. According to Exodus 6, the name "Yahweh" was not known until it was revealed to Moses. Yet in Exodus 13:7 the Dtr simply assumes that Joshua is a grown man who can go to war. However, the amount of time between the revelation of the name to Moses in chapter 6 and the appearance of Joshua in chapter 13 is hardly two months at best (compare Exod 7:25; 8:10, 20-23; 9:13, 18; 10:4, 13, 22; 12:1; 13:4; 16:1). Thus "Joshua," which is the oldest name in the Bible containing part of the deity's name, "Yahweh," would have already had this name *before* it was revealed to Moses in Exodus 6. This is another indication of complex history of the compilation and finalizing of these folktales.

Nehemiah mentions Joshua once (8:17) but spells the name "Jeshua" following other textual traditions. There also four references to Joshua in the Apocryphal literature: 1 Maccabees 2:55; 2 Maccabees 12:15; Sirach 46:1; and 4 Ezras 7:107. All of the above considerations point to the conclusion that while Joshua may have been an Ephraimite military leader remembered in popular stories, his role in the book bearing his name is a literary creation by the Dtr. The biblical description of this figure precludes anything even close to a biographical sketch. "Of the hero of this cycle of stories, Joshua, hardly anything is known. He was an Ephraimite and was buried at Timnah-Heres, in the southern part of Mount Ephraim (Josh 24:30; Judg 2:9)" (Na'aman, 257; compare Coogan 2014, 203–205).

On the surface, the book of Joshua seems to recount in a straightforward manner how Israel, under the leadership of Joshua, entered the land of Canaan from the Transjordan, opposite Jericho, and within a short time (five years or so) conquered the entire country, eliminating all of its inhabitants. Following this initial success, Joshua divided the land among the twelve tribes, and following a ceremony at Shechem, where "Israel" pledged its fealty to Yahweh, the tribes dispersed to occupy their respective allotments. Beneath this simple story line, however, lies an array of literary, historical, theological, and archaeological complexities.

This commentary will appropriate the consensus of historical critical scholarship in attempting to interpret the book. It is not my intention to convince interested readers to look at the material from a Christian perspective; rather, I encourage readers to view it from a historical critical/archaeological perspective. Neither is it my intention to alienate those who may have different beliefs about the Hebrew Bible. We all cherish our own beliefs however different they may be. None of us are fully equipped to deal with all the issues and problems raised by a critical study of the book of Joshua. None of us knows it all. If a reader completes this critical "journey" through the book and wishes to find some theological values commensurate with his or her own Christian or other religious assumptions about how things are, fine. It is to be hoped that non-Christian readers can also discover "food for thought."

The above discussion raises a serious exegetical question: what meaning(s) can fictional (or not, as the case may be) stories that are more than twenty-five centuries old have for twenty-first-century CE people living a secular democratic republic? To assume that the stories must have some contemporary meaning because they are in the "Bible" is too simplistic. At the very least, those who make such claims should be required to provide clear, rational evidence in support of them. Moreover, little, if any, of the book's contents seem to be actually used in contemporary religious contexts (see "Conclusions" below). Finally, it is hoped that any reader making it this far will find the above discussion of the many critical issues vis-à-vis Joshua helpful when beginning the "journey" through this book.

The "Israelite Conquest" of Canaan

Joshua 1:1–12:24

Preparing for the Invasion of Cisjordan

Joshua 1:1–5:15

The "Speech" of Yahweh to Joshua (1:1-9)

1 And it happened that after the death of Moses, the servant (this word can
also mean "slave") of Yahweh, that Yahweh spoke to Joshua, the son of
Nun, the assistant of Moses saying (MT: "to say"): 2 "Moses my servant (is)
dead, and now arise, cross this Jordan, you and *all* this people, into the
land that I am giving to them, to the Israelites (MT: "sons of Israel"). 3
Every place where the sole of your feet treads upon it, to you I will give it
even as I spoke to Moses. 4 From the wilderness and the Lebanon and as far
as the river Euphrates (MT: "Perat"), *all* the land of the Hittites, and as far
as the Great Sea (the Mediterranean) (where) the sun enters (idiom for "in
the west") will be your territory. 5 No man will stand himself before you
(MT: "to your faces") *all* the days of your life. As I was with Moses I will be
with you. I will not fail you and I will not leave you. 6 Be strong and be
assured, for you will cause this people to inherit the land that I swore to
your fathers to give to them. 7 Only be strong and be very bold to keep to
do ("to obey") in accordance with *all* the law that Moses my servant
commanded you. Do not turn aside from it, right nor left, in order that
you may prosper in *all* where you go. 8 The book of this law will not depart
from your mouth and you will mull over (MT: "to moan, growl") it by day
and by night in order that you will keep to do according to *all* that is
written in it. Because at that time you will make your way prosper and at
that time you will have success. 9 Have I not commanded you? Be strong
and be bold. Do not fear and do not be dismayed, for Yahweh your god
(is) with you in *all* where you go."

As already discussed above, it is all but universally accepted among critical scholars of the Hebrew Bible that the book of Joshua is the first book of the DH (but see Auld, 1998, 148–49, who questioned a "connected Deuteronomistic History") and was first composed by the Dtr during the time of King Josiah and redacted during the Babylonian Exile or shortly thereafter. If the reader has not already done so it would be useful, in order to see the forest for the trees, to stop here and read the DH in its entirety, paying close attention to the content of a character's "reported speech," especially when the speech centers on the theme of obedience to the words/laws of Yahweh (examples: Josh 1:2-9, by Yahweh; Judg 2:11-15, a "reporting speech" by the Dtr; 1 Sam 12:1-8, a "reported speech" by Samuel; 1 Kgs 2:1-4, a "reported speech" by David and so forth; beginning with the preface, the book of Deuteronomy, there are three "reported speeches" by Moses: 1:1–4:43; 5:1–26:19; 27:1–30:20).

Attention should also be paid to the emphasis given in Joshua to keeping and obeying the law commanded by Moses, which, it is claimed, he wrote in a "book" (Heb. *sepher*). This reference to a book or scroll that Moses supposedly wrote in the desert is obviously an anachronism from the time of the Dtr in the late-seventh or sixth century BCE or later. Note that v. 14 is geographically confusing. We are told that the women, children, and livestock are to stay "beyond the Jordan" while the two and half Transjordanian tribes are to cross over the Jordan with the other tribes to fight the Canaanites. From the perspective of the Joshua "character" giving this speech, "beyond the Jordan" would be in Cisjordan, which would be on the west side of the Jordan. But just the opposite was intended. That is, the women, children, and livestock were to be left in the Transjordan where, at this point in the story, they already are (compare the same geographical confusion in Deut 1:1). Through a close reading of the text, the reader should come away with some awareness of how this "history" was constructed and presented primarily through secondary, "reported speeches," accompanied by the "reporting speeches" of the Dtr (compare Polzin, 73–80, and above). Thus the book begins with a "reporting" speech by the editor(s) informing the readers that, after the death of Moses, Yahweh spoke to Joshua. How the editors knew this or knew what language Yahweh spoke we are, of course, never told (they obviously assumed that Yahweh spoke Hebrew, just as Allah spoke Arabic, and Hindu gods speak Hindi, and so forth). Also note the reiteration used by the Dtr: first he reports the death of Moses, and then has Yahweh in a "reported" speech (1: 2-9) report the death again to Joshua (compare 13:1) while commissioning him to cross the Jordan and enter Canaan. Using this technique, Joshua not only succeeds Moses as leader but also does so by the direct command of the tribal deity (compare Deut 31:7-8, 23). By using such a speech, the Dtr established Joshua as the sole earthly representative of Yahweh (for a detailed discussion of this motif see Rowlett, inter alia). According to Rowlett's argument, the Dtr employed this "rhetoric of violence" (Rowlett, 121–55) that characterizes the story of Joshua, an otherwise minor figure in the Hebrew Scriptures (see above), to justify King Josiah's bloody reformation at the end of the seventh century BCE. Joshua is "a thinly disguised King Josiah" (Rowlett, 47; for a convenient summary of the various scholarly arguments concerning the dates and redactional history of the book of Joshua, see Rowlett, 30–48).

Nevertheless, while a royal, late-seventh century BCE background (Porter 1970, 102–32) may ultimately lie behind the conquest story of Joshua, in its final redacted stage, the story is part of the whole fabric of the DH, which dates no earlier than the time of the Babylonian Exile (587/6–539 BCE). Thus in its final form, the purpose of the DH would seem to have been to edify the contemporary audience composed of the exiled Jews, as well as their future descendants (Soggin 1972, 29). In fact, it will be argued throughout this commentary that the final use of the story in Joshua was to give the Babylonian exiles and their children the hope that one day soon they would return to their homeland and reclaim the land taken from them by the Assyrians and the Babylonians. They apparently never saw the irony in this hoped-for turn of events: the land they took from the indigenous inhabitants of Canaan by violence, commanded by their god, Yahweh (the theme of Josh 1–12), had now been taken from them by violence, first by the Assyrians, and then by the Babylonians, all in the names of their "gods." To cite a modern idiom: "the chickens came home to roost."

This opening "speech" by Yahweh is followed by two speeches of Joshua, first to his "officers," (v. 11; the Hebrew word used here, *shoter*, is used elsewhere; in Exod 5:14-19 it is translated "supervisors" in the NRSV; compare Prov 6:7). The second speech by Joshua is to the Transjordanian tribes (Reuben, Gad, and the half-tribe of Manasseh, vv. 13-15), and finally a "collective" speech is given by these same tribes to Joshua (vv. 16-18). It should be obvious by now that these "speeches" are the creation of the biblical writers/editors, not the people in whose mouths they are placed.

The emphasis given the law of Moses (vv. 7-8) in this chapter clearly indicates the chapter's final compositional date: either during or perhaps shortly after the Babylonian Exile that began in 586 BCE. Prior to the exile, the emphasis of the traditions in Judah (from whose perspective the Hebrew Scriptures were written; see Finkelstein 1995, 362; 2007a, 14–20) was on the royal ideology/theology associated with the Davidic Monarchy and the Jerusalem temple, both of which were destroyed by the Babylonians during the early part of the sixth century BCE. This long "history" ends with the Dtr emphasizing that the last Judean monarch, Jehoiakin, was released from prison and allowed to dine at the king's table for as long as he lived (2 Kgs 25:27-30). Perhaps the Dtr's motivation for this poignant ending to the story was to hold on to the hope that someday the exiles would once more be led by Yahweh back to the "land of promise" just as he had led them through the wilderness to this land centuries before (at least in the story they are about to tell). This hope, of course, was never realized. Had scribes from the northern kingdom of Israel written the Bible, it would no doubt read very differently than it does. The DH, according to Finkelstein,

> . . . argued that the Davidic kings are the only legitimate heirs to the territories of vanquished Israel and the leadership over the Israelites still living in those territories, and that the cult of all Israelites should be centralized in the temple in Jerusalem. As such, the texts are highly ideological on both the political and theological levels. They represent the point of view of one elite faction of *Judahite society* (we have no idea if it ever formed the majority in late-monarchic times); they certainly do not represent the Northern Kingdom. . . . We can only imagine how different a history of Israel written by scribes from the Northern Kingdom or by other factions of Judahite society would be had it survived. (2007a, 15, my emphasis)

In Judah, David and Jerusalem were emphasized (see the "speeches" in 2 Sam 7 extolling David, note esp. v. 13, which is an oblique reference to Solomon and the building of the temple; compare Ps 89, which also dates to the exile, esp. vv. 3-4; also Ps 132, esp. vv. 11-12; Isa 6:1–9:7 [6:1–9:6 in Hebrew]). David was the "messiah," the anointed one (2 Sam 5:3). But David's throne did not last forever, and the DH is one long, complicated, and at times confusing theological attempt to explain how this could have happened: the answer, in a word, is disobedience. For the Dtr, the only way to live a successful life is to obey the laws of Yahweh and worship only him (Nelson 1997, 20.) That may sound easy enough; unfortunately, it is mostly pious and naïve rhetoric. For a clear "reporting speech" describing disobedience on the part of both Israel and Judah, read 1 Kings 17:7-23. This speech rationalizes from the theological perspective of the Dtr why both Israel and Judah (v. 19, obviously edited after the Babylonian war) ultimately failed. What now? The Dtr's solution was to go "back to Sinai," not literally of course, but figuratively through the law of Moses. It is as if seven hundred years of "Israelite" history had been swept clean. This emphasis on the law is clearly seen in Joshua 1. If further proof of this Deuteronomistic theology is needed, one only needs to read the deathbed blessing ("last words") of King David to Solomon (1 Kgs 2:1-9). As one reads read this "speech," it should be keep in mind that according to the description given David in chapter 1, David is so feeble that he cannot have sex with a beautiful young virgin and cannot remember that he, according to the prophet Nathan, had promised Solomon his throne:

> When David's time to die drew near, he charged his son Solomon, saying: "I am about to go the way of all the earth. Be strong and courageous [the same command given Joshua by Yahweh in Josh 1:6, 7, 9] and keep the charge of Yahweh your god, walking in his ways and keeping his statutes, his commandments, his ordinances, and his testimonies, as it is written in the law of Moses, so that you may prosper in *all* that you do and wherever you turn. Then Yahweh will establish his word that he spoke concerning me: 'If your heirs take heed to their way, to walk before me in faithfulness with *all* their heart and with all their being, there will not fail you a successor on the throne of Israel.'"

This pure Deuteronomic preaching from the exilic or later period is straight out of the book of Deuteronomy (Deut 4:29; 6:2; 8:6; 9:5 and more; compare again Josh 1:6, 7, 9, 18 with 1 Kgs 2:2—"Be strong and courageous" [for a lengthy discussion of this phrase see Rowlett, 156–80]—as well as the wording in Deut 6:1-2 and 8:6 with 2 Kgs 2:3 and Josh 1:7-8). Furthermore, the image of a righteous, obedient David presented in these Deuteronomistic sermons is extremely exaggerated to say the least. Far from being a man "after [Yahweh's] own heart" (1 Sam 13:13) who walked in the ways of Yahweh, "keeping my statues and my commandments" (1 Kgs 3:14), David was a ruthless, cold-hearted murderer. (Read the rest of his deathbed, "godfather" hit list speech to Solomon: 1 Kgs 2:5-9! See also Halpern's evaluation of David [2001, esp. chapter 4, "King David, Serial Killer"]; compare Miscall, 81–86.)

What does all of this have to with Joshua? A lot, I hope. Faced with the unimaginable horrible consequences of two wars (the Assyrian at the end of the eighth century BCE and the Babylonian at the beginning of the seventh century), a small percentage, and it must have been very small, of elitist Judean scribes tried to explain how the longest-running dynasty in history (according to the biblical version, David's house controlled Judah some four hundred years, minus the few years of usurpation by the Queen Mother, Athaliah, 2 Kgs 11:1-16) came to such a catastrophic end. The problem is, of course, they tried to do it theologically, and the attempt failed miserably.

A telling text case of how this Deuteronomistic theology does not work well, if at all, is the story of King Josiah himself told in 2 Kings 22:1–23:30. According to 2 Kings 22:1, Josiah's reign began around 640 BCE and lasted for thirty-one years (609 BCE). We are also told that he was eight years old when he began to reign, making him forty years old when he was killed in battle with the Egyptians. According to the theological assumptions presented in the DH, however, Josiah should have had a long, full, and peaceful reign. But once again reality trumped theology. Upon learning that Neco, the king of Egypt, was passing through Judah on his way to join forces with the Assyrians in an attempt to stop the rising influence of the Babylonians, Josiah went out to stop Neco. According to the story, their forces met in the valley of Jezreel, close to the famous city of Megiddo, and King Josiah was killed (2 Kgs 23:29; compare 2 Chr 35:20-24). He died a violent death that contradicts the words of the prophetess, Huldah, who had prophesied that Josiah would go to his "grave in peace" (2 Kgs 22:20). In the eyes of the Dtr, Josiah was the ideal, faithful king, unlike any other in Judah's history (all nineteen kings of the northern kingdom of Israel are condemned by the Dtr). Second Kings 21:24–23:30 is devoted to the Dtr's summary of Josiah's life, and 23:25 provides the following characterization of the king: "Before him there was no king like him, who turned to Yahweh with *all* his heart, with *all* his being, and with *all* his might, according to *all the law of Moses*; nor did any like him arise after him."

Josiah's untimely death posed a real problem for the Dtr. They were not the only ones bothered by this glitch in their theology. So was the author of the book of Chronicles. He tried to avoid the contradiction raised by Josiah's perfect obedience to the law and his violent death by imaging that Yahweh himself had put words into the mouth of none other than Neco! According to Neco, Yahweh had ordered him to hurry to the aid of the Assyrians and Josiah should mind his own business! "Cease for yourself provoking a god (***ᵉlohim***), *who is with me, so that he will not destroy you*" (v. 21, my emphasis). But Josiah "did not listen to the words of Neco *from the mouth of* ***ᵉlohim***, but joined battle in the plain of Megiddo" (2 Chr 35:20-24; quote from v. 22).

In the end bad things happened to Josiah—not because a foreign king killed him in battle but because Israel's god destroyed him! Neco just happened to give this god a helping hand. What lengths so-called theologians will go in order to keep from having to confess that their theology does not work! Nothing ever counts against it (compare Dawkins's description of theology above). Far more accurate of the human condition are the observations of the anonymous sage of the postexilic period (his exact dates disputed), Qoheleth (usually rendered "Ecclesiastes" in English):

> In my vain life I have seen everything; there are righteous people who perish in their righteousness, and there are wicked people who prolong their life in their evil doing. (7:15)

> Again I saw that under the sun the race is not to the swift, nor battle to the strong, nor bread to the wise, nor riches to the intelligent, nor favor to the skillful, but time and chance happen to them ***all***. For no one can anticipate the time of disaster. Like fish taken in a cruel net, and like birds caught in a snare, so mortals are snared at a time of calamity, when it suddenly falls upon them (my emphasis). (9:11-12; NRSV)

It is not "disobedient" fish and birds that get caught and presumably eaten; their destruction is simply due to "time and chance." Nowhere does this sage refer to obeying Yahweh's commandments as the key to a successful life. This omission did not escape the book's final editor (12:13-14). Not much has changed in the conservative theological world in the intervening twenty-five hundred years or so since the DH and the Chronicles were written. There are those among us today who insist on giving theological explanations for military victories/defeats, natural disasters, or whatever. Did the Christian god really send Hurricane Katrina (December 2005) to destroy New Orleans because of gays, abortionists, feminists, the ACLU, and People For the American Way, as certain Christian spokespersons have claimed (see *media-matters* in bibliography)? I wonder how many people who perished in that storm had ever given two cents worth about the ACLU, the People for the American Way, or any of the other perennial imagined enemies of the Christian right. Furthermore, does anyone know how many helpless animals, including beloved pets, also perished? Is this really the best the Christian god can do?

One more example of a modern questionable theological claim is that the devastating earthquake that struck Haiti on January 12, 2010, killing tens of thousands of humans (and one suspects many more thousands of non-human animals who never seem to matter to people who claim to know the mind and will of their god), including thousands of children, was brought on by the evangelical god of Christians because the Haitians had made a pack with the "devil" to drive out the French in the late eighteenth–early nineteenth centuries. What about the earthquakes that struck Haiti in 1751, 1842, and 1946? Where these natural catastrophes also the work of the "devil" because of Haiti's slave revolution against the hated French? This irresponsible and self-serving use of biblical texts and theology can make religion dangerous, mean, and offensive. How can one believe in a just god who destroys the righteous with the wicked, including children (compare above Craig's superficial rationalization justifying the divinely approved slaughter of children during the "conquest")? Does anyone really believe that the Assyrians or Babylonians actually separated the good from the evil before they raped, butchered, and plundered? Yet the Deuteronomistic theology expressed throughout the DH fails to take the deaths and sufferings of the innocent into consideration.

Nevertheless, this theological claim that some humans know which other humans their god wants destroyed, because this god has communicated such knowledge to them, is the theological source of Joshua's power and control. He is the god's commander on Earth and thus has not only the right but also the duty to decide who belongs to the "insiders" and who to the "outsiders," and consequently who lives and who dies. Thus, what appears at first glance to be a rather clear either/or situation quickly becomes a problem. The issue with the Transjordanian tribes; Rahab the prostitute ("outsider," Josh 2); Achan ("insider," Josh 7) from the tribe of Judah; and the story of the ruse of the Gibeonites ("outsiders," Josh 9) all challenge the objective of drawing legitimate boundaries that separate one group from another (see Rowlett's helpful discussion of this issue of "boundaries," 156–80). In fact, nowhere in chapter 1 of Joshua (nor in any other chapter in the book) is the welfare of the original inhabitants of the land (Deut 7:1, for the list) ever raised (with the two exceptions just named). What are the ethical implications of such an attitude towards "the other" (Warrior)? It is going to get worse before the Dtr is finished with his story. The "Israelites" will get the land promised to their ancestors (1:6) by killing everyone already living in it (Deut 7:1; Josh 10:40-42; 11:16-20; see below). While the phrase "holy war" is not used anywhere in Joshua (and the expression itself is nowhere found in the Bible, see discussion below), it is clearly implied. Who exactly would have read or even heard of the story now contained in the book during the time of Josiah or during the exilic/postexilic periods is unclear, as suggested previously. The survivors in exile would have known, of course, that both Israel and Judah had long been wiped off the map. The Dtr claimed it was because of disobedience: the people did not follow the law of Moses (1:7). The Hebrew word *shama*, translated as "obey," occurs over twenty times in the book of Deuteronomy, six times in chapter 28 alone. It can also be translated "listen to," "hear." This creates a convenient but questionable theology because nothing ever counts against it. From a purely political perspective, disobedience was not the reason Israel and Judah were destroyed. Assyria and Babylonia were. Israel and Judah could not have withstood the far superior armies of the ancient Assyrians and Babylonians.

Whether or not the *theological* interpretation given to these political developments by the Dtr is true, I have no way of knowing. One must believe it or not on other grounds, the discussion of which is beyond the scope of this commentary. It needs to be remembered that while the biblical writers may give the impression that "Israel" and "Judah" were unique, powerful kingdoms during their existence, they were not. They existed independently side by side for only about 200 years (c. 925–722 BCE Judah lasted alone until 586 BCE), precisely during the relatively short period when neither Egypt in the south nor Assyria in the northeast was powerful enough to control the area occupied by these two smaller states (compare Van De Mieroop, 224).

The geographical boundaries described in v. 4 include the desert to the south and east ("wilderness"), most of what was, and is, Syria to the northeast reaching to the Euphrates River, and the Mediterranean ("the Great Sea") to the west. "This Lebanon" is lacking in LXX and makes little sense since Lebanon is inside the northern boundaries. It has also been recognized by scholars that the reference to the Hittites is a later gloss that is neither in the LXX nor in the parallel account in Deuteronomy 11:24. This description of the extent of an "Israelite" empire is extremely exaggerated as well as idealistic and was never a historical reality. This includes the so-called "United Monarchy of David and Solomon," the existence and extent of which has been much debated by scholars (1 Kgs 4:21; Finkelstein 2007 b and d; Mazar 2007 b; Miller 2004). While it is unclear at what time such a far-reaching empire was conceived, it may have arisen with the grandiose efforts of King Josiah (see above), whose persona may have been the motivation for the Dtr's creation of the Joshua story as already suggested (Nelson 1981; Rowlett 1996; Finkelstein 2007d; Mazar 2007b, 54–55; and discussion above). What seems clear is that in Dtr's ideology the divine promise made to Moses (Deut 11:24) cannot be thwarted, not even by exile.

The theme of "land" is of utmost importance to the Dtr (compare Deut 9:1-23). That Israel failed to keep the land once they possessed it created a major theological concern for the authors of the story. This failure had already been anticipated in Deuteronomy (31:24-29) and accounts for one of only two references to Joshua in the entire NT (Heb 4:8). As mentioned above, in 2 Kings 17:1-41, there is a lengthy "reporting" speech by the Dtr explaining theologically why both Judah and Israel were ultimately destroyed. It must be assumed that the final editors of the DH already knew, of course, that the promises made by Yahweh to Joshua in chapter 1 were "fulfilled" only temporarily, if at all.

Israel was able to occupy the land and enjoy Yahweh's blessings when she did "according to *all* the law which Moses my servant commanded you"

(v. 7). Many scholars believe that the expression "the book of the law" (v. 8) refers to the legal material in the book of Deuteronomy, especially chapters 12–26 (compare Deut 31:9). However, as the editors of the DH will make clear in the story they are about to tell, living "according to *all* the law" is no simple task but requires constant reinterpretation and adaptation. The DH is a valiant but ultimately failed attempt to explain theologically the rise and fall of these states.

The "Speech" of Joshua to the Officers and the Transjordanian Tribes (1:10-15)

> 10 Then Joshua commanded the officers of the people saying: 11 "Pass in the midst of the camp and command the people saying: 'prepare foodstuffs for yourselves for yet in three days you are crossing this Jordan, to come in to possess the land that Yahweh your god is giving to you to possess.'" 12 And to the Reubenite, and to the Gadite and to the half-tribe of Manasseh Joshua said: 13 "Remember the word that Moses the servant of Yahweh commanded you saying: 'Yahweh your god is giving you rest and he is giving to you this land.' 14 Your women (wives), your children and your cattle (livestock) will dwell in the land that Moses gave to you beyond the Jordan, but you will cross over in battle array before your brothers; *all* the strong (ones) of the army will help them, 15 until (when) Yahweh gives rest to your brothers (relatives) as to you, and they also possess the land that Yahweh your god is giving to them. Then you will return to the land of your inheritance and you will possess it (MT: "her"), which Moses the servant of Yahweh gave to you, beyond the Jordan, (the) place of the rising sun (idiom for "in the east")."

Just as Joshua was prepared in a "speech" by Yahweh to possess the land, now the people are prepared in a "speech" by Joshua: first to the "officers" (v. 11) then the Transjordanian tribes (1:12-15.). At first reading, it seems curious that the only tribes mentioned by name here are those who historically had lived in the Transjordan and who had played an insignificant role in Israel's history. However, by referring to them directly, the Dtr anticipates a problem that will require further treatment in the story (chapter 22), namely, the status of those tribes who were *of* Israel but not geographically *in* Israel.

The "Speech" of the Transjordanian Tribes to Joshua (1:16-18)

> 16 And they answered Joshua saying: "*All* that you commanded us we will do; and every place that you send us we will go. 17 As we obeyed Moses in everything thus we will obey you. Only may Yahweh your god be with you even as he was with Moses. 18 Every man who is disobedient to your mouth

> and does not obey your words in regard to *all* that you command will be put to death. Only be strong and be bold."

The transfer of Moses' authority to Joshua is completed when the people respond. His authority will be valid only if "Yahweh your god [is] with you." With the authority of the Davidic king destroyed by exile, the Dtr reverts to a charismatic model of kingly authority (compare Deut 17:14-17). Put into the collective mouth of the Transjordanian tribes, this "reported speech" echoes the classic Dtr ideology of "obedience" as the necessary condition for success and repeats a common Dtr theme of being "strong and courageous" (v. 18; cf. 1:7,9; 10:25; 2 Sam 9:13; Rowlett). This collective speech also clearly sets forth the penalty for anyone who does not obey *all* that Joshua commands: execution (v. 18). This motif of a human who is the god's surrogate on Earth plays a significant role in the story. Both good things and bad things can happen to those who either recognize and honor Joshua's divinely appointed position (for examples of good things: Rahab and the Gibeonites), or do not (for bad things: Achan and the five kings at Makkedah; see below and the discussion by Rowlett, inter alia). The "reported speech" of the Transjordanian tribes to Joshua already alludes to the idea that bad things can, and will, happen to those who do not "obey": This idea is clearly affirmed by the words "Every man who is disobedient to your mouth and does not obey your words in regard to *all* that you command will be put to death" (v. 18). The horrible consequences wrought on this planet by those who have used this role model (whether consciously taken from Joshua or not) to claim that they are a god's chosen spokesperson and that they speak with an authoritarian voice for this god and must be obeyed else those who disobey will suffer bad consequences is one of the most evil characteristics of religions, then as well as now (think of ISIS and Boko Haram). It is also noteworthy how quickly one can become an "outsider" (also known in the modern world as "excommunication"), if one does not let such people do one's own thinking and believing when it comes to all things "religious." Thus the Dtr has already set the stage for the fate of Achan, and all that belongs to him, narrated in chapter 7, as well as all the other "outsiders" to be encountered before the "conquest" is completed.

Rahab and the Jericho Spies

Joshua 2:1-24

1 Then Joshua, the son of Nun, secretly sent out two men from Shittim
saying: "Go, see the land, and also Jericho." And they walked and they
went into a house of a woman, a prostitute, and her name was Rahab. And
they laid down there. 2 And it was reported (told) to the king of Jericho:
"Behold men have come hither from the Israelites to search out the land."
3 And the king of Jericho sent (word) to Rahab saying: "Bring out the men,
the one who came to you, who went to your house, for they came to search
out *all* the land." 4 But the woman took the two men and hid them. Then
she said: "Thus they came to me, the men, but I do not know from where
they (came). 5 And as the gate (is) to be closed at dark, then the men went
out but I do not know where the men went. Pursue after them quickly for
you will overtake them." 6 But she brought them up to the roof and she
hid them in the flax of the tree; the (flax) set in order by her upon the roof.
7 So the men chased after them on the road (to) the Jordan, to the fords.
And the gate was shut behind (them) as they came out running after them.

8 But before they themselves had lain down she went up to them on
the roof. 9 And she said to the men: "I know that Yahweh has given to you
the land and that the fear of you has fallen upon us and that *all* those who
dwell in the land melt before you. 10 For we have heard how Yahweh made
dry the waters of the Sea of Reeds (wrongly translated as "Red Sea") before
you when you came out from Egypt, and what you did to the two Amorite
kings who (were) beyond the Jordan, to Sidon and to Og, whom you
totally destroyed (MT: חרם, "devoted to the ban"). 11 And when we heard
(about it) lo our heart melted, and there did not arise a continuance of
spirit in a man because of you. Yahweh your god, he is god in the heavens
from above and upon the earth below. 12 And now, swear now to me by
Yahweh that as I showed kindness, so you will do kindness with the house
of my father. And you will give me a sign of faithfulness, 13 so that you will
preserve my father and my mother and my brother and my sister and *all*
who (are) to them and you will deliver our lives from death."

> [14] And the men said to her: "Our life for (MT: "instead of") yours (to die)! If you do not tell this matter of ours then it will be when Yahweh gives us the land that will make for you mercy and faithfulness." [15] Then she let them down with the cord through the window for her house (was) on the outer wall (portion) of the wall, and she was living in the wall itself. [16] And she said to them: "Go (MT: "walk") toward the hill-country lest the pursuers encounter you. Now hide yourselves there three days until the pursuers return, then afterwards you may go on your way."
>
> [17] And the men said to her: "Truly we (are) free from the oath that you have caused us to swear to you, [18] (if) we, we ourselves, come into the land with hope, this red cord you tied in the window with which you let us down with it and your father and your mother and your brother and *all* the house of your father you have gathered to you toward the house, [19] but (if) it be (that) *all* who go out by the doors of your house (to) the outside, his blood (will be) on his head and we ourselves (will be) innocent. But *all* who are with you in the house, his blood (will be) on our heads if a hand is (laid) upon him. [20] But if you speak of this matter of ours then we will be exempt from your oath that you caused us to swear."
>
> [21] Then she said: "According to your words so it (will be)." Then she sent them away and they went away. Then she tied the red cord in the window. [22] And they went away and came to the hill-country and they dwelled there three days, until the pursuers returned. For the pursuers had searched *everywhere* (MT: "in *all* the way") but they did not find (them).
>
> [23] Then the two men returned and they came down from the hill-country and they crossed over and they came to Joshua, the son of Nun, and they recounted to him *all* that happened to them. [24] And they said to Joshua: "So Yahweh has given into our hand *all* the land, and moreover, *all* those living in the land are melting away from before us."

After the Dtr's "sermons" of chapter 1, which emphasized taking the "land," not the extermination of its inhabitants (1:2, 4, 6, 11, 13, 14, 15), chapter 2 tells a suspenseful and ironic story. Ironic because the "hero" ("heroine") of this story is not some powerful Israelite warrior preparing to do battle with Canaanites, but a woman who is not an Israelite, much less a warrior; she is a prostitute (compare Bird, 1999)! Is this why we are told in the first verse that when the spies went into her house they laid down? For what? Maybe they were worn out from their "walk" (v. 1), but knowing human nature, sex would be my guess (see Creach's comments, 32–34). In any case, this woman is not only given a name, "Rahab"; she is also given a voice. In fact, she is the only named person in the story. Neither the spies nor the "king" have names. Oftentimes in the Hebrew Scriptures women are not mentioned by name and/or not given a voice. Gomer, for example, in Hosea 1, is named but nowhere in the prophetic book is she allowed to speak. What she supposedly thought about the arrangement between her and the prophet is left to one's imagination. On the other hand, the Levite's concubine who was raped all night (Judg 19:22-26) has neither a name nor a voice (Trible, 64–91). Another shocking example is the rape of Dinah, the daughter of Leah and Jacob (Gen 24). She has a name but no voice. What she thought about what happened to her, especially in light of Shechem's (the man who raped her) claim to have loved her and wanted to marry her (vv. 2-3), we can only try to imagine. According to the law in Deuteronomy 22:28-29, a man could rape a virgin who was not engaged and if caught in the act, pay fifty shekels of silver to her father and force her to marry him. Moreover, he could never divorce her. This is one view of biblical marriage never mentioned by those opposed to homosexual marriage "because the Bible says."

From a literary perspective, chapter 2 is complex and many scholars have long believed that originally the story related here might have had little to do with the city of Jericho. On the other hand, the story as we have it is also believed to be the work of the final redactor of the book who connected what was probably an old tradition to the story in 6:17b, 22-25. The story begins with the spies who are commanded to "go, view the land," and only the "land" is mentioned when they return (v. 24). However, in the story as told, they hardly spy out any of the land! It has even been suggested that the story of Rahab is an etiology. An etiology is a story told to explain the origin of a name, a natural phenomenon, a cult practice, and so forth. Joshua has more etiologies (12) than any other book in the Hebrew Bible: 4:9; 5:9; 6:25; 7:26; 8:28-29; 9:27; 10:27; 13:13; 15:63; 16:10. On this reading, the story of Rahab was told to explain the presence of a Canaanite family living among Israelites after the conquest was over (Miller and Tucker, 29).

Once more the issue of "boundaries" comes to the forefront. Rahab is an "outsider," with no connections to the "inner circle" of "Israelites." She has no pristine genealogy linking her to "Israel's" ancestors. But when she proclaims her fealty to Yahweh and professes him to be *'elohim* (god, vv. 8-13; I wonder what images she might have conjured up when she heard [spoke] this word? But I doubt she thought of a monotheistic "God" with upper case "G"), she and *all* her house are preserved, ostensibly violating the *ḥrm* (ban; see Rowlett's discussion, 177–80). On the other hand, Achan (chapter 7) has all of the insider connections (7:16-18) but fails in his duties and in obedience to Yahweh, and thus to Joshua, Yahweh's representative on Earth, he becomes an "outsider" and is subsequently executed. He and all that belonged to him (7:24) are exterminated. This is one of only two public executions narrated in the book of Joshua (the other is that of the five kings of the Amorites, 10:16-27; see below). In her analysis of the Achan incident, Rowlett pointed out that while the real issue in the Joshua story (also known as Josiah) was that of power and control over others in order to reestablish the monarchy of David (Josiah's predicament), this power play was masked in a kind of "false modesty" where Joshua (Josiah) claimed that Yahweh, the god, was really in charge of what was happening, while he, Joshua (again, Josiah), was merely "Yahweh's humble servant" (174; 7:19-20). Thus, ultimately it was the god who wanted these people killed, not Joshua/Josiah. Such pretense at humility, while at the same time asserting all the power they can over their followers, is no stranger to contemporary religious leaders. Without the noncritical, herd mentality of their followers, such religious self-righteous manipulation might not exist today to the extent that it does. Altemeyer (89), in his study of authoritarianism, described this mentality as "a column of army ants on the march" (compare the rhetoric now coming from some Christian quarters over the recent Supreme Court ruling allowing same-sex marriage).

Nevertheless, with this story of the spies sent out by Joshua, the Dtr begins the account of how Israel came to occupy the land of Canaan. Spy stories also occur elsewhere in the Bible and reflect their popularity. Apparently people enjoyed hearing (reading?) them. Besides Joshua 2, such stories can be found in Numbers 13–14; 21; Deuteronomy 1; and Judges 6; 7; 14; and 18. In addition to the above examples, we are told in 1 Samuel 26:4 that David sent men to spy on Saul and in 2 Samuel 10:1-5 that David's "envoys" that he sent to Hanun, the Ammonite king, are accused of having been sent by David "to search the city, to spy it out, and to overthrow it" (v. 3). Many of these stories contain similar language and seek theologically to justify taking land belonging to someone else, reflecting a "holy war" mentality. All of this requires a theological orientation that should be repugnant to twenty-first-century enlightened citizens. Unfortunately, such stories of "conquest" by a god's chosen people have characterized much of the history of Christianity and Judaism (Prior 1997, 1999; Ben-Gurion, 1990).

Other critical issues in chapter 2 need attention. One is the text itself. The textual versions of Joshua are complicated. Anyone with a working knowledge of Hebrew and Greek can consult commentaries that devote a lot of space to the textual problems (Margolis 1933–36; 1998; Butler 1983; Greenspoon 1983; Nelson 1997; Auld 1998). If, in fact, the present form of the book of Joshua was written hundreds of years after the settlement of Israel took place, primarily for theological, not historical, purposes, then the story as we have it is really a barrier to any attempt to penetrate behind it to the actual events underlying the formation of ancient Israel. This is precisely why all attempts to reconstruct the history of early Israel from the Bible have failed. The written sources simply will not bear up under such historical scrutiny. Perhaps it is time to stop trying to use these late, reworked traditions as though they were historical sources in the modern sense of that expression. What is required, as many critical scholars have come to realize, is that we must give up our attempt to maintain the "essential historicity of the conquest traditions" (Callaway 1987, 92). This observation, shared by most mainstream biblical scholars, raises the question of whether or not there is any positive value of such a book (for conservative approaches to these issues see Hoerth, inter alia; Kitchen, inter alia; Hess et al.).

Other puzzling aspects/inconsistencies to this story have captured interpreters' interests for a long time. For example, chapter 1 says that the people are to prepare to cross over the Jordan in three days (v. 11). This version of the story seems to be picked up in chapter 3 where the people are told to break camp (at Shittim) and go camp at the Jordan for "three days" (3:1-2). But according to chapter 2, the unnamed spies, to avoid being captured by their pursuers from Jericho, flee into the hills and stay "three days" (2:22). They then return to Joshua to give their report. Only then are we told that following their return the people camped out at the Jordan for three more days. Advanced mathematics is well beyond my pay grade, but third grade arithmetic would imply that, taken at face value, the story as we now have it requires not three but six days, if not longer. On the other hand, if the story comprises what were originally separate oral traditions, then it is possible that chapter 3 followed the story in chapter 1, and the conflict in the number of days is solved (well, until you stick chapter 2 back into the story). Many scholars believe this confusion is the result of a later editor who needed an antecedent story of some sort to make sense of the report in chapter 6:22-25.

Such an approach to biblical studies requires that the Bible can no longer be considered as the primary source at our disposal for trying to reconstruct the early beginnings of Israel (the bibliography relevant to this question is too long to be included here, but see Dever 1992, 2001a, 2012; Finkelstein 1988b, 1991, 2008, 2010; Finkelstein and Mazar 2007). This claim must go to archaeology, which alone can provide us with contemporary evidence from the periods that concern us the most: the end of the Late Bronze Age and the beginning of Iron Age I, circa 1250–1150 BCE (see the discussion on archaeology above and Dever 2012, 105).

The story of Rahab and Jericho also raises the troublesome issue of what is generally referred to as "holy war." According to the rules governing "holy war" (חרם), Deut 20:15-18), Israel was to "save alive nothing that breathes"

(v. 16). This concept of *hrm* is also present in the Mesha inscription that is dated to the middle of the ninth century BCE (Schmidt, 2006a, 313). In the story of Rahab, however, the spies, not Yahweh, agreed to spare her and her family for the help she gave them, ostensibly violating the ban. In chapter 7, on the other hand, Achan and his family are put to death for committing the same offense: violating the ban. How is one to understand what is going on here? It has already been suggested that the issue of "insiders" versus "outsiders" certainly played a role in the Dtr's use of the Rahab tale. The attempt by some commentators to discover some universal ideological/theological truths in this story is questionable at best. For example, according to Polzin, this story "raises two hermeneutic questions for the Israelites concerning the word of God. First, how does one interpret and apply God's command to put complete trust in him while taking over the land . . . ? Second, how does one interpret the Mosaic rules for holy war?" (86–87). Polzin argued that what we see here, then, is the Dtr's concern "to counter an authoritarian dogmatism" by telling stories that illustrate both the conditional (Rahab) and the unconditional (Achan) aspects of the Sinai/Horeb covenant (87). Thus, in the immediate story, Israel is allowed to occupy a land that she does not deserve (Deut 9:4-5), while Rahab and her family are spared deaths that they do deserve. It is then suggested that the story of Rahab can be interpreted as a variation of the Dtr's larger themes of the "justice and mercy of God vis-à-vis Israel" (Polzin, 88). This sounds a lot like special pleading to me, and, moreover, who gets to decide what is "conditional" versus "unconditional" about a covenant supposedly carved in stone? How does the annihilation of entire groups of peoples illustrate the "mercy" of a god? Furthermore, if the Israelite god can spare a non-Israelite prostitute, surely he could also forgive and spare an Israelite (Achan) who kept for himself what supposedly belonged to the deity (the "holy" part of a "holy war"; see below). The story of Rahab is an intriguing and exciting fictional short (very short) story attempt to justify an even more fictional, as well as horrifying, story: the slaughter of the original inhabitants of Canaan. In fact, chapters 1–12 could well be called "a pseudo-history of non-events" (I no longer know the source of this witticism).

That a prostitute was chosen to be the heroine of this story seems no accident. Contrary to Soggin's conclusion (1972, 39), Rahab's profession is central to the story for several reasons. First, she is said to live in the city wall (v. 15), which reflects her status as a prostitute, that is, she is portrayed as living literally on the fringes of her own society (Fewell, 66). Second, as is commonly pointed out, by virtue of her profession, neighbors would not be unduly suspicious by the presence of men in her house, and, of course, the location of her house made it easy to dispatch the spies. But most important, as a prostitute, Rahab throws into bold relief once again the issue of "insider" versus "outsider" that dominates the Dtr's concern. In this regard, Polzin made an interesting suggestion when he concluded that the story of Rahab is "really the story of Israel told from the point of view of a non-Israelite" (88). This may be well and good as far as it goes, but the fact still remains that for the "outsiders" to become "insiders," the original "insiders" must be turned into "outsiders" so they can be slaughtered as Yahweh, the god, had commanded. How does this fit into the ethical principle of "do unto others as you would have them do unto you," or "love your enemies" (compare Warrior)?

Moreover, what are we to make of the fact that the heroine of this story is a prostitute? The word in Hebrew, זונה, appears many times in the Hebrew Bible. It is the noun form of the verb *zanah* (Erlandsson). In the KJV and the 1952 RSV the word is translated as "harlot," as it is in the Jewish Publication Society's Bible called the *TaNaK* (this acronym stands for *Torah* [the Pentateuch/the first five books in the Bible], *Neviim* [the Prophets, both Former, Joshua-Kings, and Latter, the three major prophets Isaiah, Jeremiah, and Ezekiel, as well as the twelve minor prophets), and "*Kethuvim*" [the "Writings"], which includes all of the other canonical books in the Hebrew Bible). Perhaps part of the purpose of the Dtr was to provide a little comic relief from the otherwise horrible acts about to be committed (in the story line, at least). Here we have a woman, a prostitute (in other parts of the NRSV this word is translated as "whore," especially in Ezek 16 and 23), who is in control of the entire situation. She protects the unnamed spies, outsmarts a rather stupidly portrayed king, and sends his men on a wild goose chase searching for the spies. *Zona* is also used in the Bible to describe a woman who has sexual intercourse outside of an acceptable man-woman relationship, usually defined as a wife or concubine (Solomon is said to have had seven hundred wives and three hundred concubines, 1 Kgs 11:3; the Bible does not elaborate on the cause of his death, but my own suspicion is that he died from sheer exhaustion!). Samson is said to have visited a prostitute at Gaza (Judg 16:1), and Tamar, the daughter-in-law of Judah, pretended to be a prostitute in order to seduce him (Gen 38:15). Because of the subordinate position of women in the Hebrew Bible, only they are the subjects of the verb *zanah* when it is used to designate an actual sexual act between a woman and someone with whom she does not have a "formal covenant relationship" (Erlandsson, 100). On the other hand, men who had sex outside of marriage, unless it was with the wife of another man or a woman already engaged (for other sexual prohibitions, see Lev 18) were, well, just being men. The double standard between the sexes has been around a very long time! Priests are forbidden from marrying whores (Lev 21:7, 14), and in prophetic literature the prophets, unsurprisingly, condemn prostitution (Amos 2:7; Jer 5:7; Mic 1:7; Hos 1:2). Hosea's case is particularly interesting because Yahweh, the deity, commands him to marry a prostitute, and the book of Proverbs gives stern warnings to men against giving in to them (Prov 6:26; 7:10-23; 23:27-28).

Furthermore, most of the biblical imagery of prostitution or whoredom is used as a metaphor or allegory for religious idolatry on the part of the Israelites. Jerusalem is called a "whore" (Isa 1:21; Jer 3:1, 3; Ezek 16; compare Jer 2:20-22; 3:1-3), and the two states, Judah and Israel, symbolized by their capitols, Jerusalem and Samaria respectively, are portrayed as two sister whores, "Ohalibah" (Jerusalem) and "Ohalah" (Samaria), who are competing for the whore of the year award (Ezek 23; warning: Ezek 23 contains the most sexually explicit language in the Bible: read it at your own risk).

What then is the Dtr trying to do with this portrayal of Rahab, the prostitute? The traditional interpretation seems to be that the author was trying to explain how it happened that not all Canaanites were slaughtered by Moses/Joshua as commanded by Yahweh (Deut 7:1; Josh 10:40, 11:16-20).

However, from the perspective of the exilic/postexilic periods, the story of Rahab may have been understood in a different cultural context while still raising the all-important issue of "boundaries." What happens if one looks at this story from the point of view of what was taking place in the Jewish community during the exilic and postexilic periods? There was a movement recorded in the books of Ezra and Nehemiah to rid the Jewish community of mixed marriages (Ezra 9–10; Neh 13:23-29). Nehemiah 9:1 specifically mentions such foreigners as the Canaanites, Hittites, Perizzites, Jebusites, Ammonites, Moabites, Egyptians, and Amorites. Five of these are in the prohibitive list in Deuteronomy 7:1 (Canaanites, Hittites, Perizzites, Jebusites and Amorites). In Deuteronomy 23:3, two others, the Ammonites and Moabites, are also excluded from the "assembly of Yahweh." These ethnic groups rank right up there with Israelite men whose testicles have been crushed or whose penises have been cut off (Deut 23:1). They too are not allowed in the assembly of Yahweh.

By getting rid of all the foreign women and their children, Ezra–Nehemiah repeat the story in Joshua (Josh 6:21), albeit by a different method, that of expelling the wrong peoples (a.k.a. "outsiders") from the "pure" Jews (a.k.a. "insiders"; Ezra 10:44). Perhaps expulsion and abandonment (nothing is said about where these "foreigners" were sent or the fate that awaited them, including the children) is better than violent extermination. Nevertheless, just as in Joshua, Yahweh, now the god of the "Jews," is still not big enough to accept all humans despite the priestly creation myth in Genesis 1 that portrays the god as creating *ha'adam* (literally "the man, the humankind)—that is, the human race, male and female—in "his image" (vv. 26-27). (*Ha'adam* occurs some 140 times in the Hebrew Bible, all with the definite article and always in the singular. Thus, *ha'adam* is not a personal name, but a general term for the entire human race, just as is our English word, "mankind," "humankind"). You have to belong to the right ethnic/religious group (the ugly head of "ethnocentricity" pops up again!). If, in fact, Joshua as we now have it originated in the circles from which came Ezra–Nehemiah, with their obsession with the exclusiveness of the Jews at the expense of everyone else, there is no little irony in the story of Rahab. On this reading, her story could be used, seen from the time of its composition, as reinforcing this postexilic exclusive attitude so clearly spelled out in Ezra–Nehemiah. The primary message of the book would then seem to be that if the "Jews" in exile would go back to "Sinai," metaphorically speaking, in terms of "obeying" the laws of Yahweh mediated through Moses, they would get their land back, which was now in the hands of "foreigners," namely the Babylonians and Persians. From this perspective, perhaps the Dtr made up the Rahab story to support the genocide of the inhabitants of Canaan. Crenshaw has made the suggestion that the book of Joshua did, in fact, originate in the "circles that produced Ezra and Nehemiah. The intention of the book would therefore be to promote an exclusive attitude toward non-Israelites by offering an *imaginary* reconstruction of the settlement in Palestine" (1986, 114, my emphasis).

Such ethnocentricity reflected in the Ezra–Nehemiah faction should be as repugnant and unacceptable to modern sensibilities as is the description of genocidal slaughter described in Joshua. The postexilic book of Jonah was written in opposition to such attempts at "ethnic cleansing." For the author of Jonah, the mercy of and acceptance by Yahweh, the god of Israel, was extended to all peoples, even the hated Ninevites, including their animals! This universal message of Jonah is placed in the mouth of the king of Nineveh himself:

> By the decree of the king and his nobles: the *adam* (human being), the cattle, the herd, the flock, will not taste anything. They will not feed, and they will not drink water. The *adam* and *the animals* shall be covered with sackcloth, and they shall cry mightily to god(s) ('^{e}*lohim*). Everyone will turn from his or her evil ways and from the violence that is in their hands.

> Who knows? The god ('^{e}*lohim*) may relent and change his mind; he may turn from his fierce anger, so that we do not perish. (3:7-9; my emphasis)

There you have it. Not only all the people (*haadam*) but also all the sheep, goats, cows, chickens, asses, camels, and so forth repent from their evil and violent ways in sackcloth! And according to the very last verse in Jonah (4:11), the animals were many! In Joshua 2:9-13, Rahab also gives a "speech" comparable in some ways to the "speech" placed in the mouth of the king of Nineveh:

> I know that Yahweh has given you the land, and that the dread of you has fallen on us, and that *all* the inhabitants of the land melt in fear before you. For we have heard how Yahweh dried up the water of the Reed Sea before you when you came out of Egypt, and what you did to the two kings of the Amorites that were beyond the Jordan, to Sihon and Og, whom you utterly destroyed. As soon as we heard it, our hearts melted, and there was no courage left in any of us because of you. Yahweh, your god, is indeed god (MT*: '^{e}lohim is '^{e}lohim*) in heaven above and on earth below. Now then, since I have dealt kindly with you, swear to me by Yahweh that you in turn will deal kindly with my family. Give me a sign of good faith that you will spare my father and mother, my brothers and sisters, and *all* who belong to them, and deliver our lives from death.

Whatever the case may be, her "confession," as it were, was not lost on the author of the New Testament book Hebrews, where Rahab, along with other notables such as Abraham and Moses, is listed in the "roll call of faith" (Heb 11:31). Moreover, her story, however fictional it may be, may serve as a counter-example to the "final solution" described in such vivid detail in the rest of the story in Joshua. "Outsiders" could become "insiders" if they professed a belief in the tribal deity, Yahweh. (If word got out, you would think all of the "Canaanites" would convert. "Conversion" sounds a lot better than "killing everything that breathes"! How does this ideology differ from that of the modern-day organizations such as ISIS and Boko Haram?)

There is also the issue of Rahab's lying to the unnamed king in vv. 4-5. Deceit, often in the form of lying, is a common motif in the Hebrew Bible. And it begins with none other than Yahweh himself, the tribal deity. In Genesis 2:16-17, Yahweh warns humankind not to eat of the tree of knowledge of good and bad. "For on the day you eat from it, you shall surely die." When the serpent shows up and the woman tells him what the god had said, he responds, "You will not die; for '^{e}*lohim* (literally, "gods") knows that when you eat it your eyes will be opened and you will be like the gods (the same word, *'ᵉlohim*) knowing good and bad" (Gen 3:4-5). After the god discovers what has happened he reports back (to other *'ᵉlohim*?): "Now the human (*haadam*) has become like us to know good and bad" (Gen 3:22). Not only does humankind not die; Yahweh, the deity, also quotes the serpent who told the truth! Go figure.

There are many examples of someone lying to someone else in the stories that follow. Abraham lies to the Egyptian pharaoh to save his own hide (Gen 12:10-20), placing his wife, Sarah, in great danger. Jacob lies to just about everyone—first to his father, Isaac (Gen 27:18-20), managing at the same time to use the name of Yahweh in vain, violating what would later be forbidden in the Mosaic Law (Exod 20:7; Deut 5:11). The stories that follow his fleeing from the wrath of Esau, his brother, to his uncle, Laban, back in Mesopotamia are filled with one episode after another where these two Arameans make a living trying to out-lie and out-trick the other. Much of it is filled with wonderful humor such as Laban tricking Jacob into marrying his oldest daughter, Leah, first (Gen 29:21-30). What Leah thought about this arrangement we are never informed, but being the oldest daughter she may have accepted it gladly. Here is another story that illustrates the "biblical view of marriage." The same man can marry sisters while they both are alive. However, this practice will be condemned in Leviticus 18:18. (For more stories of deceit and lies see chapter 31.) In an ironic twist, Jacob's own sons lie to their father over the fate of another son, Joseph (Gen 37).

There are other examples of lying by biblical characters to achieve their goals. Two are, of all people, prophets! The court prophet, Nathan, apparently coached Bathsheba, one of David's wives, how to lie to David so she could secure the throne for her son, Solomon, after David's death (1 Kgs 1:11-30, see above). Centuries after David's death, King Zedekiah summoned the prophet, Jeremiah, to ask his advice concerning the circumstances brought on by the Babylonian war. When they finished their conversation, Zedekiah warned Jeremiah not to let anyone know what they had said or he (Jeremiah) would die. When the officials came and asked Jeremiah what he had told the king, he told the lie that the king told him to tell (Jer 38:14-28; note esp. vv. 24-28).

Seen in the broader context of the use of the "lying motif" to advance a story line, secure desirable ends, and create dramatic tension, Rahab's lie fits perfectly well with how the Dtr dramatizes her predicament. Most of the lying helps secure the survival of the liar. Such behavior also dramatically illustrates the ambiguity and irony often accompanying biblical folktales, making them at the same time entertaining and very exciting.

Crossing the Jordan

Joshua 3:1-17

1 Then Joshua rose early in the morning and set out from the Shittim and
they came to the Jordan, he and *all* the Israelites. And they remained there
before they crossed over. 2 And it happened at the end of three days that
the officers passed through the camp, 3 and they commanded the people
saying: "When you see the ark of the covenant of Yahweh your god and the
Levite priests carrying it, then you will set out from your place and you will
follow after it, 4 but only at a distance. There will be a space between you
and between it of about two thousand cubits in measure. You will not
approach toward it! In order that you will know the way that you are going
in regard to it (ark) for you have not crossed passed by this way recently."

5 Then Joshua said to the people: "Consecrate yourselves for
tomorrow Yahweh will do wonderful things in your midst." 6 Then Joshua
said to the priests: "Pick up the ark of the covenant and pass on before the
people." So they picked up the ark of the covenant and they walked in
front of the people.

7 Then Yahweh said to Joshua: "This day I will begin to make you
great in the eyes of *all* Israel that may know that even as I was with Moses
so I will be with you. 8 For you will command the priests carrying the ark
of the covenant saying: 'when you come to the border ("banks") of the
waters of the Jordan, in the Jordan you will stand.'"

9 Then Joshua said to the Israelites: "Come here and hear the words of
Yahweh your god." 10 And Joshua said: "By this you will know that *El* is
alive in your midst and you will surely dispossess the Canaanite, and the
Hittite, and the Hivite, and the Perizzite, and the Girgashite, and
the Amorite, and the Jebusite from your presence. 11 Lo the ark of the
covenant of the lord (*adon*) of *all* the earth is passing before you in the
Jordan. 12 And now take twelve men (MT: "man") from the tribes of Israel,
one man of each tribe. 13 And it will happen that when the soles of the feet
of the priests carrying the ark of the covenant of Yahweh, lord of *all* the
earth, (come to) rest in the waters of the Jordan, the waters of the Jordan

> will be cut off (from) the waters descending from above and they will stand in one heap."
>
> [14] And it happened that when the people set out from their tents to cross over the Jordan, the priests carrying the ark of the covenant (were) in front of the people, [15] and when those carrying the ark of the covenant came, and the feet of the priests carrying the ark dipped into the edge of the waters, that the Jordan was full on *all* its banks, *all* the days of the harvest. [16] And the waters coming down from above stopped, rising into one heap, very far away at Adam, the town that is beside Zarethan, and those (waters) descending toward the sea of the Arabah, the Salt Sea ("Dead Sea"), were finished, cut off. And the people crossed over opposite Jericho. [17] While the priests carrying the ark of the covenant of Yahweh stood on dry ground in the middle of the Jordan, to be set up, *all* Israel passed over on dry ground until the whole nation crossed over the Jordan.

The story in Joshua 3–5 will quickly be seen to contain three major themes or motives: a "miracle" story of how the Israelites crossed the River Jordan (ch. 3); the stone memorial(s) set up to commemorate the crossing (ch. 4); and the cultic act of Passover (including circumcision, ch. 5; on Passover in general see Vanderkam, 2009). That said, however, these tales are filled with textual and literary complexities that clearly suggest that different versions or parts of versions of these stories have been combined by the final redactor of DH to produce the story as we now have it. Because of these complexities, scholars have had a field day trying to locate and identify the basic elements and functions of the varied parts. These materials have been labeled as a "cultic legend" (H.-J. Kraus, 152–65), as a "sacred drama" (Soggin 1972, 54), and, chapter 3, as a "foundational myth" (Nelson 1997, 55–60). Arguments can be made, and obviously have been, for all of these suggestions as well as others. Note especially v. 10 where the god of Israel is now called *El* (אל; Cros), which is another Hebrew word with the meaning of "god." *El* is also the name of the high god of the Canaanite pantheon, originally worshiped by Isra-*el* (on *El* see above and below).

The comparison here between Moses/Joshua (v. 7) and Reed Sea/Jordan River (vv. 14-16) appears fairly obvious. Just as Yahweh was with Moses at the Reed Sea, now he is with Joshua, and the Jordan becomes dry land just as the sea did (Exod 14:21c). The Reed Sea/Jordan stories are totally mythologized in the Psalms (66:6; 114:1-8). When the literary structure of the story in 3:1-17 is appreciated, questions of its historicity become superfluous. One of the major differences, however, between the story told here and that in Exodus is the presence of the ark of the covenant in the former. The ark (always a different word in Hebrew from the ark of Noah) seems originally to have been associated with war (Num 10:35). Its fortunes in Israel prior to the monarchy are not clear, but it was the symbol par excellence of Yahweh's presence among his people (Birch). This lack of agreement among critical scholars (see for example Kraus, Soggin, and Nelson above) should create caution in anyone trying to make sense out of the material contained in these chapters. The ambiguities and complexities encountered here include the following (Nelson 1997, 55–62).

Confusing Chronological Data

The problem with chronological issues, especially concerning the number of days involved, has already been raised (above). According to 1:11, the people are told that they have "three days" to prepare for the river crossing. But according to 2:22, the spies hide out "three days" before reporting back to Joshua. Chapter 3 begins with the early rise of Joshua, who immediately set out for Shittim with "all of the Israelites," one assumes without breakfast! Joshua seems to have enjoyed getting up early (see also 6:12; 7:16; 8:10). Arriving at the Jordan, they camped before crossing the river. In 3:2, the three-day motif appears again. Does this include the day the people "camped," or are we now talking about four days? Add the three days of the hidden spies and it is up to seven days! It gets worse. In v. 5, in a Joshua speech, the people are told to "sanctify themselves, for tomorrow Yahweh will do wonders among you." Now how many days has it been? Three? Four? Five? Seven/eight? (See Nelson 1997, 60.)

The Story of the Ark

The story included by the Dtr regarding the ark is hopelessly confused and confusing. The ark itself is referred to in a variety of ways:

- "The ark of the covenant of Yahweh your god" (3:3).
- "The ark of the covenant" (3:6, 8, 14, 17; 4:9, 15).
- "The ark of the covenant of Yahweh" (3:11, 17; 4:18).
- "The ark of Yahweh" (3:13; 4:11).
- "The ark" (3:15; 4:10).

Adding to the confusion is the description of the ark in relationship to the people. We are told that the people must stay a minimum of two thousand cubits away from this object (3:4)! A cubit is usually figured to be around eighteen inches (measured from one's elbow to the tip of the middle finger). Two thousand cubits would then be about three thousand feet, well over a half-mile! At this distance, the ark would hardly have been visible! The story is incoherent and unbelievable as written. It has even been suggested that whoever wrote this story had never actually seen the Jordan River (Rösel, 61)! The obvious reason for this exaggerated distance between the box and the people is the assumed holiness of the ark. Thus it was dangerous for common people to be near it, much less make physical contact with it, as the story of Uzzah in 2 Samuel 6:1-11 clearly illustrates. This assumed holiness is also the reason why only Levitical priests could carry it around. As a symbol for the presence of the tribal deity, Yahweh, it is not surprising that the oldest traditions in the Bible concerning the ark all relate it to war (Num 10:35-36; 14:44; 1 Sam 4-7; cf. Ps 132:8). Yahweh is a man of war (Exod 14:14; 15:3; for a general discussion of the ark of the covenant see Birch).

The Carriers of the Ark and Where They Stand

There seems to be considerable confusion over where the priests carrying the ark are supposed to be standing while the people pass over the river. Some texts imply that the priests are standing on the edge of the river (2:8, 13, 15), while other verses suggest that they stand in the middle of the river (3:17; 4:18). Such inconsistencies only add to the incoherency of the story.

Unfulfilled Command

The command given to the Israelites to "sanctify" themselves (3:5) is nowhere said to have been obeyed. Nor is there any suggestion of how the people were to carry out such a ritual act. In fact, this verse interrupts the discussion concerning the ark that began in 3:2.

What happened at the Jordan is also ambiguous. Some texts suggest that the water of the Jordan was "cut off" (3:13, 16) while at the same time claiming that the water "stood still" (3:16). On the other hand, 4:22, based on analogy with one version of the Exodus myth (Exod 14:21c), claims that Yahweh "turned the sea into dry land." Moreover, the mention of the "twelve" men (3:12) who carry the stones abruptly interrupts the story of the ark and river crossing and is not explained until 4:1-9. The number, no doubt, was used by the Dtr to stress that all of the "events" described in this story involved "*all Israel.*"

Hagilgal and the Circle of Stones

Joshua 4:1-24

1 And so it happened that as the whole nation finished in crossing over the
Jordan that Yahweh spoke to Joshua saying: 2 "Take for yourselves from the
people twelve men, one man from each tribe, 3 and command them saying:
'take for yourselves from here out of the middle of the Jordan from the
place (where) the feet of the priests were fixed, twelve stones and cross over
with them and set them down in the lodging place where you will remain
tonight."

4 Then Joshua called the twelve men, a man whom he had secured
from the Israelites, one man from each tribe. 5 And Joshua said to them:
"Pass on before the ark of Yahweh your god into the middle of the Jordan
and lift up for yourselves each a stone on his shoulder for the number of
the tribes of the Israelites, 6 in order that this may be a sign among you.
When your sons ask in time to come saying: 'What (are) these stones to
you?' 7 Then you will say to them that the waters of the Jordan were cut off
from the ark of the covenant of Yahweh. When it crossed over in the
Jordan, the waters of the Jordan were cut off; and these stones (will be) for
a memorial to the Israelites into the far future."

8 *And the Israelites did so even as Joshua commanded. And they carried
twelve stones from the middle of the Jordan* even as Yahweh had spoken to
Joshua, according to the number of the tribes of the Israelites (my
emphasis). And they passed over with them to the lodging place and set
them down there.

9 *Then Joshua set up twelve stones in the middle of the Jordan* below the
standing place of the feet of the priests carrying the ark of the covenant
(my emphasis). And they are there even to this day. 10 Then the priests
carrying the ark were standing in the middle of the Jordan until everything
that Yahweh had commanded Joshua to say to the people was completed.
And the people hastened and crossed over. 11 And it happened that as *all*
the people finished crossing over, the ark of Yahweh and the priests crossed
over in front of the people.

> 12 Then the sons of Reuben and the sons of Gad, and the half-tribe of Manasseh crossed over in battle array before the Israelites even as Moses had spoken to them. 13 About forty thousand who were equipped for the war crossed over before Yahweh for battle, to the plains of Jericho. 14 On that day Yahweh caused Joshua to be great in the eyes of *all* Israel and they feared him even as they feared Moses *all* the days of his life.
>
> 15 Then Yahweh spoke to Joshua saying: 16 "Command the priests carrying the ark of the testimony [not "covenant"] and they will come up out of the Jordan." 17 And Joshua commanded the priests saying: "Come up out of the Jordan." 18 And so it was that as the priests carrying the ark of the covenant of Yahweh came out of the middle of the Jordan and the soles of the feet of the priests were drawn to the dry ground, the waters of the Jordan returned to their places and they came as they were before on *all* its banks.
>
> 19 So the people came out of the Jordan on the tenth day of the first month; and they encamped at Hagilgal on the east border of Jericho. 20 And these twelve stones that they took from the Jordan, Joshua set up at Hagilgal. 21 Then he said to the Israelites: "When your sons ask their fathers in time to come saying: 'What (mean) these stones?' 22 Then you will let your sons know, saying: 'On dry ground Israel cross over the Jordan.' 23 For Yahweh your god made dry the waters of the Jordan from before you until you crossed over, even as Yahweh your god did to the Reed Sea, which he made dry from before us until we crossed over, 24 in order that *all* the people of the earth might know that the hand of Yahweh (is) mighty, so that you might fear Yahweh your god *all* the days."

Hagilgal is referenced some forty times in the Hebrew Bible and is always accompanied with the definite article, *ha* ("the") in the Hebrew text meaning literally, "the gilgal," except in Joshua 5:9 (see below). The reason for the definite article is not known (just as in the case of *Ha'ai*, translated in English usually as "'Ai" or simply "Ai" in chs. 7 and 8; see below). This phenomenon is known elsewhere in Joshua (19:18-20, and so forth). In the following discussion, in order to avoid confusion and at the same time stay as close as possible to the original Hebrew, the word (and even with the definite article it is still one word in Hebrew) will be transliterated as "Hagilgal." Its importance in pre-monarchic Israel has long been noted (Miller 1990, 332), but the traditions preserved about this site in Joshua have proven to be extremely difficult to interpret. Soggin argued that the textual confusion encountered here over the two traditions of the twelve stones makes a "more thorough study impossible" (1972, 64). Polzin's literary solution, namely that the tradition of Joshua's setting up the twelve stones in the middle of the

Jordan (v. 9) is a Dtr device to enhance the "interpretive role of Joshua" with regard to Yahweh's word seen from the perspective of Josiah's reformation, may make some sense. Thus, all the non-Israelites in the land (this Hebrew word, ארץ, is commonly translated as "earth") will know the power of Yahweh and fear him all their days (v. 24). Of course, Yahweh's power is exercised, once again, through his chosen earthly representative, Joshua. Thus the legitimacy of the reformation to centralize power in the hands of King Josiah at the end of the seventh century BCE is once more affirmed as divinely approved. It is noteworthy that in v. 14 the people are said to have feared Joshua just as they had feared Moses. (The verb, ירא, has the basic meaning of "fear," "be afraid"; the translation in the RSV and the NRSV, "stood in awe of," misses the point. When you can be killed for disobeying Joshua [1:18], Moses, and/or Yahweh [Deut 13:1-11], "awe" is hardly the appropriate emotional response.)

Memorial Stones (4:1-8, 9)

These etiologies concerning the twelve stones raise a critical/literary problem. There are two etiologies here: the first (vv. 1-8) claims that Joshua, by the command of Yahweh, selected twelve men to carry twelve stones from the middle of the Jordan to the camp site (presumably Hagilgal). The other, very puzzling etiology claims that Joshua set up the twelve stones in the middle of the Jordan (v. 9). How stones set up in the middle of a river could still be seen "to this day" (v. 9) is not clear (no pun intended). These stones were to be a memorial to the people of Israel forever (v. 4). Thus Yahweh's promises could not be destroyed by time or by exile and, apparently, not by muddy waters! The usage of stones in cultic contexts is quite common in the Hebrew Bible, and another stone story occurs in Joshua 24:26-27 (see below and Laughlin 2001).

This episode ends with the Dtr reporting the response of the inhabitants of Canaan (v. 24), exaggerated as the claim that "the people of *all* the land (or earth)" would know and fear Yahweh (v. 24; here the RSV and the NRSV translate the verb, *yr'*, correctly with the English word, "fear"! Compare Deut 13:4). Polzin observed that as an "omniscient observer," the Dtr frequently penetrates "the psychological consciousness of *all* his characters" (102). In other words, the Dtr made up all the "reported speeches" of his characters!

How Many Warriors? (4:12-13)

According to 4:12-13, the warriors of the two and a half Transjordan tribes, Reuben, Gad, and Manasseh, also crossed over the Jordan. They are said to have numbered "about forty thousand." The number of warriors of the other nine and a half tribes is not given. If one assumes that the other tribes would have had roughly the same number of fighting men (which averages out to about sixteen thousand warriors per tribe), a fighting force of some one hundred and ninety two thousand warriors are envisioned here! By the time the women, children, and old men who cannot go to war anymore are added to this group, a population of well over a half million people is suggested! The point is that the story implies everyone crossed rather quickly. The tale seems highly embellished, as are similar biblical stories involving large numbers (compare Exod 12:37; Num 1:44-46).

All of these issues, and others, point to the complex and muddled nature of these traditions (Nelson 1997, 66). Nevertheless, the intent of the Dtr seems clear: the people called "Israel" became a "nation" (3:17) not by their own machinations but by the miraculous crossing of the Jordan where they would ultimately come into possession of land. Nelson called this story Israel's "foundational myth." Such a story from the Dtr's perspective may have justified "outsiders" becoming "insiders," which is typical Dtr theology that is clearly reflected in the closing speech of chapter 4 attributed once more to Joshua:

> For Yahweh your god made dry the waters of the Jordan from before you until you crossed over, even as Yahweh your god did to the Reed Sea, which he made dry from before us until we crossed over, in order that *all* the people of the earth might know that the hand of Yahweh (is) mighty, so that you might fear Yahweh your god *all* the days."

This is the story that future generations are commanded to tell when their children ask, "What do these stones mean?" (4:6, 21). The story serves theologically to justify the land-grabbing schemes by one group over others who are already in the land. The horrible historical consequences of such a self-serving theology cannot be fleshed out here (but see Gunn; Prior 1997, 1999; Warrior; Ben-Gurion). The major theological problem with this story, of course, is that it ignores totally the fact other peoples already "possessed the land" (3:10).

While chapters 3 and 4 serve primarily to emphasize the crossing of the Jordan (Nelson 1997, 67), the story also serves a secondary intention of explaining a circle (?) of stones at a site called "Hagilgal," first mentioned in

Joshua 4:19. (Deut 11:30 may refer to some other site with the same name; also the LXX has "Galilee" for Gilgal in Josh 4:19. Note also that the references to Gilgal in Josh 15:7 and 2 Kgs 2:1 do not agree with the traditional location of this site.) The traditions recounted here of the crossing of the River Jordan and the activity associated with Hagilgal are filled with textual and literary difficulties that have led to various proposed historical reconstructions (Soggin 1972, 47–67; for a helpful list of some of the textual difficulties in this story see Boling 1982, 156–58; de Vaux, 598–603). Many years ago H.-J. Kraus suggested that this complex of traditions makes up a "cultic legend" (152–65). Others have called these stories a "liturgical narrative" (Polzin, 92) and a "sacred drama" (Soggin 1972, 54).

In this folktale, Hagilgal (maybe meaning "the circle [of stones]") becomes the first site where the first national monument (stones) was erected. The place is mentioned some forty times in the MT. It has been suggested that "Hagilgal" may originally have referred to several "circles of stones," with the one preceded by the definite article considered the most important and/or best known (Ely). All of this confusion is due to the complexity of the tradition(s) about this site and the transmission history of the biblical text. Whatever term one chooses to categorize this section in Joshua, it seems highly likely that as it now stands it represents a historicizing of ritual acts involving the themes of Passover and conquest. Originally this ritual reenactment may have involved only the tribe of Benjamin, in whose territory Hagilgal was located. Miller and Tucker succinctly summarized the critical issues raised by this story some forty years ago (41–42):

> Any attempt to outline or to summarize the story [in chapter 4] reveals inconsistencies and repetitions which must have resulted from the combination of several traditions and the work of more than one writer. We are hard pressed to state precisely what is supposed to have happened, or to list without contradictions the sequence of events.

According to traditions preserved in 1 Samuel, Hagilgal was an important earlier Israelite cultic center (Laughlin 1989). Samuel is said to have worked here as a Judge (1 Sam 7:15-16), and here Saul was both reaffirmed publicly as "king" (1 Sam 11:14-15) and condemned by Samuel (1 Sam 13:5-15). Furthermore, one of the most violent "cultic" acts described in the Hebrew Scriptures took place here: the hacking into pieces of Agag, the king of the Amalekites, by Samuel (1 Sam 15:32-35). The close association of Hagilgal with both Samuel and Saul may indicate that at first Hagilgal was an important Benjaminite site. It is also claimed that David chose Hagilgal as a rallying place for reuniting his supporters after Absalom's revolt was crushed (2 Sam 19:15, 40; [vv. 16, 41 in MT]).

The last references to the site in the Hebrew Scriptures are from the eighth century BCE prophets, Hosea, Amos, and Micah. Hosea (4:15; 12:11) and Amos (4:4; 5:5) condemn Hagilgal for its cultic excesses, which, among other things, seem to have included cult prostitution (see esp. Hos 4:14). The only positive reference at this time comes from Micah (6:5), who lists what happened at Hagilgal among Yahweh's saving acts.

The site itself has never been discovered. The geographical references to it seem to locate it somewhere east of Jericho (Josh 4:19). All attempts to locate it have failed, and if the description of Hagilgal as a "camp" (Josh 10:6, 15, 43 and elsewhere) is to be taken at face value, there may be little or nothing to find at this late date (Muilenburg 1955; 1962). By the time of the writing of the DH, Hagilgal had become a symbol of all Israel (twelve men; twelve stones), but played no role after the eighth century BCE. Other "Gilgals" such as those mentioned in Deuteronomy 11:30, 2 Kings 2:1, and Joshua 15:7, as already mentioned, are believed to refer to other sites. But even in these exceptions, the noun is preceded by the definite article. Scholars usually emend the "Gilgal" in the Hebrew text of Joshua 12:23 to read "Galilee" based on the reading in the LXX.

Circumcision and Passover

Joshua 5:1-12

[1] And it came about when *all* of the kings of the Amorites beyond the Jordan toward the sea [the Mediterranean], and *all* the kings of the Canaanites by the sea heard that Yahweh had made the waters of the Jordan dry up before the Israelites while they were crossing over, their hearts melted and there was not still in them a spirit because of the Israelites.

[2] At that time, Yahweh said to Joshua: "Make for yourselves knives of flint [MT: "swords of rock"] and turn and circumcise the Israelites a second (time)." [3] So Joshua made for himself knives of flint and he circumcised the Israelites at Gibeath-haaraloth (MT: "the hill of the foreskins"; a.k.a. "Mount Foreskins"!). [4] And this is the reason Joshua circumcised *all* the people who came out of Egypt; the males, *all* the men of war, had died in the wilderness on the journey in their coming out of Egypt. [5] Even though *all* of the people coming out had been circumcised but *all* the people, the ones born in the wilderness after coming out from Egypt were not circumcised. [6] For forty years the Israelites walked in the wilderness until *all* the nation, the warriors (MT: "men of war"), the ones who came out of Egypt perished, because they did not listen to the voice of Yahweh. For Yahweh swore to them that they would not see the land that Yahweh swore to their fathers to give to us, a land flowing with milk and honey. [7] Thus it was their sons he (Yahweh) raised up instead of them (in their place) that Joshua circumcised, for they were uncircumcised, because they were not circumcised on the way.

[8] So it was that when the circumcision of the entire nation was completed, they remained below them in the camp until they were healed (MT: "alive"). [9] Then Yahweh said to Joshua: "Today I have rolled away the shame of Egypt from upon you." And the name of the place itself was called Gilgal (without the definite article: *ha*) unto this day.

[10] While the Israelites were encamped at Hagilgal (with the definite article, *ha*) they kept the passover on the fourteenth day of the month in the evening in the plains of Jericho. [11] And they ate the produce of the land

> on the morrow of the passover [the day after passover], unleavened breads and roasted grain (LXX; MT: "bone"). [12] Then the manna stopped on the morrow of their eating from the produce of the land. And there was no manna again for the Israelites. Now they ate from the produce of the land of Canaan in that year.

This chapter begins with an interesting motif that cannot be fully explicated here. It is the motif of "hearing." "When *all* the kings . . . heard that Yahweh had dried up the waters . . . ." How all the kings *heard* is never disclosed. This motif has already been encountered in Joshua 2:10, in the "speech" by Rahab. It will appear again in 9:1, 10:1, and 11:1. It also appears in other contexts (for example see 1 Kgs 12:2; the reader is never informed concerning the medium of such "hearings").

Moreover, the origin and meaning of circumcision as practiced in later Israel cannot be discussed here (Polhill, 156–57; Soards). However, the reason given in 5:4-7 that the circumcision of those born in the wilderness could not have been done prior to the present context seems contrived at best. Perhaps it was intended to link the rite of circumcision with that of Passover, which immediately follows in this story (compare Exod 12:48). By juxtaposing the themes of the crossing of the Jordan with Passover (5:10), the tradition of the exodus from Egypt has been connected with that of the entry into the land. Moreover, according to the story told in Exodus 12:43-49, men who participated in the Passover festival had to be circumcised. Women, apparently, never participated in the Passover rite. Nowhere does the Hebrew Scripture offer regulations vis-à-vis female participation. The connection here between Passover and circumcision is, however, unclear (compare Halpern 1983, 81–94; 1992a, 89–113). In fact, the rather detailed explanation of why the male Israelites who crossed the Jordan had to be circumcised (5: 2-9) is literarily disconnected from the description of Passover in 5:10-12, as is the extremely weird story with which the chapter ends.

All three pericopes appear to be artificially connected chronologically. The circumcision story begins with the ambiguous reference, "at that time . . ." (5:2). What time, exactly? The Passover story also begins with another ambiguous phrase: "While the Israelites were camped at Hagilgal" (5:10). The final episode of the chapter begins with still another vague time reference: "once when Joshua was by Jericho" (or "when Joshua was in Jericho"). It would appear that the connection of all three of these vignettes is the editorial work of the Dtr. Consequentially, in all likelihood the entire scenario is fictional, a product of the imagination of the Dtr (see quote from

Miller and Tucker above). Nevertheless, the story's connection with Passover would seem to be strengthened by the use of the verb *'br* ("to pass," "passover"), which appears some eight times in chapter 3 alone (vv. 1, 4, 6, 11, 14, 16).

In a detailed literary analysis, Polzin (91–110) argued that the biblical narrator used this ritual drama to illustrate once again the fulfillment of the word of Israel's deity. Nevertheless, the way the story is told here seems artificial and contrived. Note that there is no hint here that the rite included infants as it ultimately would (the P tradition in Gen 17 is dated by many scholars to the exile or later). Moreover, v. 2 seems to imply that the "sons of Israel" were being circumcised a "second time"! Furthermore, the etymological etiology in v. 9 for "gilgal" is forced and served only as a popular meaning of the word. The Hebrew word, גלל (*gll*), has the meaning of a large rolling stone (Ezra 5:8; 6:4; in Isa 28:28 this same word is translated as a "cart wheel") and has the same consonants as "gilgal"; Laughlin 1989). But the practice of circumcision and its symbolic meaning of belonging to the family of Abraham and thus being an heir to the promises that Yahweh, the tribal deity, had made to him, would have found receptive ears among the exiles. Furthermore, the reference to Passover anticipates the claim that King Josiah renewed the Passover celebration as part of his reforms in Judah at the end of the seventh century BCE (2 Kgs 23:21-23).

The reference to "rolling" away the "reproach of Egypt" (v. 9) has also elicited a variety of responses. Polzin's suggestion that Joshua 5:9 is the Dtr's response to Deuteronomy 9:20 (111) seems a stretch. Moreover, according to Exodus 12, the first circumcision took place while the "Hebrews" were still in Egypt. Perhaps it was a botched attempt and the current circumcision of all the males born while in the wilderness (Josh 5:2-7) made up for it (Soards). Actually, given the fantastic numbers of the people supposedly involved in the exodus (which would have been in the millions; Exod 12:37; compare Num 1:45-47), the infant mortality rate thousands of years ago, and the conditions of a desert environment, the entire collection of "exodus/conquest" stories should probably be read as folktales with little or no historical veracity. Scholars continue to debate these controversial issues and, barring new and decisive evidence, will no doubt continue to do so. While the stories of the exodus out of Egypt and the conquest of Canaan by the Israelites are among the best-known stories of the Bible, there is no or little direct archaeological evidence that supports taking the stories at face value (Dever 2010, 356; Finkelstein and Mazar 2007, 41–65; Grabbe 2007, 84–88; Finkelstein and Silberman 2001, 62–64; Frerichs and Lesko 1997).

This lack of archaeological evidence for an exodus of biblical proportions is a very important issue. If there was no "exodus," there certainly was no "conquest" as described in the Bible (Halpern, 1992b). It has often been said, in the face of the absence of archaeological evidence to support these biblical stories, that "absence of evidence is not evidence of absence." Perhaps this is a clever witticism, and proving a negative is usually impossible. For example, I do not believe that "ghosts" exist, but I cannot prove that they do not exist. I do not have to. It is up to the people who do believe that ghosts exist to provide the supporting evidence. To quote Christopher Hitchens once more, "What can be asserted without evidence can also be dismissed without evidence" (150). Nevertheless, sometimes absence of evidence may very well be evidence of absence, especially when one has every right to find evidence if what is being claimed actually exists or happened. Regarding the question of an "exodus" out of Egypt of biblical proportions, no one has expressed the significance of the lack of evidence supporting such a claim more clearly than Finkelstein and Silberman in their book, *The Bible Unearthed*:

> Some archaeological traces of their generation-long wandering in the Sinai should be apparent. However, except for the Egyptian forts along the northern coast, *not a single campsite or sign of occupation from the time of Ramesses II and his immediate predecessors and successors has ever been identified in Sinai.* And it has not been for lack of trying. Repeated archaeological surveys in all regions of the peninsula including the mountainous area around the traditional site of Mount Sinai, near Saint Catherine's Monastery . . . , have yielded only negative evidence: not a single sherd, no structure, not a single house, no trace of an ancient encampment. One may argue that a relatively small band of wandering Israelites cannot be expected to leave material remains behind. But modern archaeological techniques are quite capable of tracing even the very meager remains of hunter-gathers and pastoral nomads all over the world. Indeed, the archaeological record from the Sinai peninsula discloses evidence from pastoral activity in such eras as the third millennium BCE and the Hellenistic and Byzantine periods. There is simply no such evidence at the supposed time of the Exodus in the thirteenth century BCE.
>
> The conclusion—that the Exodus did not happen at the time and in the manner described in the Bible seems irrefutable when we examine the evidence at specific sites where the children of Israel were said to have camped for extended periods during their wandering in the desert (Numbers 33) and where some archaeological indications—if present—would almost certainly be found. According to the biblical narrative, the children of Israel camped at Kadesh-barnea for thirty-eight of the forty

> years of the wanderings. The general location of this site is clear from the description of the southern border of the land of Israel in Numbers 34. . . . Yet repeated excavations and surveys throughout the entire area have not provided even the slightest evidence for activity in the Late Bronze Age, *not even a single sherd left by a tiny fleeing band of frightened refugees.* (62–63, my emphasis)

One might add to the above observations that, according to the Bible, it was not a "relatively small band of wandering Israelites" that left Egypt but a large horde numbering in the millions (Exod 12:37; Num 1:45-47)!

A Visit from a Commander of Yahweh's Army

Joshua 5:13-15

> [13] Now it happened that Joshua was close to Jericho and he lifted up his eyes and, behold, he saw a man standing in front of him with a drawn sword in his hand. And Joshua walked up to him and said to him: "(are) you for us or our foes?" [14] And he said: "No, (it is) because I am a captain of the army of Yahweh that I have now come." And Joshua fell on his face (MT: "faces") to the earth and prostrated himself and said to him: "What, my lord, are you saying to his (Yahweh's) servant?" [15] And the captain of the army of Yahweh said to Joshua: "Take off your sandal from upon your foot, for the place on which are standing is holy." And Joshua did so.

The ambiguous nature of this pericope has given rise to many interpretations. The most common suggestion is that something has fallen out because it seems to anticipate some sort of a command to Joshua other than to take his sandals off (v. 15; compare Exod 3:5). It has been suggested that 6:2-5 is the actual command, given by Yahweh himself and not by some intermediary divine army commander, whatever that is (Nelson 1998, 80–83). What seems certain is the Dtr is once again confirming Joshua's legitimacy as the successor of Moses. The order given to Moses, "remove the sandals from your feet, for the place on which you are standing is holy ground," is repeated verbatim to Joshua in 5:14, minus the word "ground" that occurs in Exodus 3:5. What possible connection this story could have with the preceding Passover story is anyone's guess. It is almost as if the Dtr had a weird yarn about an encounter between Joshua and some otherworldly military commander and decided to stick it someplace in his story. This abrupt lack of continuity points once more to the complex transmission of this tale before its literary fixation. Moreover, what made the place where Joshua stood in the story "holy"? It has been suggested that the "holy place" was in Jericho itself. The beginning of v. 13 could be translated as, "when Joshua was in Jericho." But such a translation would imply that the city had already been taken by the Israelites, and, in any case, considering the fate of Jericho in this story, what would make it a "holy" place? This short vignette raises far more questions than there are satisfactory answers. It has been suggested (for example, Polzin, 110–13) that the ambiguities in this story are a deliberate creation of the Dtr. Just as Yahweh's relationship with Israel was not automatic, neither were Israel's struggles to understand the ambiguities of faith. Why "faith" can only be faith if cloaked in ambiguities in the first place, Polzin did not bother to explain. As always in such theologizing, the goods of mystery always trump the goods of clarity.

The "Conquest" of Canaan

Joshua 6:1–12:24

Introduction: Archaeology and the "Conquest" of Canaan

As already noted (see above) a literal, naïve reading of the traditions contained in these chapters would force the conclusion that roughly forty years after the people left Egypt with Moses, their descendants, under the command of Joshua, marched into the land of Canaan from the region of the Transjordan and in a relatively short period (five years or so) annihilated all of its inhabitants, beginning with the miraculous destruction of Jericho. This paraphrasing of the story, as though it were a real historical event, was rejected many years ago by mainstream biblical historians and archaeologists (Dever 2003a, 41). Now recent archaeological discoveries, already discussed above, have confirmed this judgment. The issues involved here were succinctly focused by the late P. de Vaux many years ago: "The problem raised by the settlement of the Israelites in Canaan and the growth of the system of the twelve tribes is the most difficult problem in the whole history of Israel" (475; compare Mendenhall, 66; Mazar 1990, 281). There are too many critical issues with which to deal adequately here. The interested reader is encouraged to pursue these questions through the references given in the more detailed section dealing with archaeology above (see above, Archaeology and the Book of Joshua, pp. 29–43).

The full implications of this emerging new synthesis for understanding the origin of the Israelite religion and its worship of the local deity, Yahweh, have yet to be clarified (K. McCarter, Jr. 1992, 119–36; Smith 2002). It should also be emphasized that given the above critical discussion of what happened in the central-hill country of Canaan during Iron Age I, the word "conquest" is a misnomer as is reflected in the title of one of Finkelstein's most influential books: *The Archaeology of the Israelite Settlement.* There was no "conquest" of biblical proportions regardless of what date(s) one wishes to use. In other words, if there were no "conquest," there obviously is no date for a "conquest." I hope the detailed discussion of the stories now to be discussed will justify such a conclusion.

The Fall of Jericho

Jericho 6:1-27

1 Now Jericho was shut up and closed because of the Israelites. No one came out and no one went in. 2 And Yahweh said to Joshua: "See, I have given into your hand Jericho with her king (and) the mighty men of courage. 3 Now you will go around the city, *all* the men of war surrounding the city one time. This you will do six days, 4 and seven priests will carry seven rams' horns in front of the ark. On the seventh day you will go around the city seven times, and the priests will blow on the horns. 5 When there is drawn-out horn (blast) of the ram's horn, when you hear the sound of the horn, *all* the people will raise a shout, a great shout, and the wall of the city will fall flat and the people to a man will go up facing it."

6 Then Joshua, the son of Nun, called the priests and said to them: "Carry the ark of the covenant and seven priests will carry seven horns of rams' horns before the ark of Yahweh." 7 Then he said (*qere*) to the people: "Pass over and go around the city; and the one equipped (for war) will pass over before the ark of Yahweh." 8 And so as Joshua spoke to the people, then the seven priests, the ones carrying the seven horns of the rams' horns before Yahweh, passed on, and they blew on the horns and the ark of the covenant of Yahweh following behind them. 9 And the one equipped (for war) was walking in front of the priests who were blowing the horns; and the one bringing up the rear was walking behind the ark, to go and to blow on the horns.

10 Then Joshua commanded the people saying: "You will not shout nor let your voice be heard, and you will not let a word come out of your mouth until the day I say to you to shout. Then you will raise a shout." 11 So the ark of Yahweh went around the city, going around one time. Then they went into the camp and remained in the camp.

12 Then Joshua rose early in the morning, and the priests lifted up the ark of Yahweh. 13 And the seven priests carrying the seven horns of the rams' horns in front of the ark of Yahweh, the ones who were walking, and they were blowing the horns. And the one equipped (for war) was walking in front of them, and the one bringing up the rear was walking behind the

ark of Yahweh, and with the horns blowing proceeded. 14 And they went around the city on the second day one time then returned to the camp. Thus they did this for six days. 15 Then it happened on the seventh day that they rose early so to rise at dawn and they went around the city after this judgment seven times. Only on that day did they go around the city seven times.

16 And so it was on the seventh time the priests blew the horns and Joshua said to the people: "Shout! For Yahweh has given to you the city. 17 And the city and *all* that is in her will be devoted (put to the ban: *herem*) to Yahweh. Only Rahab the prostitute will live; she and *all* who (are) with her in the house because she hid the messengers that we sent. 18 But only you keep away from the devoted (things) lest you cause to destroy and you take from the devoted (things), and you make the camp of Israel into a devoted (thing) and you make trouble for us. 19 But *all* silver and gold, and vessels of copper (bronze) and iron (are) sacred to Yahweh. It will go (into) the treasury of Yahweh."

20 Then the people raised a shout and they blew on the horns. And it happened as the people heard the sound of the horns that the people raised a shout, a great shout, and the wall fell down below. Then the people went up toward the city, a man in front, and they captured the city. 21 And they put to the ban (*herem*; exterminated) *all* who (were) in the city, both man and woman, both young and old, and even cattle (oxen) and sheep, and ass with the edge of the sword.

22 Then to the two men who spied out the land, Joshua said: "Go into the house of the woman, the prostitute, and bring out from there the woman and *all* the belongs to her, even as you swore to her." 23 So the young (men) who spied brought out Rahab and her father and her mother, and her brother, and *all* who belonged to her; *all* her kindred they brought out, and they put them outside the camp of Israel. 24 Then they burned the city with fire and *all* that was in her. Only the silver and gold, and the vessels of copper and iron, they put into the treasury in the house of Yahweh (MT: בית יהוה, *beit Yahweh*).

25 But Rahab the prostitute, and the house of her father, and *all* who belonged to her, Joshua let live. Thus in the midst of Israel, even up to this day, she has dwelled, because she hid the messengers whom Joshua sent to spy on Jericho. 26 Joshua then swore this oath saying: "cursed be the man before Yahweh who arises and builds this city, Jericho. With his first born he will establish her and with his youngest he will cause to stand her doors (gates)." 27 And Yahweh was with Joshua, and his report (fame?) was in *all* the land.

In light of the preceding archaeological discussion, the historical problem raised by the conquest stories of Jericho (as well as *Ha'ai*, see below) can be summed up succinctly: the site of Jericho was not occupied at the end of the Late Bronze Age-Iron Age I. The secondary literature on the story of Jericho is vast, but suffice it to say that while the archaeological evidence for this ancient city is sometimes ambiguous (Kenyon 1957; see Holland and Netzer with bibliography and Levine), it is abundantly clear that no Late Bronze Age city of any size existed during the time most scholars would date the first appearance of the "Israelites" in Canaan. Rationalizations to explain this absence (such as rain or wind erosion; the questioning of the identification of Tel es-Sultan as Jericho; the suggestion that it happened during the Middle Bronze Age) are all examples of Dever's "wishful thinking" (1992, 84). The story of Jericho is no more and no less than a "miracle" story in which a deity, in this case, Yahweh, does all the work and all the Israelites have to do is obtain a parade permit and march around the city a few times, blow rams' horns, and shout at the top of their lungs.

John H. Hayes, in his book, *Introduction to Old Testament Study*, argued that the story of Jericho shows "a remarkable religious orientation" (1979, 220). The cultic characteristics present in this story include the emphasis on the priests, the ark of the covenant, the blowing of horns and shouting, as well as the number seven associated with the marching around the city by the Israelites. "The entry into the promised land is depicted as a religious processional" (Hayes, 220). Consequently, the cultic ("religious") characteristics of this story make it difficult, if not impossible, to recover with any certainty actual historical events that might be associated with it (see Mitchell's discussion of Joshua 6 where he calls the story "A Cultic Miracle at Jericho," 51–66). Furthermore, close literary analysis reveals that the story as we have it is filled with duplications and ambiguities. Even the beginning of the story is puzzling. Chapter 5 ends with Joshua standing barefoot on "holy ground," "close to Jericho" (5:13). The story in chapter 6, however, begins with the "Israelites" already at Jericho with no word concerning when or how they got there.

A close, critical reading of the MT also reveals several confusing duplications (Miller and Tucker, 53–55). Both vv. 16 and 20 report the final blasts of the ram's horn while vv. 21 and 24 both report Jericho's destruction. In v. 21 it is by the application of the ban (*herem*) where all living creatures are slaughtered with the edge of the sword (see Lohfink). In v. 24, on the other hand, we are told that the city and all who were in her were destroyed by fire. Moreover, two different signals are given for when the "Israelites" were to raise a war shout: the first is the horn blast (v. 5), but in vv. 10 and 16 we are informed that the "shout" was to commence on the order of Joshua, not at the sound of the horns. Shouting or a "war cry" is a frequent motif in "holy war" (1 Sam 4:5; 17:20, 52; 2 Chr 13:15; Jer 14:16; von Rad 1958, 41–51). Finally, vv. 22-23 and 25 report twice the saving of Rahab. The idea of a "holy war" is very troublesome (or probably should be) to our modern age. An entire cottage industry has revolved around it (von Rad, Niditch).

Other ambiguities also abound in this story. Did the walls of Jericho "fall flat" when the people shouted (vv. 16, 20) or at the sound of the rams' horns or both (vv. 16, 20)? Speaking of the horns, who blew them? Verses 4 and 16 clearly claim the priests were the horn blowers, but vv. 9b and 13b imply it was the rearguard following behind the ark. In v. 20a, we are simply told that "they blew the horns." The only subject preceding the verb "to blow" is *hā'am*, "the people." In fact, *hā'am*, the only subject in this verse, occurs four times! Then there are the insertions concerning Rahab. Joshua 2:15 locates Rahab's house on the "outer side of the city wall." Thus it would seem to be fair to conclude that when we are informed in 6:20 that when the people shouted and the horns blew "and the wall fell down below," that included the house of Rahab. How is it then that not until vv. 22-23, after the collapsing walls, are we informed that the two spies are ordered by Joshua to go into the house of the "woman" and bring out her and her family. Are we supposed to conclude that they survived the collapse of the city walls and were found safe in a pile of rubble after the destruction of the city was completed? To make matters even worse, v. 25 seems to be an altogether different version of the rescue of Rahab and all that belonged to her. Such textual difficulties clearly indicate that this story consists of radically different versions of what supposedly happened at Jericho. Perhaps this reflects the telling and retelling of this folktale before becoming fixed in a literary form.

Another critical issue is how to understand the story in chapter 6 in relation to another story of the destruction of the city reported in 24:11a. In this latter version (see below), we are told in barely a third of one verse that "when you went over the Jordan and came to Jericho, *the citizens of Jericho fought against you . . .*" (my emphasis; for a tortuous attempt to salvage some historicity of the Jericho story see Hess 2008).

The Hebrew Bible mentions the city of Jericho itself over fifty times. In almost fifty percent of these (26 times), the mention of the site is for geographical location/orientation. Thus, the expression "across the Jordan from Jericho" often occurs (Num 22:1; 26:3, 63; 31:12; 33:48, and so forth). Sometimes the expression refers to the "plains of Jericho," as in Jeremiah 39:5 and 52:8. Ten times "Jericho" appears in reference to its king (Josh 2:2, 3; 6:2; 8: 2; 10:1, 28, 30; 12:9). Moreover, as just mentioned, there are two different versions of what happened to the city. The more famous one, with the tumbling walls, is found only in chapter 6. But there are no few curiosities to this story. After mentioning the city by name in the opening two verses of the chapter, "Jericho" is never mentioned again until v. 25. There is no mention of any king after v. 6 and, perhaps even more puzzling, no mention of any resistance on the part of the city's inhabitants (Coogan 1990a).

The story in 24:11, however, is a much more cryptic account that links the defeat of Jericho with that of other peoples including the "Amorites" and "Canaanites." This summary passage also specifically relates that the "citizens of Jericho fought against" Israel (24:11b). Conspicuously absent, however, is any mention of marching around, blowing horns, walls falling flat, rescuing prostitutes, or imposing the "ban" (6:17). Stuck in the larger "Shechem renewal speech" by the biblical editor(s), this version of the capture/destruction of Jericho seems to come from a very different source than that preserved in chapter 6.

Both stories, whatever their ultimate origin, seem to be literary creations of the Dtr. Coupled with the archaeological data now known from Jericho, the fictitious nature of the stories should be abundantly clear. All archaeological discussion of this site must now deal with the work of the late Kathleen Kenyon (see the bibliography in Holland and Netzer). While subsequent archaeological analysis of the site has demonstrated some Iron Age I activity on the tel, nothing has been discovered to indicate that a city (town) of biblical proportions existed there during this time. Kenyon showed that although some tenth century BCE pottery sherds were found in a tomb, the site of ancient Jericho, modern Tel es-Sultan, was for the most part abandoned from the Late Bronze Age I period (14th century BCE) to Iron Age II (7th century BCE).

The story of the miraculous fall of the city's walls would then have been added at some point in the usage of this tradition by later Israelites celebrating the "conquest." It is no little curiosity that such a dramatic story is nowhere else mentioned in the entire Bible. As Coogan has pointed out, there is no biblical reference to this tumbling wall story outside its present location, indicating that the story was "a local tradition incorporated only at a fairly late date into the biblical recital" (1990a, 21). No prophet ever makes reference to it and neither does any psalm or any other postexilic book.

The "House of Yahweh" (6:24)

This reference to the temple is obviously anachronistic (see also Exod 23:19 and 1 Sam 1:7, 9, 24; note Samuel uses "house" of Yahweh [vv. 7, 24] and "temple" [v. 9] to describe the same structure) and refers to the practice of bringing the booty of holy war for dedication to the deity. What became a later practice in Israel is simply assumed here. Moreover, where such a "house" (temple) would have been located at this time is ambiguous. According to later tradition, the first "house (temple) of Yahweh" was not built until the time of Solomon (1 Kgs 6:1-37). It has been suggested that perhaps this reference to a temple in Jericho was inserted by a scribe from a much later period (Miller and Tucker, 57).

Another Story of the Saving of Rahab and Her Family (6:25)

The story in this one verse seems to pick up an unexpected reference to Rahab in v. 17b. This fragment abruptly interrupts Joshua's instructions to the Israelites for what is about to happen to Jericho, her inhabitants, and the "devoted" things. In this obscure reference to Rahab, the two men sent by Joshua as "spies" in 2:1 are no longer identified as "spies" but as "messengers," just as they are in v. 25 (both the roles of "messenger" and "spy" could be combined in the same person; 2 Sam 10:3). This would seem to indicate that the main point of the Rahab-Jericho pericope had more to do with the "message," in the form of Rahab's "confession" (2: 8-13), that the men supposedly brought back to Joshua than spying out the land, which they never do (Nelson 1997, 95). In other words, the "confession" put into the mouth of Rahab served perfectly the Dtr's purposes.

Joshua's Curse on Jericho (6:26-27)

This curse by Joshua seems to be a prophecy after the fact ("prophecy ex eventu") based on the story in 1 Kings 16:34. Curiously, in the Kings story we are told that someone named Hiel from Bethel rebuilt Jericho. The theological rationale here seems to be that since the city was destroyed under the ban, it belonged to Yahweh (vv. 18-19). Thus, it could not be rebuilt, and a curse was put on anyone who did. Nothing is said in the story of Hiel about how effective the curse was! Jericho, for the most part, lay in ruins from the fourteenth to the tenth-ninth centuries BCE. The story in Kings takes place during the reign of Ahab, a ninth-century Israelite king (1 Kgs 16:29–22:40). The Dtr obviously viewed the practice of burying one's children beneath the foundation of a city as an abomination.

The Story of Ha'ai (et-Tell), or "Trouble" and "Death"

Joshua 7:1–8:29

This story is divided into two chapters in standard translations of the Bible, but it will be translated here as the one story that it actually is.

7:1 Now the Israelites acted unfaithfully with regard to the *herem* (devoted
things). For Achan, the son of Carmi, the son of Zabdi, the son of Zerah,
of the tribe of Judah, took from the devoted (things), and the anger of
Yahweh was kindled against the Israelites. 2 Then Joshua sent men from
Jericho to Ha'ai, which is near Beth-aven ("house of iniquity"), east of
Beth-el ("house of god"), and said to them saying: "Go up and spy out the
land." And the men went up and spied on Ha'ai. 3 And they returned to
Joshua and said to him: "All the people do not need to go up. Let about
two thousand men (MT: "man") or three thousand man go up and let
them destroy Ha'ai. Do not let *all* the people toil up there, for they are
few." 4 So they went there about three thousand man from the people, and
they fled from before the men of Ha'ai. 5 And the men of Ha'ai killed them
about thirty-six men and chased them from the front of the gate as far as
Shebarim and they killed them on the slope. And the heart of the people
melted and became like water. 6 Then Joshua tore his garments and fell on
his face on the ground before the ark of Yahweh until the evening; he and
the old men of Israel. And they lifted up dirt to their head. 7 Then Joshua
said: "Alas, lord Yahweh, why have you caused this people to pass over the
Jordan to give us into the hand of the Amorite in order to destroy us?
Would that we had been willing and lived beyond the Jordan! 8 I pray, my
lord, what can I say now that Israel has turned (his) back before her
enemies? 9 Now the Canaanite will hear and *all* those living in the land,
and they will surround us and they will cut off our name from the earth.
Then what will you do for your great name?"

10 Then Yahweh said to Joshua: "Stand up! Why is this one, even you,
falling on your face? 11 Israel has sinned; and moreover they have transgressed (MT: "passed over") my covenant that I commanded them. And
also they have taken from the devoted (things); and moreover they have

stolen, and have deceived, and have put (them) in their baggage. [12] Thus the Israelites are not able to stand before their enemies. They turn (their) back before their enemies because they have become as *herem* (devoted to destruction). I will not again be with you if you do not exterminate the devoted (things) from your midst. [13] Arise, consecrate the people and say, 'consecrate yourselves for tomorrow.' For thus says Yahweh, the god of Israel: "(There are) devoted things among Israel; you will not be able to stand before your enemies until you take away the devoted things from among you." [14] So in the morning you will come near according to your tribes, and it will be the tribe that Yahweh takes (who) will approach by clans, and the clan from which Yahweh takes her will approach by households, and the household that Yahweh takes him will come near according to the men (LXX: "man"). [15] And it will be that the one taken in regard to the devoted things will be burned with fire, him and *all* that he has, for he has transgressed (MT: "passed over") the covenant of Yahweh and for he has done a disgrace in Israel."

[16] So Joshua rose early in the morning and brought Israel near according to tribes and the tribe of Judah was taken. [17] Then he brought near the clan(s) of Judah and took from the clan(s) the Zerahite, and he brought near the clan of the Zerahite according to the men and Zabdi was taken. [18] And he brought near his house according to the man ("man by man"), and Achan, the son of Carmi, son of Zabdi, son of Zerah, belonging to the tribe of Judah was taken. [19] Then Joshua said to Achan: "My son, give (MT: "set") now glory to Yahweh, the god of Israel and give thanksgiving to him. Tell me now what you have done; do not hide (it) from me." [20] Then Achan answered Joshua and said: "Truly I have sinned against Yahweh the god of Israel. And according to this and according to that I did (LXX: "thus and thus"). [21] When I saw among the spoil a cloak from Shinar (probably Babylonia), one that was good, and two hundred shekels of silver, and one bar (MT: "tongue") of gold, fifty shekels in weight, and I desired them and I took them. Now, behold, they are hidden in the ground in the middle of my tent and the silver is underneath."

[22] Then Joshua sent messengers and they ran to the tent and behold it was hidden in the tent with the silver underneath. [23] And they took them from the middle of the tent and they brought them to Joshua and to *all* of the Israelites. And they cast them out before Yahweh. [24] And Joshua took Achan, the son of Zerah, and the silver, and the cloak and the bar of gold and his sons and his daughters and his cattle and his ass and his sheep and his tent and *all* that was his, and *all* Israel with him, and he brought them to the valley of Achor ("trouble"). [25] And Joshua said: "Why have you troubled us? Yahweh will trouble you on this day." And *all* Israel stoned him, with a stone, and they burned them with fire and they stoned them with stones. [26] Then they raised upon him a great heap of stones (that are there)

even to this day. Then Yahweh turned from his burning anger (MT: "from
the burning of his nostril"). Thus the name of the place is called "The
Valley of Trouble" (Achor) even to this day.

8:1 Then Yahweh said to Joshua: "Fear not and be not dismayed. Take with
you *all* the people of war ("fighting men") and arise, go up to Ha'ai. See, I
have given the king of Ha'ai, his people and his city and land into your
hand. 2 Now you will do to Ha'ai and to her king even as you did to
Jericho and her king. Only her (Ha'ai) spoil and her livestock you may take
for yourselves. Set yourself lying in wait ("ambush") regarding the city from
behind her."

3 So Joshua arose and *all* the people of war, to go up (against) Ha'ai.
And Joshua chose thirty thousand fighting men (MT: "man") from the
army and sent them by night. 4 And he commanded them saying: "See,
you are lying in wait with regard to the city, from behind the city. Do not
be very far from the city, but *all* of you be determined. 5 Then I and *all* the
people with me will approach the city. And when it happens that they
come out to encounter us even as before, we will flee from them. 6 They
will come out after us until we draw them away from the city, for they will
say, 'they are fleeing from us even as before' (MT: "as the first [time]"). We
will flee from them 7 (and) you will arise from the lying in wait (ambush)
and you will take possession of the city, for Yahweh your god will give her
into your hand. 8 And it will happen when you have seized the city you
will burn the city with fire according to the word of Yahweh, you will do.
See, I have commanded you."

9 So Joshua sent them out and they came to the ambush (place), and
they remained (there) between Beth-el and between Ha'ai, toward the sea
(Mediterranean) from Ha'ai. But Joshua remained that night among the
people. 10 And in the morning Joshua rose early and he mustered the
people and he went up, he and the old (men) of Israel, before the people of
Ha'ai. 11 And *all* the people of war who (were) with him went up and they
drew near, and came in front of the city. And they camped on the north
(side) in relation to Ha'ai, with a valley between it and between Ha'ai.
12 And he took about five thousand men (MT: "man"), and he put them in
ambush ("lying in wait") between Beth-el and between Ha'ai, west of
Ha'ai. 13 And they placed the people and *all* the camp that was north of the
city and its rear ("hind-part") west of the city. But Joshua stayed (MT:
"walked") that night in the midst of the valley.

14 And it happened that when the king of Ha'ai saw (this) they
hastened and rose early, and the men of the city went out to meet Israel for
battle, he and *all* his people, at the appointed place, in front of the Arabah.
But he did not know what was lying in wait for him behind the city.
15 Then Joshua and *all* Israel pretended to be defeated before them and

they fled on the road (toward) the wilderness. [16] And *all* the people who were in the city (*qere*; *kethib* reads "in Ha'ai") assembled in order to pursue after them. And they did pursue after Joshua and were drawn away from the city. [17] There was not a man left in neither Ha'ai nor Beth-el who did not go out after Israel. So they left the city open and they chased after Israel.

[18] Then Yahweh said to Joshua: "Stretch out with the javelin that (is) in your hand toward Ha'ai for into your hand I will give her." So Joshua stretched out with the javelin that (was) in his hand toward Ha'ai. [19] Then the one lying in wait arose quickly from his place, and they ran quickly as Joshua (MT: "he") was stretching out his hand. And they went into the city and they captured her and hastened, and burned the city with fire. [20] When the men of Ha'ai turned back after them, they looked, and behold, the city was going up in smoke toward the heavens. And there was not in them hands to flee ("they had no power") this way or that way, for the people who were fleeing to the wilderness turned around toward the pursuer.

[21] When Joshua and *all* Israel saw that the one lying in wait had taken the city and that the smoke of the city went up, then they turned back and they killed the men of Ha'ai. [22] Then those came out from the city to encounter them and they were, with regard to Israel, in the middle of those from this (side) and those from that (side), and they (Israelites) killed them until no one remained and no survivor escaped. [23] But the king of Ha'ai was seized alive and they brought him to Joshua.

[24] So it happened when Israel had finished killing *all* of those who were living in Ha'ai, (and) in the open field in the wilderness where they pursued them in it, when *all* of them had fallen by the edge of the sword until they were consumed (finished), then *all* Israel returned to Ha'ai and they struck her down with the edge of the sword. [25] And it was so that *all* who fell on that day both man and woman was twelve thousand; *all* the people (MT: "man") of Ha'ai. [26] For Joshua did not draw back his hand with which he stretched out the javelin until *all* the inhabitants who lived in Ha'ai had been exterminated ("put to the ban"). [27] Only the animal (livestock) and the spoil of that city Israel plundered for themselves according to the word of Yahweh with which he had charged Joshua. [28] Then Joshua burned Ha'ai, and made her a tel (a "ruin/heap") for a long time, a waste (place) until this day. [29] And the king of Ha'ai he hung on the tree until evening time, and as the sun was going in (sunset), Joshua commanded and they took down the corpse from the tree and they threw it down at the entrance to the gate of the city and they raised over it (MT: "him") a great heap of stones. (There they are) even to this day.

From an archaeological perspective, the history of Ha'ai is as troublesome as that of Jericho. Ha'ai (modern et-Tell; MT: "the heap/ruin," which is always preceded by the definite article, *ha* [הָ]; in English translations of Joshua the term is usually translated simply as 'Ai or Ai) is located a few miles north of Jerusalem, about one mile east of another important biblical site, Bethel (modern-day Beitin). Garstang, of Jericho fame, also excavated here and again claimed to have found evidence of a 1400 BCE destruction. But later excavations by Judith Marquet-Krause in the 1930s and by my own teacher, Joseph Callaway, in the 1960s and early 1970s, have clearly shown that no Late Bronze Age city at Ha'ai existed here (Callaway 1972, 1980, 1985, 1987, 1988). In fact, they concluded that the site had lain in ruins (hence its name: Ha'ai= "the ruin/ heap") from about 2400 BCE to around 1200 BCE or later. If Joshua lived during the thirteenth century, as many scholars today believe, there was simply no city or town here for him to destroy despite the dramatic biblical story. Certainly if Kenyon was right, there was an even greater miracle than the crumbling walls of Jericho: Joshua would have had to be at Jericho in the fourteenth century and at Ha'ai in the twelfth. He would have been nearly three hundred years old! As one scholar put it, from the way the story of Ha'ai is recounted in Joshua it is clear that a "tall tale is being told" (Stager 1998, 96).

The biblical site of Ha'ai was abandoned for more than twelve hundred years after its destruction in the Early Bronze Age. Beginning around 1200 BCE, a small farming village was built on the site (Callaway 1976, 18–30). There are still attempts by some scholars to find other antiquity sites to fit with what is now known from the archaeological remains at et-Tell. Such attempts are motivated more by the searchers' theological assumptions than by archaeology. Consequently, they are compelled to find some archaeological site, apparently any site whose remains will "fit" with the known archaeological evidence. All such attempts are grasping after straws (for a recent unconvincing example of such an attempt see Wood, 2008).

Moreover, such attempts are, at best, circular arguments. Even Callaway himself (d. 1988) began his excavation of et-Tell expecting to find archaeological evidence that would in some way support the biblical story. Since et-Tell had neither Middle nor Late Bronze Age remains, Callaway at first tried to argue that the "conquest" occurred during Iron Age I (c. 1200–1050 BCE), the date of the earliest remains discovered on the site following its Early Bronze Age destruction. When his circular argument was pointed out to him (by his close friend and well-known biblical historian, J. Maxwell Miller), Callaway, an ordained Southern Baptist minister, changed his mind and concluded that the evidence from et-Tell "does not support at any point the account of the conquest of Ai in Joshua 7–8" (Callaway 1987, 97; Callaway had tremendous integrity and publically gave J. M. Miller credit for pointing out the logical fallacy in his argument, Callaway 1987, 92). Furthermore, one of Israel's most prominent historical geographers, A. Rainey (d. 2011), after viewing all the evidence available, concluded that the most likely site for Ha'ai is still et-Tell (Rainey and Notley 2006, 125). Until there is clear archaeological evidence forthcoming that can convince reasonable archaeological skeptics that et-Tell is not the location Ha'ai, such conclusions as those of Callaway and Rainey must be taken seriously. While the exact location of antiquity sites mentioned in the Bible (or non-biblical texts, for that matter) has always been a legitimate issue for archaeologists, to seek to identify a site based primarily on prior theological/ideological assumptions about the Bible (which characterize most of Wood's argument referenced above) is misdirected.

Moreover, while the Dtr may have believed he was telling an accurate "historical story," it is his own literary construct of the story created to serve his theological agenda that is the real issue here. That agenda is anticipated in Joshua 6:18, where Joshua warned the "Israelites" to keep away from the "devoted things" lest they make "the camp of Israel into a devoted thing and you make trouble (from עכר; compare 7:25) for us" (6:18). Now, in 7:1 we are informed that the "Israelites" acted unfaithfully with regard to the *herem*, all because of the actions of one person, Achan, who had taken the booty and hidden it in his tent. By his "unfaithfulness" the entire camp is infected. The consequences that follow include, first, the defeat of the "Israelites" by the men of Ha'ai. The second horrible consequence of such faithlessness is the execution of Achan and everything that belong to him, including his family and animals (this is the first of two public executions narrated in the conquest story; the second one is the execution of the five kings at Makkedah reported in 10:16-27; see below). Thus Achan's actions infected the entire Israelite community (7:10-12), and therefore the community ("*all Israel*," v. 23) participates in the executions. As Rowlett has argued, Achan violated Joshua's authority given to him by Yahweh himself and is punished not only by Joshua but also by the people (176–77). Once again the Dtr illustrates the importance of "obedience to the laws of Moses," as interpreted and put into practice by Yahweh's earthly representative, Joshua. Following this public spectacle we are informed that Yahweh turned from "his burning anger" (7:26). Seen from the perspective of the time of Josiah or the exile, the Dtr's ideology would have been easily recognized: only by blind obedience to the covenantal commands (7:11) and the human put in charge of them can the anger of the tribal deity be quelled and the kingdom of David be restored its formal glory (Nelson 1997, 103). That such simplistic black/white theology never quite works out in practice is overlooked, and no one is supposed to ask questions (compare once more the life of Josiah, the most praised king in the Bible, who was killed at the ripe old age of thirty-nine; see above; 2 Kgs 22:1; 23:25-29). The fact that historically speaking it is most unlikely that any such execution took place as described in Joshua 8 does not justify the Dtr tale. Yahweh is once more portrayed as a killer god, and when he commands such horrible acts, they are "morally right." Thus the notion of *herem*, the extermination of holy things devoted to Yahweh, is invoked again.

Furthermore, we are not told how, with tumbling walls and a conflagration that consumed the city of Jericho, such booty could have been found and stolen in the first place. In addition, the idea that a "house of Yahweh" (that is, a temple) was somewhere nearby is hardly likely at such an early date as assumed here. That agenda seems to be the meaning and application of the rule of *herem* or the ban within the context of holy war (Deut 20:16; the same notion of *herem* is found on the Mesha inscription; see Schmidt 2006a, 315). The publications on the issues/questions concerning the portrayal of the Israelite deity as a warrior god who kills on behalf of Israel are far too many to list here (see von Rad 1958, 135–66; Jones, 1975; Polzin, 113; Niditch 1993; Rowlett, 51–65; Nelson 2007). Just as the story of Jericho illustrates how the rules of holy war could be ignored to spare those under the ban (Rahab and her family), the story of Ha'ai illustrates just how complex and dynamic the interpretation and application of these rules could be. As Nelson observed, the story of Rahab serves as an example of fidelity, and the Achan debacle, infidelity (1997, 102–103). We are told that Achan and his family were destroyed for breaking the rules relevant to *herem* (7:1, 16-26). This is the idea that some things belong to Yahweh that must be set apart from normal things. The way the things that are set apart are given to Yahweh, especially living things, humans and animals, is by killing them (sacrifice is just a euphemism). How many human and animal lives have been killed through the millennia to satisfy such a barbaric religious idea is, of course, unknown.

Another issue this story raises has to do with the idea of "collective sin" whereby the whole is sacrificed because of the failure of the part. This rationale is denied elsewhere in the Bible (Ezek 18:1-32). Following Achan's execution we are told (8:2, 27) that the rest of the Israelites were granted permission by their god to take the spoil and livestock as booty for themselves. Polzin's rather bland attempt to justify such acts is worth quoting here: "There seems to be no doubt at all that the narrative (the Ai episode) is intent upon outlining some of the possible hermeneutic situations that could arise in the continued understanding, interpretation, and application of divine commands" (114–15).

The theological problem here, of course, is who gets to "understand," "interpret," and "apply" what some god commands? To read the Bible naively as the "word of a god" eventually leads to "cherry picking." One picks what fits with one's own beliefs and ignores all the rest.

The archaeological/historical problems raised by the excavations of Jericho and et-Tell with regard to the nature of the "Israelite conquest" are but symptomatic of the problems in general when archaeological data are compared with the biblical stories. It has already been argued that there is no way to reconcile the archaeological data now readily available for study with a literal reading of the Jericho-et-Tell stories.

The reference to a "heap of ruins" ("tel") in 8:28 is probably the source of the story told here whatever the real etymology of the name, "Ha'ai" (compare Mazar 2003).

The Altar on Mount Ebal

Joshua 8:30-35

> 30 At that time, Joshua built an altar to Yahweh, the god of Israel, on Mount Ebal, 31 as Moses, the servant (slave) of Yahweh, had commanded the Israelites, as it is written in the book of the law (torah) of Moses: "an altar of perfect (unhewn) stones on which iron has not been wielded upon it." Then they offered upon it a whole burnt offering to Yahweh, and they sacrificed peace offerings. 32 And he (Joshua) wrote upon the stones a copy of the law of Moses, which he had written before the Israelites. 33 Then *all* Israel, both its old ones and officers and its judges, stood, from this side and that side (that is, "both sides") of the ark in front of the Levitical priests carrying the ark of the covenant of Yahweh, also the alien as well as the citizen, half in front of Mount Gerizim and half in front of Mount Ebal even as at the first (when) Moses, the servant of Yahweh, had commanded regarding the blessing of the people of Israel. 34 And after this Joshua (MT: "he") read *all* the words of the law, the blessing and the curse, according to *all* that is written in the book of the law. 35 There was not a word of *all* that Moses commanded that Joshua did not read in front of *all* the assembly of Israel, and the women, and the children, and the sojourner who was walking among them.

This story of an altar constructed on Mount Ebal is what is called a "floating pericope." It occurs in three different locations in the ancient texts. In the MT it occurs at the end of the story of the victory at Ha'ai, before 9:1-2. In the Old Greek (OG) the story is found after 9:1-2. In the Dead Sea Scrolls (4QJosha) the story occurs before 5:2 following the crossing of the River Jordan but before the note concerning circumcision. It has been suggested that the OG version makes more sense because it connects the story of the kings mentioned in 9:1-2 with Israel's victory at Ha'ai in chapter 8 (Nelson 1997, 116–20). This logical connection is interrupted by the altar pericope as found in the MT. Its present location there may have been determined by the ideological/theological agenda of the Dtr. Wherever one chooses to locate the story, it is "manifestly disconnected from its context whichever of the three possible locations one chooses" (Nelson 1997, 117). J. Alberto Soggin, in his 1972 commentary on Joshua, made the suggestion that this story bests fits between 24:27 and 24:28 (230–31). This would have made the story of the altar fit within Joshua's covenant renewal speech, the subject of chapter 24. N. Na'aman has also argued for a Shechem setting for this story, created by the Dtr after the fall of the first temple (6th century BCE). According to Na'aman, the story was fabricated with the purpose "of substantiating the central position of the cultic site at Shechem" (2006, 354). It may also be the case that this altar was influenced by the memory of King Josiah. Secon Kings 23:1-3 reads,

> The king directed that *all* the elders of Judah and Jerusalem should be gathered to him. The king went up to the house of Yahweh, and with him went *all* the people of Judah, *all* the inhabitants of Jerusalem, the priests, the prophets, and *all* the people, both small and great; he read in their hearing *all* the words of the book of the covenant that had been found in the house of Yahweh. The king stood by a pillar and made a covenant before Yahweh, to follow Yahweh, keeping his commandments, his decrees, and his laws, with *all* his heart and *all* his being, to perform the words of this covenant that were written in this book. *All* the people joined in the covenant.

Joshua 8:32-35 portrays Joshua as a royal figure who wrote a copy of the law on stones and read the law to "*all Israel*" (vv. 33, 35), including women and children as well as the "aliens who resided among them" (v. 35). Compare this with the story of Josiah where we are informed "that *all* the people both great and small" (2 Kgs 23:2) and "all the people joined in the covenant" (23:3). If, as already suggested, Josiah was the role model for the Dtr's creation of the Joshua character that then justified ideologically King Josiah's bloody reformation (Nelson 1981; Rowlett, inter alia), perhaps the Dtr placed the altar story in its present location in the MT to fulfill as quickly as possible the Mosaic directive in Deuteronomy 27:2-8. In so doing the stage was set for the major thrust of the conquest (Nelson 1997, 115–20).

There are also additional problems with its present location. Mount Ebal is more than thirty miles from the Jordan, yet we are told in Deuteronomy 27:2 that Moses and the "elders of Israel" commanded "all the people" (not just Joshua), "on the day that you cross over the Jordan into the land that Yahweh your god is giving you, you shall set up large stones and cover them with plaster." It is unlikely that a motley group of any size that included "all the people," which, according to Joshua 8:35, extended to women and children and aliens, could have walked thirty miles in one day. That would be a feat even for a military force moving on foot. Moreover, in Deuteronomy, it is "the people" (not Joshua) who are ordered to set up the stones, cover them with plaster, and write upon them "all the words of the law" (Deut 27:3).

This story, as already mentioned, follows 9:2 in LXX and seems to interrupt the flow of the narrative that continues in 9:3 in MT. Moreover, the base of operations at this point in the story is Hagilgal, not Shechem (cf. 9:6; 10:15, 43). The argument that has erupted over the claim that the remains of this altar have actually been found only serves to illustrate the extreme difficulty of correlating archaeological remains with biblical texts (Zertal 1985; Rainy 1986; Dever 1992, 32–34, 76–78, 84–85).

In 1980, during a regional survey of the territory traditionally associated with the biblical tribe of Manasseh, an Israeli archaeologist (A. Zertal) from Haifa University discovered the remains of a stone structure that he dated to the Late Bronze Age/Iron Age I (1250–1150 BCE; Zertal, 1993, 1994). Associated with this structure were ashes, bones, and an assortment of ceramic remains. It is also noteworthy that the site is located in a remote, isolated place. Zertal excavated here from 1982–1989. Most scholars, especially archaeologists, who have offered an opinion about this discovery seem to agree with Zertal that the site may have been used for "cultic" activities for the people who used it (Coogan 1987; Mazar 1990, 348–50; Mazar 2007a). After several seasons of excavating, Zertal concluded that these remains, which had gone through two periods of use (called "strata"), belonged to the Mount Ebal altar that Joshua is said to have built in 8:30-35. However, while others have defended the cultic function of this structure, the final interpretation of what it really was, who used it, and for what purpose(s) is still open. Without assuming the historicity of the biblical story in advance (and there is no rational reason to do so), it is currently impossible to link the physical remains discovered here with any specific ethnic group, such as "Israelite" or "Canaanite." Moreover, the religious rituals practiced here, if any, and to what deity or deities, are totally unknown (Coogan 1987; Ahlström 1991, 120–21; Van der Steen, 67; Block-Smith and Nakhai, 71; Killebrew 2005, 159). Other suggestions for these remains include an isolated farmhouse or fort (Dever 2001; idem, 2003, 88–90, where Dever, facetiously, suggested that the structure was a huge picnic site used for barbecues[!]; for the argument that it was a fort or watchtower see Kempinski, 1986; for Zertal's response to Kempinski, see Zertal, 1986; for the perspective of evangelical scholars see Hawkins, 184–87; Kitchen, 232–34).

More serious is the fact that, so far, almost nothing has been recovered from these Iron I settlements suggesting any kind of religious beliefs of the settlers, not even a single cemetery. Burial practices can be important in providing clues relevant to the religious beliefs or lack thereof of the people involved. As Dever put it, "It is as though a lot of people lived in the 12th-11th centuries B.C., but no one ever died" (2003, 126). Moreover, there is no archaeological evidence of any worship of the god Yahweh during this period, and no comparably sized altar has ever been found from the entire Iron Age (1200–597 BCE; Mazar 2007a, 90). The recent suggestion by the Israeli archaeologist, A. Faust, that the lack of burial remains is due to the "egalitarian" nature of the *early Israelites* who used simple, non-elaborate tombs during the Iron Age I period is another example of a circular argument where the identity of the people(s) who settled the central-hill country is assumed to have been *Israelite* to begin with (2013). Furthermore, the origin of Yahwism itself is a still much-debated issue (Smith 2001, 2002). It is no little curiosity that the people called "Isra*el*" were named after the high god of the Canaanites, "*El*" (or "*Elyon*"), not "Yahweh" (see discussion above and Smith 2001, 142–43). In Deuteronomy 32:8-9, Yahweh is a minor god who is allotted Jacob ("Israel") by El! But in the MT, Deuteronomy 32:8b reads, "he (Elyon) fixed the boundaries of the peoples according to the number of *the sons of Israel*" (that is, "the Israelites," my emphasis). But in the OG, as well as texts from the Dead Sea Scrolls, the word "Israel" is missing. In its place is the word "*'elohim*" ("gods"). By changing this one word the Masoretes changed the entire meaning of the verse. Originally the text referred to the assembly of the gods of which, in Deuteronomy 32:8, Yahweh, the tribal deity of Jacob, was only one among others (compare Ps 29:1, "Ascribe to Yahweh, sons of gods; MT: "*'elohim*"; see also Ps 82:1, 6). Emanuel Tov, an internationally known authority in textual criticism as well as a Septuagint expert, described the change from "gods" in Deuteronomy 32:8 to "Israelites" in the MT as an "anti-polytheistic alteration" (Tov, 269). Apparently the same "alteration" also occurred in Psalm 96:7 (compare Ps 96:7 with Ps 29:1). The original reading means that "Yahweh" is not the "presider god" in Deuteronomy 32:8-9 but "one of his sons" (Smith 2001, 49).

A rather literal translation of Deuteronomy 32:8-9, using the wording suggested by the OG and the Dead Sea Scroll, would read like this: "When Elyon gave out (the) nations, when he divided (the) sons of adam (humankind), he fixed (the) boundaries of peoples according to (the) number of (the) gods (*'elohim*). Thus the portion of Yahweh (is) Jacob, (the) territory of his inheritance" (compare Smith 2001, 143; 2002, 32). The original god of the people who would become "Israel" was the high god of the Canaanite pantheon, *El(yon)* (compare Gen 14:19; 16:13; 17:1; 32:28; 33:20; 35:27). Genesis 33:19-20 is especially significant for this discussion. After Jacob is said to have purchased a plot of land from the Shechemites, he built an altar and named it, "*El-elohe-Israel.*" That is, "El, the god of Israel." Here "El" is a proper name and is clearly identified as the god (the meaning of *elohe*) of "Isra-el." The translation of this text at the bottom of the page in the NRSV is totally misleading: "God, the God of Israel." The point of all this is that the people called "Israelites" in the Bible worshiped the Canaanite god, El. At what point in time would there have been an ethnic group in Canaan who worshiped a god named Yahweh, what was the origin of this deity, and when El(yon) and Yahweh merged into one god is still unknown. Mark Smith, in his thorough study of these questions, has suggested a pre-monarchic date for this merger (2001, 139–41). Another way to look at this is the fact that while personal names in Genesis contain the epithet "El," such as "Ishma-*el*" (Gen 16:15) and, of course, "Isra-*el*," (Gen 32:27), not a single name occurs with the epithet "Yah" as would later occur in such names as "Adonijah," identified as the brother of Solomon (2 Sam 3:4; 1 Kgs 1:5ff.). The name means "my lord is Yah(weh)."

What these arguments mean for the story of the altar in Joshua 8:32-35 is simple. Without presupposing the final theological formulation of the Bible, including especially the move to a monotheistic religion that did not take place any earlier than the exilic or postexilic period (Smith 2001, 153), there is absolutely nothing in the archaeological remains that Zertal uncovered that should lead anyone to say, "Yahweh was worshiped here." Moreover, as already noted, this story about an altar seems totally out of place. It has been argued that the entire altar story in Joshua was composed from a combination of materials found in the book of Deuteronomy (Coogan 2014, 204; Rösel, 134). This can be clearly seen in the following table that illustrates, in places, the identical wording of the story.

Joshua 8:30-35	**Deuteronomy 27:2-8; 36:9; 29:10-11; 27: 12a, 13a; 11:29; 31:11-12**
(30) Then Joshua built an altar to Yahweh, the god of Israel, on Mount Ebal (31) as Moses the servant of Yahweh had commanded the people of Israel, as it is written in the book of the torah (law) of Moses, "an altar of complete (unhewn) stones upon which iron has not been wielded upon it." Then they offered upon it a whole burnt offering to Yahweh, and they sacrificed peace offerings.	(4) And it will be when you have crossed the Jordan you will set up these stones which I, myself, am commanding you today on Mount Ebal . . . (5) And you will build an altar there to Yahweh your god, an altar of stones you have not wielded upon them an iron tool. (6) [With] complete stones you will build an altar to Yahweh your god and you will offer upon it a whole burnt offering to Yahweh your god. (7) And you will sacrifice peace offerings . . .
(32) And he (Joshua) *wrote* upon the stones a copy of the law of Moses, which he had written before the Israelites.	(8) And you will write upon the stones *all* the words of this torah (law) to make thoroughly clear
(33) Then *all* Israel, both its old ones and officers and its judges stood from this side and that side of the ark in front of the *Levitical priests carrying the ark of the covenant of Yahweh,* also the sojourner as well as the citizen, half in front of *Mount Gerizim* and half in front of *Mount Ebal* even as at the first (when) Moses, the servant of Yahweh, had commanded regarding the blessing of the people of Israel	(36:1) Then Moses *wrote down* this torah (law) and he gave it to *the priests, the sons of Levi, the ones carrying the ark of the covenant of Yahweh,* and to *all* the old ones of Israel. (27:12a) These will stand on *Mount Gerizim* to bless people when you have crossed the Jordan . . . (27:13a) . . . and these will stand for the *curse* on *Mount Ebal* . . .
(34) And after this Joshua (MT: "he") read *all* the words of the law, the *blessing and the curse* according to *all* that is written in the book of the torah.	(11:29) . . . you will give the *blessing* on Mount Gerizim and the curse on Mount Ebal
(35) There was not a word of *all* that Moses commanded that Joshua did not read in front of *all* the assembly of Israel, and the women, and the children, and the sojourner who was walking among them.	(31:11-12) Assemble the people—the men and the women and the children and the sojourner who is in your gates in order that they may hear and fear Yahweh your god and keep to do *all* the words of this torah.

After his own comparison, Rösel concluded, "It is now clear that Joshua 8:30-35 is wholly Deuteronomistic and *has no earlier base*" (135, my emphasis). Without assuming the historicity of the Joshua story in advance, nothing in the archaeological remains would remotely suggest that this was an "Israelite" altar constructed by someone named "Joshua." To do otherwise is to engage in a circular argument. This is exactly what Zertal did. His interpretation of the structure as an Israelite altar was based solely on his use of the biblical account and a Jewish tradition found only in the Mishnah (*Sotah* 7.5).

Additionally, Na'aman has suggested that the command to build the altar on Mount Ebal and the description of its construction belongs in the larger context of the story of the cult site located at Shechem. Na'aman's suggestion is supported by Soggin's argument (see above) that the story of the altar fits better if inserted between Joshua 24:27 and 28. According to Na'aman's argument, the altar story was created during the exilic period and placed at the beginning of the conquest story "with the purpose of substantiating the central position of the cultic site at Shechem" (Na'aman 2006, 339–58; quotation, 354). The "most important feature of this narrative," according to Polzin (115), is the way Joshua interprets and applies the law of Moses in his new situation (cf. Deut 11:29; 27:1-26). Actually, it is "the way" the Dtr applies his understanding of the "law of Moses" through the Joshua character. Rowlett has made another compelling suggestion that the ceremony described in the MT Ebal story "functions as another communal identity" (157) and thus its "meaning in its literary context" (157) is more important than historical questions relative to an actual religious ceremony. She concluded her argument by suggesting four themes that are linked by the Dtr's use of this story: (1) this ceremony immediately follows a military victory that in itself emphasizes those who are included in the community from those who are excluded; (2) the ceremony emphasizes the community's bond with Yahweh, their god; (3) this acclaimed sovereignty of Yahweh is "linked" by "proxy" to the power of the community's leaders "in hierarchical order: Joshua, the elders, officers and judges" (v. 33); (4) and most important for Rowlett's analysis is the emphasis in the story given to the role of Moses. "Therefore, obedience to the hierarchical chain of command is linked with faith in the deity and the heritage of the law, all of which converge in the person of King Josiah at the time of the composition of the DH" (157). Finally, Nelson (1997, 115–20) has suggested that the placement here of the altar story that emphasizes formal ceremonies celebrating the covenant linked to Moses served as a bracket for the beginning of

"Israel's" possession of the land, just as another covenant ceremony in Joshua 24 served as the closing bracket after the distribution of the land.

Introduction:
The Ruse of the Gibeonites

Once more the Dtr's preoccupation with the interpretation of the Mosaic law is clearly in view in this next story. According to Deuteronomy 20:10-18, Israel could offer peace to a city that was not located in Canaan, but all the inhabitants of Canaanite cities were to be put to death:

> When you draw near to a town (this word עיר [*'yr*], is frequently translated as "city" in the Bible) to fight against it, offer it terms of peace. If it accepts your terms of peace and surrenders to you, then *all* the people in it shall serve you at forced labor. If it does not submit to you peacefully, but makes war against you, then you besiege it; and when Yahweh your god gives it into your hand, you shall put to the sword *all* of its males. You may, however, take as your booty the women, the children, livestock, and everything else in the town, *all* of its spoil. You may enjoy the spoil of your enemies, which Yahweh your god has given you. Thus you shall treat *all* of the towns that are *very far from you*, which are not the towns of the nations here (Deut 20:10-15, my emphasis)

However, for the towns that are "not very far away" but are located in Canaan, another fate awaits:

> Only from the towns of these people that Yahweh your god is giving you (as an) inheritance you will not leave alive any who has breath. For you will utterly exterminate them . . . just as Yahweh your god has charged you. . . . When you besiege a town for many days to wage war against it (MT: "her"), to seize it you will not destroy her trees (MT: "tree") by welding an ax upon it. But from it you may eat but you will not destroy it. For (is) the tree in the field as the human (MT: *ha'adam*) to come under siege from you (MT: "from your faces")? Only a tree that you know that (it is) not a tree for food, you may spoil it and cut it down and build a siege ramp

> against the town (city) that is making war with you until it (MT: "she") comes down. (Deut 20:16-17, 19-20)

Of course, trees are not human beings. In this case the fruit bearing trees are to be spared, while those that do not bear fruit are to be cut down and used to build the siege work against the very city that is being attacked (Deut 20:20)! Such is the lunacy of "holy war." Furthermore, women of the enemy located in towns outside of Canaan are considered to be nothing more than sex objects and can be raped. If the city does not resist the "Israelites," all of its inhabitants are to become slaves. However, if they resist, all the males are to be killed. All of this commanded by a god who supposedly had just freed his own people from slavery in Egypt (the Hebrew Bible contains a delicious amount of irony)! Those not from "far away" are to be butchered, but not food-bearing trees. Does anyone really believe that women whose husbands, other family members, and friends had just been slaughtered would willingly have sex with the very men who had committed such an atrocity? The moral injunction envisioned here is not "do unto others as you would have them do unto you" but "do unto others as you think your god commands regardless of how horrible and terrible it may be." I do not know how many "Bible-believing" people actually know that such stories as this exist in the Hebrew Bible. We seem to have become desensitized to what would or should be totally revolting behavior if found in some other book besides the Bible. The Bible speaks with many voices, and the portrait of Yahweh presented here has come under harsh judgment (Dawkins 2006b, 31).

The Gibeonite Story

Joshua 9:1-27

1 Now it happened when *all* of the kings who (were) beyond the Jordan, in the hill-country and the lowland and in *all* the coast-land of the Great Sea toward the Lebanon, the Hittites and the Amorites, the Canaanites and the Perizzites, the Hivites and the Jebusites, 2 that they gathered together to fight Joshua and the people of Israel altogether, as one mouth. 3 So when those who were living in Gibeon heard what Joshua had done to Jericho and to Ha'ai, 4 they did also the same in craftiness, and they walked and went as messengers and they took worn-out sack-cloths for their asses, and skins of wine, worn-out and ripped open and tied up, 5 with worn-out and patched sandals on their feet, and worn-out garments on them, and *all* bread, their provisions were dry, were crumbled. 6 And they went to Joshua at the camp at Hagilgal and they said to him and to the men (MT: "man") of Israel: "From a land *far away* we have come, so now make (MT: "cut") for us a covenant." 7 But the man of Israel said (on the meaning and usage of *qere*, see p. 55) to the Hivite: "Perhaps in my midst you are living; so how can I make a covenant with you" (*qere*)? 8 And they said to Joshua: "We are your slaves." And Joshua said to them: "Who are you? And from where do you come?"

9 And they said to him: "From a land *very far away*, your slaves have come, because the name of Yahweh your god, for we have heard a report of him, of *all* that he did in Egypt 10 and *all* that he did to the two kings of the Amorites who (were) beyond the Jordan, to Sihon, king of Hesbon, and to Og, king of Bashan who lived in Ashtaroth. 11 So our old (men) said to us, as well as *all* who dwell in our land, saying: 'Take in your hand food for the journey, and go to meet them, and say to them: "We are your servants. So now make (MT: "cut") a covenant with us. 12 This (is) our bread; (it was) hot when we supplied ourselves with it on the day we brought it out from our house for the journey to you; but now, behold, it is dry and crumbled. 13 And those skins of wine, when we filled (them were) new, but, behold, they have burst open; and these garments and sandals of ours are worn-out from the very long journey." 14 So the men

took their food but they did not ask for advice from Yahweh (MT: "ask the mouth of Yahweh").

[15] And Joshua made peace with them and he made a covenant with them for their lives; and the chiefs of the congregation swore an oath to them. [16] Then it happened after the end of three days, when they had made a covenant with them, that they heard that they were near to them (MT: "him"), and that they were living among them. [17] Then the Israelites set out and they came to their cities on the third day. And their cities (were) Gibeon, and the Chephirah, and Beeroth and Kiriath-jearim. [18] But the Israelites did not kill them because the chiefs of the congregation had sworn to them by Yahweh, the god of Israel. And *all* the congregation murmured against the chiefs. [19] So *all* the chiefs said to *all* the congregation: "We swore to them by Yahweh, the god of Israel, so now we are not able to touch them. [20] This we will do to them, in order to let them live so that wrath will not come upon us because of the oath that we swore to them." [21] Then the chiefs said to them: "Let them live." And they became cutters of wood and drawers of water for *all* the congregation, even as the chiefs had said to them.

[22] Then Joshua called to them and said to them saying: "Why did you deceive us saying: 'We are very far from you,' when you are living among us? [23] Now you are cursed and a slave will not be cut off from you and you (will be) cutters of wood and drawers of water for the house of my god."

[24] And they answered Joshua and said: "Because it was truly told to your servants that Yahweh your god had commanded Moses, his servant, to give to you *all* the land, and to exterminate *all* the inhabitants of the land from before you, so we were in much fear for our lives by reason of you, so we did this thing. [25] So now, behold, we are in your hand. Do to us what is good and right in your eyes to do." [26] So he (Joshua) did thus to them and he delivered them from the hand of the Israelites, and they did not kill them. [27] But on that day, Joshua made them cutters of wood and drawers of water for the congregation and for the altar of Yahweh, even to this day, at the place that he chooses.

To pull off their deception, the Gibeonites lied and claimed, at first, that they had come from a "*far country*" (Josh 9:6). But, as if someone in the group remembered the "correct" answer, they changed their story in v. 9 to a "*very* far country" (compare Deut 20:15). The fact that the Israelites were deceived by a ruse (just as they had deceived Jericho [the Rahab episode] and Ha'ai [8:1-23]) does not allow them to violate their oath to spare the Gibeonites (9:19). The situation under which Gibeon is allowed to live is analogous to Israel's: Gibeon should have been devoted to the *ban*, but was spared by a "covenant" made with Joshua (9:15). Israel should also have been destroyed for her unrighteousness and stubborn heart, but was spared because of a covenant Yahweh made with their ancestors (Deut 9:1-29). Gibeon and Israel, then, both exist not because they deserve to but because of sworn covenants. Once more, boundaries are redrawn to include "outsiders" who now become "insiders" by swearing allegiance to Joshua and to his god, Yahweh. To people in the days of Josiah and/or the exile, the meaning of this story would be clear: because of the deity's promises to their ancestors, they, undeserving as they might be, once more had the possibility of becoming his people ("insiders") in the reoccupation of the land. But does pandering to hopeless exiles justify such violent behavior? Both the "reported speech" by the Gibeonites and "reporting speech" by the Dtr that close the chapter (9:24-27) reflect clear Deuteronomistic theology.

Note once more the emphasis on the inclusiveness of the land and the peoples: *all* the land is given to the Israelites, and *all* the indigenous inhabitants are to be put to death. The Gibeonites are saved by their trick but condemned to be "hewers of wood and drawers of water for the congregation and for the altar of Yahweh, to continue to this day, in the place that he should choose" (v. 27). Whatever place this may have implied in the oldest version of this story, as it now stands, most scholars believe that from the time of Josiah, at least, it refers to the temple in Jerusalem.

The longstanding identification of Gibeon with the site of el-Jib, located a few miles southwest of Ha'ai, need not be disputed. However, that Gibeon does not seem to have existed in the Late Bronze Age is another indication of the literary construction of the book of Joshua. Moreover, one should appreciate the irony in this story. Just as the "Israelites" acted out a ruse with the citizens of Jericho (ch. 6) and Ha'ai (8:10-17), leading the latter into a deadly trap, the Gibeonites tricked the Israelites into making a covenant with them!

The Southern Campaign

Joshua 10:1-43

There are actually three episodes or stories in this chapter that have been combined: the attack against Gibeon and its miraculous deliverance (vv. 1-15), the five kings in the cave of Makkedah (vv. 16-27), and the attacks against certain cities in the southern part of Canaan (vv. 28-43). The chapter is also filled with textual difficulties with the MT often at variance with the LXX and other versions. Thus, chapter 10 is a complex literary production.

The Attack against Gibeon (10:1-15)

> [1]And it happened when Adoni-zedek ("my lord is righteous"), the king of
> Jerusalem, heard how Joshua seized Ha'ai and destroyed her (MT: "devoted
> her to the ban, *hrm*") even as he did to Jericho and her king so he did to
> Ha'ai and her king, and how the inhabitants of Gibeon made peace with
> Israel and were among them, [2] then he was very fearful because Gibeon
> (was) a great city, like one of the cities of the kingdom and because she was
> larger than Ha'ai and *all* her men (were) mighty. [3] So Adoni-zedek, the
> king of Jerusalem sent to Hoham, the king of Hebron and to Piram, the
> king of Jarmuth and to Japhia, the king of Lachish and to Debir, the king
> of Eglon saying: [4] "come up to me and help me let us destroy Gibeon, for
> she has made peace with Joshua and with the Israelites."
>
> [5] So the five kings of the Amorites—the king of Jerusalem, the king of
> Hebron, the king of Jarmuth, the king of Lachish, the king of Eglon,
> assembled themselves and went up with *all* their armies and they camped
> about Gibeon and they waged war against her. [6] Then the men of Gibeon
> sent to Joshua at the camp of Hagilgal saying: "do not relax your hand
> from your servants (slaves). Come to us quickly and save us, and help us
> for *all* the kings of the Amorites who dwell in the hill-country are gathered
> against us."
>
> [7] So Joshua went up from Hagilgal, he and *all* the people of war
> ("warriors") with him and *all* the mighty (ones) of the army. [8] Then
> Yahweh said to Joshua: "Do not fear them for into your hand I have given

> them—not a man will stand before you." 9 And Joshua came upon them
> suddenly for he went up the whole night from Hagilgal. 10 And Yahweh
> confused them before Israel and they slew them with a great slaughter at
> Gibeon and they chased them by the way of the ascent of Beth-horon and
> they killed them as far as Azekah and Makkedah. 11 And it happened as
> they fled before Israel on the slope of Beth-horon, that Yahweh threw on
> them large stones from the heavens as far as Azekah. And they died! There
> (were) many more who died from the hailstones than whom the Israelites
> killed with a sword.
>
> 12 At that time Joshua spoke to Yahweh on the day Yahweh gave over
> the Amorites before the Israelites and he (Joshua) said in sight (MT: "in the
> eyes") of Israel: "Sun, at Gibeon, be silent, and moon in the valley of
> Aijalon." 13 Then the sun was silent and the moon stopped until (the)
> nation took vengeance on his enemies (MT: "hostile ones"). Is this not
> written in the book of Jashar ("straight," "righteous")? And the sun stopped
> in mid-heaven (MT: "in the half of the heavens"), and did not hasten to go
> in ("set") for a whole day. 14 There has not been like this a day before or
> after with regard to Yahweh's hearing concerning a man's voice, for Yahweh
> fought for Israel. 15 And so Joshua returned and *all* Israel with him to the
> camp at Hagilgal.

This story has some connection to chapter 9, especially the first three verses. There we are told that the kings of Canaan began to unite having "heard" of Israel's initial military success. Now, with Gibeon in Israel's hand (either by ruse, MT; or simply by going over to Israel's side, LXX), and because it was a "great city" (v. 2), the kings unite at the behest of Adonizedek of Jerusalem (in the LXX this king is called Adonibezek, as in Judg 1:5-7). The five kings are Adonizedek in Jerusalem; Horam in Hebron; Piram in Jarmuth; Japhia in Lachish; and Debir in Eglon. However, originally there must have been six kings, not five (Soggin 1972, 130). It has been suggested that the names of the kings of Debir and Eglon either dropped out or were always absent. According to the story related in vv. 28-39, six cities, Makkedah, Libnah, Lachish, Eglon, Hebron, and Debir, were with their (unnamed) kings. The only named king, Horam from Gezer, is killed along with "his people," but Gezer itself is not said to have been destroyed. There is also a strange note attached to the report of the killing of the king of Makkedah: "and he [Joshua] did to the king of Makkedah as he had done to the king of Jericho." Nowhere in Joshua is the specific claim made that the king of Jericho was killed, much less are there specifics about how the killing was accomplished. This same claim is made two more times in the story: vv. 28 and 30. Since all of the cities claimed to have been destroyed were in the tribal territory of Judah (Josh 15:39-54), it has been argued that this tradition of the destruction of the six cities came from Judah, and not Benjamin (Miller and Tucker, 88).

Moreover, Debir, identified as a king in v. 3, is the name of a city in vv. 38-39. It is not mentioned again in the accounts of the five unnamed kings (vv. 16, 17, 23). Making Debir a king in v. 3 may represent a later attempt to harmonize the story with the tradition of five kings. It would also seem that the original name of the king of Eglon was lost in the transmission of the story. Probably the only part of the story in this chapter that is remembered by the general public, if at all, is the claim that Yahweh threw down stones upon Israel's enemies and the sun and moon stood still over Gibeon (10:11-14). If it were not for the serious theme of a god once more killing on behalf of one group of people against another, this tale of a god hurling "huge" heavenly stones upon Israel's enemies and the sun and moon stopping in their orbits would simply amount to "comic relief" in an otherwise revolting story. This is not the place to discuss the total scientific improbability of such a scenario having ever happened in the history of this planet (but for a good scientific critique of such a supposed event, see Sagan). In Jewish legends, when Joshua commanded the sun to stand still he used the Hebrew verb *dom* (דום—"be silent") because the sun would sing praises to Yahweh while it (MT: "he") was moving. He (the sun) agreed to stop only after Joshua promised that he, himself, would sing praises to Yahweh (Hirsch)! The original context and meaning of this mythological fragment is unknown. One also notes the ambiguous introduction to this story: "at that time" (v. 12). The point of the Dtr is, as always in the Joshua stories, that Yahweh fought for Israel. Thus the outcome of the battle with the five kings was already preordained.

Whatever the solution to the ambiguities in this story, it was told by the Dtr to emphasize his belief that Israel's victories were due less to her own military prowess than to her god's merciful intervention (v. 11). Moreover, the quote from the Book of Jashar ("Upright," vv. 12-13; cf. 2 Sam 1:18) has evoked numerous and, for the most part, questionable rational explanations. In the first place, in context, Joshua's command to the sun and moon comes after the battle had already been won and Yahweh had already stoned everyone to death (v. 11)! Thus there was no need for extra daylight to extend the battle as the gross literalizing of the poetic verses (vv. 12-13) clearly implies. In the second place, the quotation may originally have had to do with an entirely different event than the one recorded here (Soggin 1972, 122). Whatever the case may be, the story now serves the theology of the Dtr: Israel succeeded only because of an act of divinely led war; it was

Yahweh's victory, not Israel's (cf. also the memo in Josh 10:15). We are told that after the rout of the coalition, "Joshua returned and *all* Israel with him, to the camp at Hagilgal." Again, the distances said to have been traveled here are suspect. Perhaps the author of this story had no idea how far these towns were from Hagilgal. Moreover, even though the site of Hagilgal (and it is always *hagilgal* in the MT) has yet to be identified for certain, the biblical tradition locates it somewhere east of Jericho. Furthermore, in the story that follows (vv. 16-27), when the "Israelites" and Joshua returned from pursuing the armies of the five captured kings, they returned to the "camp at Makkedah" (v. 21), not Hagilgal. Consequently, even though 10:15 has "Joshua and *all* Israel" returning to Hagilgal, the story of the cave begins with no note that Joshua and his warriors had gone back up from Hagilgal (v. 7).

The Five Kings and the Cave of Makkedah (10:16-27)

16 Then these five kings fled and hid themselves in the cave at Makkedah.
17 And it was told to Joshua saying: "The five kings have been found
hiding in the cave at Makkedah." 18 So Joshua said: "Role large stones
against the mouth of the cave and appoint for her men to watch them.
19 But you, you yourselves, do not stay, pursue after your enemies and cut
them off. Do not let them get set to enter their cities (or towns) for Yahweh
your god has given them into your hand."

20 So it happened that Joshua and the Israelites completed their killing
them (with) a very great slaughter, until they were finished. But the
survivors escaped from them and had gone into the fortified cities. 21 *All*
the people returned in peace to the camp with Joshua at Makkedah. No
one sharpened his tongues against the Israelites, to a man (that is, no one
spoke ill of anyone).

22 Then Joshua said: "Open the mouth of the cave and bring them out
to me, the five kings from the cave." 23 And they did so. And they brought
out to him these five kings from the cave: the king of Jerusalem, the king
of Hebron, the king of Jarmuth, the king of Lachish, the king of Eglon.
24 And it happened when they brought out these kings to Joshua that
Joshua called to every man of Israel and said to the chiefs of the warriors
(men of the war), the ones who were with him: "Come near; put your feet
on the necks of these kings." And they came near and they put their feet
on their necks. 25 Then Joshua said to them: "do not fear and do not be
dismayed; be strong and assured, for thus Yahweh will do to *all* your
enemies when you are fighting against them."

26 Then after this Joshua struck them down and he killed them and
hung them upon five trees. And they were hanging on the trees until the
evening. 27 And it happened at the time the sun went in ("sunset"), Joshua

commanded and took them down from upon the trees and they threw them into the cave where they had hidden themselves and they set large stones against the mouth of the cave. Until this day this stuff (MT: "bone," "self") (is) there.

The fleeing kings, no longer named, are captured in the cave, publically humiliated, (v. 24), and killed (how all of the "chiefs" of the warriors could put their feet on five necks at the same time is never described; perhaps we are to imagine that there were only five to begin with or it was a symbolic act). Along with the story of the public execution of Achan (see above), this is the only other story of a public execution in the book of Joshua. The story may have originated to explain a pile of stones "which remain to this very day" (v. 27, a loose translation; compare v. 18). The precise location of the site of Makkedah is unknown, though Khirbet ("village") el-Qôm has been suggested (Dever 1990, 57). If Khirbet el-Qôm is indeed the site of biblical Makkedah, the story in Joshua appears once more to be a literary composition made up long after the event supposedly happened. W. G. Dever excavated the site in 1967–1971. He found a walled village and dozens of Iron Age tombs. One tomb contained an inscription that reads, "Yahweh and his Asherah," the Canaanite mother goddess. But he found no archaeological evidence of a settlement predating the late tenth to ninth centuries BCE and no flourishing town until the eighth century. He found no evidence of a Late Bronze Age-Iron Age I Canaanite occupation that could be associated with any "conquest" by the "Israelites" or anyone else (Dever 2003a, 65).

The Southern Campaign: The Destruction of Six Cities and the Gezerites (10:28-43)

[28] And Joshua took Makkedah on that day and he killed her king with the
edge of a sword; he utterly destroyed (*hrm*) them and *all* the persons who
were in her. He did not leave a survivor. And he did to the king of
Makkedah even as he had done to the king of Jericho. [29] Then Joshua
passed on and *all* Israel with him, from Makkedah to Libnah; and he
fought with Libnah. [30] And Yahweh also gave her into the hand of Israel
and her king. Then he (Joshua) struck her down with the edge of a sword,
and every person in her. He did not leave in her any survivor. Also he did
to her king even as he did to the king of Jericho.

[31] Then Joshua, and *all* Israel with him, passed on from Libnah to
Lachish. And he lay siege against her and fought against her. [32] And
Yahweh gave Lachish into the hand of Israel and he captured it on the

> second day and struck it down with the edge of a sword. And every person in her just like *all* he did to Libnah.
>
> 33 At that time, Horam, king of Gezer went up to help Lachish, and Joshua struck him and his people down so as to leave him no survivor.
>
> 34 Then Joshua and *all* Israel with him, passed on from Lachish toward Eglon. There he camped against her and fought against her. 35 And they took it on that day and they struck her down with the edge of a sword and every person who was in her. On that day he exterminated (*hrm*) them just like *all* that he did to Lachish.
>
> 36 Then Joshua went up with *all* Israel with him from Eglon toward Hebron and they waged war against her. 37 And they took her and struck her down with the edge of a sword, her king, and *all* her towns, and every person who (was) in her. He did not leave a survivor just like *all* he did to Eglon. Thus he exterminated her and *every* person who (was) in her.
>
> 38 Then Joshua turned back, and *all* Israel with him, to Debir and he waged war against her. 39 And he captured her and her king, and *all* her towns, and they struck them down with the edge of a sword; and they exterminated *every* person who (was) in her. He did not leave a survivor. Just as he had done at Hebron so he did to Debir and her king, just as he did to Libnah and her king.
>
> 40 So Joshua defeated *all* the land; the hill-country and the Negeb and the lowland (the Shephelah), and the slopes and *all* their kings. He did not leave a survivor. *All* that breathed he utterly destroyed (*hrm*) just as Yahweh, the god of Israel, had commanded. 41 So Joshua struck them down from Kadesh-barnea as far as Gaza and *all* the land of Goshen and as far as Gibeon. 42 And *all* these kings and their land Joshua took at one time because Yahweh, the god of Israel, fought for Israel. 43 Then Joshua and *all* Israel with him, returned to the camp at Hagilgal.

It is doubtful that the traditions recorded here preserve any real historical memory. Older attempts (Albright, 1949, 109, 112; 1957, 276–90, for example) to identify Late Bronze Age destruction layers discovered at some of these sites with a "conquest" by "Israelites" have been totally discredited except among the most evangelical conservative scholars. Furthermore, Eglon (if it is Tell el-Hesi) and Hebron have revealed no evidence of any such destruction as described here, at least not during the Late Bronze-Iron I periods. The location of Libnah remains uncertain, thus its fate during this time is still unknown. Jerusalem has been excavated more times than all the other sites put together, and no evidence for a Late Bronze Age destruction has ever been uncovered. Lachish was destroyed in the late thirteenth century BCE and again around 1150 BCE, but by whom is unknown. Debir, now identified with modern Khirbet Rabud, has not revealed any evidence of a

Late Bronze-Iron Age I destruction (Dever 2003a, 54–74). Moreover, while Joshua 10:33 does not state specifically that Joshua destroyed the major Canaanite city of Gezer, 12:12 claims explicitly that Joshua killed the king of Gezer. The excavations of the site by W. G. Dever in 1964–1973 found no archaeological evidence that could be correlated with the biblical story. Additionally, while Joshua 10:33 claims that Joshua "struck him (the king of Gezer) and his people, leaving him no survivors," 16:10 states that the Ephraimites did not "drive out the Canaanites who live in Gezer: so the Canaanites have lived within Ephraim to this day" (compare Judg 1:29).

There are also insurmountable problems related to where all of these battles were taking place with regard to Hagilgal. According to 10:15, Joshua and "*all* Israel with him" returned to the camp at Hagilgal, but according to 10:21, the camp was at Makkedah. Verse 15 is probably a gloss of some sort, especially since the entire verse is missing in the LXX. Hagilgal is one thousand feet or more below sea level (the lowest point on earth is the northern end of the Dead Sea, which is nearly 1300 feet below sea level). Jerusalem is some 2,500 feet above sea level. As the crow flies, the distance between Jericho, believed to be located southwest of Hagilgal, and Jerusalem is around fifteen to sixteen miles. But one cannot get there flying like a crow! Reconstructing the road system that existed in Israel during the Iron Age is difficult (Dorsey; for an older, but still useful, discussion of roads in ancient Israel see Aharoni, esp. pp. 39–57). The ancient road going from Jericho up to Jerusalem, like the modern one, was steep and probably very winding. For a military force of any size to walk up such a steep incline would be an arduous and time-consuming undertaking. This is especially true during hot weather. Weather conditions are never mentioned in these stories. Yet the story in Joshua implies that the Israelites left Hagilgal, came to Gibeon, over thirty miles away (altitude over 2,400 feet above sea level), fought against the coalition, and then routed their enemies. They then marched on to the city of Makkedah (if K. el-Qôm, v. 20), some twenty miles from Gibeon (and over fifty miles from Hagilgal), then on to Libnah (identification unknown). From Libnah, so the story goes, the Israelites went to Lachish, some eight miles from Makkedah, and then to Eglon (v. 34), which is nearly eight miles from Lachish. From Eglon they advanced to Hebron, a good twelve to thirteen miles away (v. 36), and then turned around and went to Debir (if identified with Khirbet Rabud), some fifteen miles in the opposite direction (v. 38). We are then told, after the nice "reporting speech" of the summary of the conquest in the south by Joshua (vv. 40-42), that "Joshua returned, and *all* Israel with him, to the camp at Hagilgal" (v. 43). Nothing is said about the time lapse between these marches and battles. Everything is telescoped to give the impression that all the battles happened in quick succession. Little or no day-to-day practical issues, such as feeding, resting, or hygienic needs, are ever mentioned. The result is the stringing together of one battle report after another that has an artificial feel to it. Moreover, Hagilgal, even though its exact location is unknown, would have been over sixty miles as the crow flies from Debir, through the rugged, barren Judean desert. By ancient roads it would be much farther, of course.

In his thorough study of the road systems in ancient Israel, David Dorsey listed two reasons why so little has been written on this subject: the lack of archaeological evidence and the fact that "biblical and contemporary extra-biblical sources say almost nothing about the specific characteristics of the roads of their day" (2). It should be noted here that, at present, no archaeological remains of open roads dating to the Iron Age have been discovered in Israel (Dorsey, 2). The book of Joshua may contain three or four references to public roads. Joshua 2:7 mentions *derek hayyarden*, "The Jordan (River) Road," while 8:15 refers to *derek hammidbar*, "The Road of the Wilderness" (compare Exod 13:18; Dorsey, 202, where Dorsey suggests that part of this road may have been found during a survey by archaeologists in the early 1980s). Joshua 10:10 refers to *derek ma'aleh bet horon*, "The Road of the Ascent of Beth (house of)-horon." Finally, a fourth road may be found in Joshua 12:3: *derek beth-hayeshimoth*: "The Road of The Beth (house of)-hajeshimoth." However, in English translations, the fact that these may have been known roads (in Hebrew, the word דרך is often translated as "road" or "way") is often obscured. For an example, the NRSV translates Joshua 2:7 not as "The Jordan (River) Road" but simply as "on the way to the Jordan." There must have been an ancient road leading from Jericho to Jerusalem, sometimes referred to in the Bible as "The Arabah Road" (2 Kgs 25:4; Jer 39:4; 52:7; Dorsey 204–206; compare 2 Sam 10:1-5, 15-17; 19:15-34). The point here is that moving armies around to do battle requires roads. The Dtr was not interested *per se* in elucidating which roads were supposedly used by the "Israelites" for the period in which he placed his stories, nor apparently, was he interested in other practical issues. Furthermore, the numbers of warriors claimed to have been available to fight seem greatly exaggerated: Joshua 7:3 claims "two or three thousand," and Joshua 4:13 claims "forty thousand." And they all are said to have come from only the two and a half Transjordanian tribes! All of these figures suggest the artificiality of these stories (Judg 20:17 states that the Israelites could raise an army of 400,000 warriors!).

All of the day-to-day activities that had to take place in order to move, feed, and otherwise support such large numbers of troops are nowhere described. This absence of detail is not unexpected given the theological motivations for telling the story in the first place. However, if the stories are taken at face value, such critical questions need to be raised. One other question that needs to be considered has to do with how far an army could travel in a day's march. There is no evidence that these supposed military forces traveled by horse or chariot, only on foot (for biblical references to traveling on foot see Deut 8:4; 11:24-25; 29:5; Josh 1:3; 3:13, 15, and so forth). We are told that the Gibeonites came to Joshua and the Israelites "with worn-out, patched sandals on their feet" (9:5), clearly implying that they were walking. They used donkeys to transport their provisions (9:4). Such telescoped stories as these raise important issues concerning the logistics of moving military forces and their provisions, keeping supply lines open, and a host of other issues necessary to the success of winning battles. The biblical stories describe none of these critical issues. Who built the ancient roads? How wide were they (Dorsey, inter alia)? Three main roads leading from the highlands of Jerusalem and Benjamin to Jericho have been identified (Dorsey, 202, Map 15), but whether the stories of Joshua assume any or all of these roads is unclear. The exact course of any army marching from the plains of Jericho into the highlands of Iron Age I Israel is also unknown. It has been suggested that an army might make fourteen to fifteen miles a day, although the forces of Thutmose averaged only about six to seven miles a day (Dorsey, 13). Such telescoping of these battles makes it impossible to begin to extract any actual "history" of such claims. The Dtr's theological summary in vv. 40-42 again reflects only the holy war construct within which Israel's conquering of the south has been placed. It may be no coincidence that the territory taken in this account closely corresponds to the reinhabited area of the returning exiles in the sixth century BCE.

Hazor and the Northern Campaign

Joshua 11:1-23

1 And it happened when Jabin, the King of Hazor heard (about this) that he sent to Jobab, the king of Madon, and to the king of Shimron, and to the king of Achshaph, 2 and to the kings who (were) from the north in the hill-country and in the Arabah south of Chinneroth, and in the lowland and in Napoth-dor by the sea; 3 the Canaanites in the east and in the west, and the Amorites, the Hittites and the Perizzites, and the Jebusites in the hill-country, and the Hivites under Hermon in the land of Mizpah. 4 And they came out and *all* their armies with them, a great multitude, like the sand that is on the sea shore, in regard to the multitude, and with a great force of horse and chariot. 5 And *all* these kings assembled and they came and encamped together by the waters of Merom to fight against Israel.

6 Then Yahweh said to Joshua: "Do not be afraid before them, for at this time tomorrow I will hand over *all* the people of war ("warriors"), slain, to Israel. Their horses you will hamstring, and their chariot you will burn with fire." 7 So Joshua and *all* the people of war came upon them suddenly by the waters of Merom and they fell among them. 8 And Yahweh gave them into the hand of Israel and they struck them down and chased them as far as Great Sidon and as far as Misrephoth-maim ("by the sea"), and as far as the valley of Mizpeh in the east. Then they struck them down until there did not remain a survivor among them. 9 And Joshua did to them just as Yahweh had said to him. He hamstrung their horses and burned their chariots with fire.

10 Then Joshua returned back at that time and he captured Hazor, and her king he struck down with the sword. Before, Hazor was the head of *all* these kingdoms. 11 And they struck down *every* living person who (was) in her with an edge of a sword, to exterminate (them). There was not left any that breathed, and they burned the city with fire. 12 And *all* the towns of these kings and *all* their kings, Joshua captured, and he struck them down with an edge of a sword; he utterly destroyed (*hrm*) them even as Moses, the servant of Yahweh had commanded. 13 Only *all* of the towns standing upon tels Israel did not burn them, only Hazor alone did Joshua burn.

> 14 And *all* the spoil of these towns and the animal(s) the Israelites took for themselves. Only *all* the humans (*ha'adam*, the humankind) did they strike down with an edge of a sword until they had annihilated them. They did not spare any that breathed. 15 Just as Yahweh had commanded Moses, his servant, so Moses commanded Joshua, and so Joshua did; he did not take away a thing from *all* that Yahweh had commanded Moses. 16 And Joshua took *all* this land, the hill-country and *all* the Negeb and *all* the land of Goshen, and the lowland (Shephelah) and the Arabah and the hill-country of Israel and its lowland, 17 from Mount Halak that goes up to Seir, as far as Baal-gad ("god of fortune") in the valley of Lebanon before Mount Hermon. And he seized *all* their kings and struck them down and killed them.
>
> 18 A long time (MT: "many days") Joshua made war with *all* these kings. 19 There was not a city that made peace with the Israelites except the Hivites, those living in Gibeon; they (Israelites) took everyone in the war. 20 For (it was) Yahweh's doing to harden their heart so that they would come out to do battle against Israel in order that they might be utterly destroyed so that there would not be for them a supplication for favor, in order that they would be exterminated even as Yahweh had commanded Moses.
>
> 21 And at that time Joshua came and destroyed the Anakim from the hill-country, from Hebron, from Debir, from Anab, and from *all* the hill country of Judah and from *all* the hill-country of Israel. Joshua exterminated (*hrm*) them with their towns. 22 No one of the Anakim was left in the land of the Israelites. Only in Gaza, in Gath, and in Ashdod did they remain. 23 So Joshua took the whole land according to *all* that Yahweh had spoken to Moses and Joshua gave her for an inheritance to Israel according to their divisions of their tribes. And the land was quiet from war.

Chapter 11 is one of the clearest examples of the ideology lying behind the DH found in the entire book of Joshua. Unfortunately, oftentimes the literary clues to his ideology are lost in modern translations. There is only one "reported speech" in the chapter, and that is the speech of Yahweh in verse 6: "And Yahweh said to Joshua: 'Do not be afraid of them, for tomorrow at this time I will hand over *all* of them, slain to Israel; you shall hamstring their horses, and burn their chariots with fire.'"

The rest of the chapter is the "reporting" (or editorial) speeches by the Dtr. When reading this chapter, as well as all the others, particular attention should be paid to the "reporting speeches," and to the use of the Hebrew word *kol*, which is repeated no less than twenty-two times in this chapter alone (for a detailed discussion of this word see above). This chapter reflects the entire ideology of holy or divine war. Yahweh sanctioned it, and Yahweh guaranteed the outcome before the battles even began (v. 6). Joshua and the Israelites had only to perform perfunctory duties. All the language of holy war is here:

1. "Yahweh handed them over" (v.8)
2. "they attacked them" (v. 8)
3. "they chased them" (v. 8)
4. "they struck them down" (v. 8)
5. "they struck its king down with the sword" (v. 10)
6. "they put to the sword . . . exterminated them" (v. 11)
7. "struck them down with the edge of the sword, utterly destroying them" (v. 12)
8. "*all* the spoils of these towns . . . they took for booty" (v. 14)
9. "*all* the people they killed with the sword" (v. 14)
10. "they left none breathing" (v. 14)
11. "he left nothing undone of *all* that Yahweh had commanded Moses" (v. 15)
12. "he took *all* their kings, struck them down, and put them to death" (v. 17)
13. "*all* were taken in battle" (v. 19)
14. "Yahweh hardened their hearts" (v. 20)
15. "that they be devoted to destruction" (the *herem*, v. 20)
16. "and receive on favor" (v. 20)
17. "but be devoted to destruction" (the *herem*, v.20)
18. "wiped out the Anakim" (v. 21)
19. "exterminated them with their towns" (v. 21)
20. "took the whole land, according to *all* Yahweh spoke to Moses" (v. 23)

All told, there are some thirty-two verbs in these twenty-three verses describing the fighting, killing, slaughtering, looting, burning, and otherwise the total destruction of towns, kings, and the indigenous populations of Canaan by the invading "Israelites" as commanded and approved by their tribal deity, Yahweh. Clines's question needs to be repeated: "what ethical responsibility do I have if I help keep this story alive" (1998, 286)?

However, the quickness with which all of this seems to have taken place is contradicted by the observation recorded in v. 18: "Joshua made war a long time (MT: 'many days') with all these kings." This tension contradicts the implication found elsewhere in the story that the "conquest" lasted for only a few short years. In Joshua 14:7-10, Caleb, in a "reported speech," claims he was forty years old when Moses sent him to spy out the land (of

Canaan). According to Deuteronomy 2:14, thirty-eight years later the "conquest" began, making Caleb seventy-eight years old. According to the details told in Joshua 14:10, he was eighty-five years old when the conquest ended. Simple math gives us seven years for the duration of the conquest. Perhaps v. 18 was added to the story by the later editor(s) to deal with chronological implications of such texts as Joshua 13:1-6 and Judges 1:1-2 (Nelson 1997, 154–55). Both texts indicate that a much longer period was required for the "conquest." Other texts also support the conclusion that the "conquest" was not as swift as implied in Joshua. Moreover, the rationale given in these texts is unexpected: if the indigenous populations are killed off too quickly, the wild animals will experience a population explosion that will threaten the Israelites! The texts speak for themselves:

Exodus 23:29-30
29 I will not drive them out from before you in one year *lest the land become a devastation and the animal of the field multiply against you.*
30 *Little by little I will drive it (the enemy) from before you until (when) you bear fruit (reproduce) and you possess the land.*

Deuteronomy 7:22
22 And Yahweh your god will clear away these nations *little by little. You will not be able to finish them quickly lest the animal of the field multiply against you.*

Compare the above texts that imply a much longer process for the taking of the land with the following passage in Deuteronomy 9:1-3:

> Hear, Israel, you are crossing today the Jordan to come in to dispossess greater and mightier nations than you, (and) great cities (towns), unassailable in the heavens; a people strong and exalted, sons of the Anakim whom you know. And you have heard it said: "who can stand before the sons of Anak?" But you know today that Yahweh your god, he is the one crossing before you, an eating (devouring) fire; he will exterminate them and he will subdue them before you and you will dispossess them and *you will destroy them quickly* even as Yahweh spoke to you. (my emphasis)

The Archaeological History of Hazor

The excavations of the imposing site of Hazor, the largest Canaanite city tel so far discovered in Israel (during its height in the Middle Bronze Age, the city enclosed more than 200 acres, which is exceptionally large for a Canaanite city), have long been used to suggest the historical credibility of the story told here in Joshua (one of the best-known Israeli archaeologists who excavated Hazor back in the late 1950s and advocated this position was the late Yigael Yadin [d. 1984]; see Zuckerman, 2007). But alas, not only does the archaeological evidence not give the story credibility (Finkelstein 1988a, 301), but the story in Judges 4–5 also contradicts the version reported in Joshua 11. Hazor was a flourishing Middle and Late Bronze Age city, and its political and economic importance is reflected in several extra-biblical sources. These include the Egyptian Execration Texts that date to the nineteenth century BCE (*ANET*, 329), as well as texts from New Kingdom documents from the time of Thutmose III (1479–1425 BCE), Amen-hotep II (late fifteenth century BCE) and Seti I (thirteenth century, *ANET*, 242). The Tel el-Amarna texts (fourteenth century BCE) also mention both Hazor and its king, ʿAbdi-Tirshi. Finally, the Papyrus Anastasi I dated to the time of Ramses II (thirteenth century BCE) mentions Hazor once more. These many extra-biblical texts attest to the importance that Hazor achieved through the centuries (for a detailed description of the references to Hazor in the non-biblical texts, see Rainy and Notley 2006, inter alia). But during the last half of the thirteenth century, the city deteriorated and was violently destroyed and abandoned for over a century before a small settlement was established there during Iron Age I (Zuckerman; Ben-Ami). The current excavations of Hazor, under the direction of Israeli archaeologist A. Ben-Tor, were begun in 1990. A senior member of this renewed excavation is Doran Ben-Ami of the IAA (the Israel Antiquities Authority). In a recent article in which Ben-Ami summarized his conclusions from a study of the Iron Age I remains (1200–1000 BCE) found on top of the destroyed LBA city, he drew the following cautious conclusion: ". . . this destruction [of the Late Bronze Age Canaanite city] *probably should not be directly associated with the settlement of the early Israelite population of the site*" (103, my emphasis). This again is a somewhat circular argument, even after factoring in Ben-Ami's weasel word, "probably." Without taking the biblical story at face value before the discussion even begins, what is there in the physical remains from this period that says, "*early Israelite*"? Ben-Tor's own co-director, Sharon Zuckerman, has voiced a much more nuanced conclusion suggesting other possibilities for the city's Late Bronze Age destruction: "The final destruction [of Hazor] itself consisted of the mutilation of statues of kings and gods. *It did not consist of signs of war or any kind of fighting.* We don't see weapons in the streets like we see in other sites that were destroyed by foreigners" (2008, my emphasis).

Her own suggestion for the destruction of Hazor at the end of the thirteenth century was an internal revolt by the rank-and-file Canaanites against their elitist overlords. At the moment, who destroyed Late Bronze Age Hazor is still debated, and as of yet there are no unequivocal answers. Perhaps further excavations will provide valuable evidence that can settle this issue once and for *all* (if there is ever a final answer to such things). Furthermore, the identity of the people who squatted on the abandoned site in Iron Age I period (eleventh century BCE) is still an open question. While it is possible that some group later to be associated with "Israel" may have been part of the peoples who occupied the site, to call them "Israelites" based exclusively on the story in Joshua 11 is premature. Moreover, given the present critical understanding of the (non) "conquest of Canaan" now current among leading biblical historians and archaeologists apropos the literary nature of the book of Joshua, it is unlikely that the account of an "Israelite" destruction of this Late Bronze Age Canaanite city should be taken at face value. None of these "ugly facts," of course, detract from the use of this story by the Dtr, which is to affirm that Joshua did all that Moses and Yahweh commanded him to do (v. 15). According to the story, the Israelites destroyed only Hazor. The other cities on mounds (the Hebrew word is *tel*, literally "ruin," "heap"; see Deut 13:17; Josh 7:28) were spared and only the inhabitants were destroyed—lucky for the buildings! The Israelites were also to take for themselves booty (Achan should have waited just a little longer!). One should also note the reference to both Judah and Israel in v. 21. The *terminus post quem* (earliest possible date) for such a reference to both of these states is late tenth to ninth century BCE, when, according to the Bible, the Davidic monarchy split into these two small, independent states long after the destruction of Hazor.

Conclusion of the "Conquest" (11:16-23)

The Dtr's Summary of the "Conquest" (11:16-20)

These verses provide a Dtr summary to the completion of the "conquest," although v. 18 strikes a note of reality in suggesting that the process was much longer than the preceding stories might imply (see above). That Yahweh "hardened their hearts" that they might receive no mercy (compare Exod 9:12; 10:1; and so forth) is the capstone of a holy war mentality. This summary makes no sense, of course, in light of the current critical synthesis of modern scholarship. The implications of this for the usage of this tradition to support modern wars by some conservative groups cannot be detailed here. But obviously such usage is misguided at best (see Conclusions below).

The Anakim (11:21-23)

The story of the Anakim preserves an independent tradition of this legendary race of giants (compare Num 13:32-33; Deut 1:28; 9:2). It has only a tenuous connection to the preceding stories and contradicts what has already been narrated (according to 10:36-39, Joshua had already destroyed Hebron and Debir). The date of this tradition is uncertain (Soggin thought that it was "ancient," 1972, 141), but in its present form it can date no earlier than the late tenth or the first half of the ninth century since it presupposes the two independent states of Judah and Israel referred to above (v. 21). The three cities mentioned where the Anakim could not be destroyed, Gaza, Gath, and Ashdod, were three of the Philistine pentapolis. The other two were Ekron and Ashkelon.

This chapter concludes with another sweeping summary of the totality of Joshua's victories and prepares the way for the story of the distribution of the land detailed in chapters 13–19. In its present context, the summary reinforces the Dtr's purpose to portray Joshua as having done "*all* that Yahweh had spoken to Moses" (v. 23): "And Joshua took *all* the land according to *all* that Yahweh had spoken to Moses. And Joshua gave it (MT: "her") for an inheritance to Israel according to their divisions by tribes. And the land was quiet from war."

What one should expect following such a summary "reporting speech" is a reported "farewell speech" and a note on the death and burial of Joshua. And such a speech was created for the occasion, but it does not occur until chapter 23. According to the grammatical construction of 11:23 in the phrase, "and Joshua gave it for an inheritance," the verb ("gave") describes a completed action (this is called an imperfect vav consecutive in Hebrew). This means that from the perspective of whoever wrote this verse, the land was already divided among the various tribes at this time. The "conquest" was completed, as Yahweh had promised, and Joshua divided the land as commanded. What one expects at this point in the story is a "farewell speech" by the hero, Joshua, and a note about his death. And this is exactly what we get, but not until twelve chapters later (see below).

The List of Conquered Kings

Joshua 12:1-24

1 Now these are the kings of the land whom the Israelites struck down and
their land that they (Israel) took possession of beyond the Jordan toward
the east (MT: "the place where the sun rises"), from the wadi Arnon as far
as Mount Hermon, and *all* the Arabah toward the east. 2 Sidon, king of the
Amorites who lived in Hesbon, ruling from Aroer, which is upon the edge
of the wadi Arnon, and from the middle of the wadi (or valley) and half of
Hagilead (in the east) as far as the Jabbok river (wadi), (on) the border of
the sons of the Amorites; 3 and the Arabah as far as the sea of Chinneroth
in the east and as far as the sea of the Arabah and the Sea of Salt ("Dead
Sea"), toward the east, on the way to Beth-jeshimoth, and from Teman in
the south beneath the slopes of Pisgah.

4 And the border of Og, the king of the Bashan, (who was) among the
remnants of the Rephaim, who lived in Ashtaroth and at Edrei, 5 who
ruled over Mount Hermon and over Salecah and in *all* of the Bashan as far
as the border of the Geshurites and the Maacathites, and half Hagilead,
(to) the border of Sidon, king of Hesbon.

6 Moses, the servant of Yahweh, and the Israelites, struck them down.
And Moses, the servant of Yahweh, gave land (MT: "her") to the
Reubenites, and to the Gadites, and to the half-tribe of Manasseh. 7 And
these are the kings of the land whom Joshua and the Israelites struck down
beyond the Jordan toward the sea (the Mediterranean), from Baal-gad in
the valley of the Lebanon and as far as Mount Halak, the one rising up
toward Seir. And Joshua gave the land (MT: "her") to the tribes of Israel as
a possession according to their divisions, 8 in the hill-country, in the lowland, and in the wilderness, and in the Negeb, the Hittites, the Amorites,
and the Canaanites, the Perizzites, the Hivites, and the Jebusites:

9 The king of Jericho-one; the king of Ha'ai, which is close to Beth-el-
one

10 the king of Jerusalem: one; the king of Hebron-one

11 the king of Jarmuth: one; the king of Lachish-one

12 the king of Eglon: one; the king of Gezer-one

13 the king of Debir-one; the king of Geder-one
14 the king of Hormah-one; the king of Arad-one
15 the king of Libnah-one; the king of Adullam-one
16 the king of Makkedah-one; the king of Beth-el-one
17 the king of Tappuah-one; the king of Hepher-one
18 the king of Aphek-one; the king of Lasharon-one
19 the king of Madon-one; the king of Hazor-one
20 the king of Shimon-one; the king of Achshaph-one
21 the king of Taanach-one; the king of Megiddo-one
22 the king of Kedesh-one; the king of Jokneam in Carmel-one
23 the king of Dor at Naphath-dor-one; (the) king of goiim in Gilgal-one
24 the king of Tirzah-one
All their kings (numbered) thirty and one.

Chapter 12 presents many problems for the modern reader, including textual issues created by the differences between the MT and the LXX (Miller and Tucker, 101–103; Nelson 1997, 158–59). Verses 7-24 have been characterized as an "enigma" (Nelson 1997, 162). Furthermore, while the king of Bethel is listed as one of the kings whom Joshua defeated, the destruction of the town itself is not narrated until Judges 1:22-26. At first glance the chapter seems to be little more than a kind of statistical summary of the preceding victories. However, while half the towns listed here, such as Jericho and Ha'ai, as well as Arad and Hormah, appear earlier in the conquest story (Josh 6–8 and Num 21:1-4, respectively), other listed sites appear only in this summation (Rainey and Notely 2006, inter alia; Miller and Tucker, 189–200). The number of towns whose kings are said to have been defeated is also confusing. The MT lists thirty-one conquered kings, while the OG only twenty-nine. Nelson, based on the occurrence of the number "thirty" elsewhere in the Bible, amended the list to thirty kings (he cites 2 Sam 23:18-38; Prov 22:20; the number 30 appears 133 times in the Hebrew Bible; first in Gen 5:3 and last in Zech 11:13). Nelson also concluded that the repeated number "one," is probably not original since it is missing in the OG (1997, 159).

The first six verses of chapter 12 summarize Moses' own military victories east of the Jordan River, the Transjordan (compare Num 21:21-35; Deut 2:24–3:11). The Sea of Chinneroth (sometimes spelled "Kinneret") and the Salt Sea mentioned in v. 3 are references to the Sea of Galilee and the Dead Sea respectively. Verses 7-24 recount Joshua's victories west of the Jordan (Cisjordan). The main importance of this list is that it mentions places "conquered" that do not occur in any other account, as mentioned above.

Actually, many of these cities were not occupied or controlled by Israel until the time of David or later. Soggin has argued that much of this list is very old because that is the only way to explain its appearance in this chapter since it does not appear in any other conquest list. On the other hand, perhaps at the time of the actual writing down of this list during or following the exile, the Dtr deliberately included these towns anachronistically (assuming he had access to some list). This seems especially attractive when one considers that all of these towns are said to have a king. What better way for the Dtr to emphasize the completeness of the "conquest" to the people during the time of Josiah and the exiles in Babylonia? Whatever the original background of this list, it has been baptized into the framework of the DH. This can be easily seen by the language used to describe both Moses' and Joshua's victories:

> **Moses** (12:6)
> Moses, the servant of Yahweh, and the Israelites struck (from נכה, *nakah*) them down (the kings listed in vv. 1-5), and Moses the servant of Yahweh (this duplication is probably a result of dittography) gave it (from the root נתן : *natan*; MT: "her," that is the "land") as an inheritance to the Reubenites and to the Gadites and to the half-tribe of Manasseh.
>
> **Joshua** (12:7-8)
> And these are the kings of the land that Joshua and the Israelites struck down (*nakah*) from the other side of the Jordan, toward the sea (the Mediterranean), from Baal-gad in the valley of Lebanon and rising toward Seir. And Joshua gave (*natan*) to the tribes of Israel an inheritance according to their divisions in the hill-country and in the Shephelah and in the Arabah and in the slopes and in the wilderness, and in the Negeb, the Hittites, and the Amorites, and the Canaanites, the Perizzites, the Hivites, and the Jebusites.

Perhaps the Dtr's real purpose for this list was to convince the exiles that just as Moses and the Israelites "struck down" the kings in the Transjordan, so Joshua and the Israelites "struck down" all the Canaanite "kings" in Cisjordan. Once more Joshua is portrayed as the "mirror image" of Moses. Soggin, in discussing the above texts, concluded that "the redactor did not want to give us so much *an account of historical facts*, as to bear witness to the mighty acts of Yahweh in history, the conquest being one of the most important of these mighty acts" (1972, 144, my emphasis).

How nonhistorical "facts" about a fictional conquest can be the "mighty acts" of Yahweh or any other deity, for that matter, Soggin did not bother to explain. Moreover, from an archaeological perspective there are several "ugly facts" (Dever 2003a, 54) about this listing that need to be pointed out. First, many of the towns/cities listed here did not exist during the time assigned any "conquest/settlement" period now accepted by most scholars (1250–1150 BCE). Second, many of the other listed towns have never been identified and/or excavated. Among the former, as already discussed, are the prominent sites of Jericho, et-Tel (Ha'ai) and Arad. Sites whose identification with ancient tels are uncertain or unknown include Hormah, Libnah, Makkedah (although there is general consensus among experts today that this is modern Khirbet el-Qôm), Lasharon, Mador, Shimron-moran, and Goiim (this word, which literally means "nations," is found in the LXX; the MT reads "Hagilgal" ["the Gilgal;" Nelson 1997, 158]).

Other sites have been identified with archaeological ruins but are awaiting excavation. These include Geder (Khirbet Jedur), Addulum (Khirbet 'Addullam), Tappuah (Tell Sheikh Abu Zarad), and Hepher (Tell el-Muhaffer; Dever 2003, 56–57). Other listed towns whose identifications are known show little or no evidence of Late Bronze–Iron Age I destruction. Among these are Hebron, Eglon, Debir (if Tell es-Rabud), Achshap, and Tirzah. To this list also belongs the city of Jerusalem. It should be remembered that any or perhaps all of this current assessment could change with the strike of an archaeologist's pick on any given site. However, at the present time, the list in chapter 12 seems to reflect the imagination of the writer/editor and not historical reality. It is not practical in a publication such as this one to go into the many historical/archaeological issues about most of the towns/cities mentioned in the book of Joshua. There are well over 180 sites listed, nearly a third of which are still unidentified (Miller and Tucker, 189–200; Nelson 1997, 285–89). Nevertheless, it should be understood by any interested reader that to assess critically such claims as made in the book of Joshua, such details are essential. (The curious reader can find individual entries for many of these sites in the following publications: *NIDB*; *ABD*; *NEAEHL*; the recently published [2006] biblical atlas by Rainy and Notley, though not the easiest book to read [each page consists of three columns of small print], will repay well those who persevere.)

The Distribution of the Land

Joshua 13:1–19:51

Introduction

The boundary descriptions and city lists in these seven chapters have a long, complicated history of composition and transmission. Their origin, dates, and purpose are not clear, and they represent a different version of the "conquest" from that told in chapters 1–12 (Hess 1996b). In fact, in the past many scholars have denied Deuteronomic authorship to these chapters and dismissed them as fanciful speculations dating to the time of the exile or later. Moreover, for today's readers these lists may seem to be of little use if not totally boring. However, since the "land" and its distribution to the "tribes" are the main concern of these chapters, perhaps this material, whatever its ultimate source or usage, was ideologically and/or theologically useful to the author. Seen from the perspective of the Judeans from the time of Josiah or the exile, perhaps once more their hope of repossessing the "land" and resurrecting Israel's past glory was revived. Yahweh had promised the entire land, described in detail here. Even though they had lost the land because of "disobedience," it would be theirs once more when they learned their lesson and turned again in obedience to Yahweh's covenantal demands. Of course, such theology never works. If "Israel" ever had a glorious past, and this is debatable, such hopes put forth by the Dtr or whoever never materialized, at least not on the grand scale recounted in these stories. They were false hopes. It is hard to escape the conclusion that these distribution lists are artificially constructed and never represented reality "on the ground."

On the other hand, Polzin argued that the narrator used this section as an ironical exposé on the sweeping claims made by the voice of "authoritarian dogmatism" such as that found in Joshua 21:43 (Polzin, 126–34). None of these considerations answers questions concerning the date and function of the lists that originally were probably independent of their present context. Zvi Gal, based on his archaeological surveys of Lower Galilee, concluded that the border descriptions and city lists for Zebulun,

Asher, Naphtali, and Issachar could not be any earlier then the tenth century BCE (98–106). Furthermore, of the more than forty-five cities listed in chapter 21 (see below) said to have been given, with their pasture lands, to the Levites, it has been shown that not before the eighth century BCE (Boling) were all of these towns occupied at the same time. Others would date the entire list no earlier than the time of Josiah (late seventh century). The origin(s) and purpose(s) of these place name lists have been much discussed in the literature (Hess 1996b with earlier sources).

The Division of the Land Begins

Joshua 13:1-33

Soggin, in his 1972 commentary, divided this chapter into four sections: (1) vv. 1-7 contain a catalog of unconquered land in Cisjordan (west of the Jordan River); (2) vv. 8-14 summarize the division of the land by Moses in Transjordan (east of the Jordan); (3) vv. 15-28 contain a detailed description of the Transjordanian lands given to Reuben and Gad; and (4) vv. 29-33 describe the land given to the half-tribe of Manasseh, and include another note concerning the Levites (151–59). By comparing the following translation of this author with another English version of Joshua, the reader will quickly come to realize just how this tradition of the lands given to Reuben and Gad and the half-tribe of Manasseh has been chopped up.

A Different Version of the Story (13:1-7)

1 Now Joshua was very old (MT: "had come along in the days"). And
Yahweh said to him: "You are very old, yet the land left over (is) much to
possess. 2 This is the land that is remaining: *all* of the territories of the
Philistines and *all* of the Geshurites.
3 From the Shihor which is over (near) in front of Egypt and as far north as
the border of Ekron, this is accounted as Canaanite: the five lords of the
Philistines: the Gazites, the Ashdodites, the Askelonites, the Gitties, and
the Ekronites, also the Avvim. In the south, 4 *all* the land of the Canaanite,
and Mearah that belongs to the Sidonians, to Aphek, as far as the border of
the Amorites, 5 also the land of the Gebalites, and *all* of the Lebanon,
toward the east (MT: "place of the rising sun"), from Baal-gad below
Mount Hermon to Lebo-hamath.

6 *All* the inhabitants of the hill-country from the Lebanon to
Misrephoth-maim, *all* the Sidonians. I, I myself, will dispossess them from
before the Israelites; only let it fall to Israel with regard to an inheritance
even as I commanded you. 7 And now divide this land for an inheritance to
the nine tribes and the half-tribe of Manasseh."

The chapter begins with a "reported speech" by Yahweh himself. Notably, once again the human author assumes that he knows the very mind of the deity, as is the case, of course, of all such "reported speeches" placed into the mouth of Yahweh and human characters throughout the entire book of Joshua. This speech by Yahweh relates that Joshua is very old and yet much land remains to be possessed (v. 1). This observation contrasts sharply with the summary of Joshua's efforts recounted in 10:40 and 11:16-20. Furthermore, according to Joshua 11:23, Joshua had already given the land as an inheritance to Israel "according to the divisions of their tribes" (compare the claims made in 12:7-8 and 21:43-45). Yahweh's speech highlights the major concern of this part of chapter 13: the allotment of land to the nine and a half tribes who lived west of the Jordan. The major point of the author seems to be that Yahweh gave the land to the *people*, not to kings or the wealthy and powerful. Thus Yahweh's will would not be accomplished until he had given Israel "all the land which he swore to give to their fathers" (21:41). The successful occupation of this land, based on this reading, was conditional upon the peoples' obedience to Yahweh's laws, the theological main theme of the DH (for a conservative discussion for such theological rationalization see Butler, 207–208).

The territories described in these opening verses are more ideal than real and in most cases presuppose the kingdom of David and Solomon in its most idealistic form (compare Josh 1:3-4; 1 Kgs 4:21 [5:1 in MT]). All of the above considerations imply that the descriptions of the division of the land into tribal allotments are speculations dating to the time of Josiah/exile or later. Soggin concluded many years ago that vv. 2-6 are an "interpolation on the part of a redactor," (152; compare Nelson 1997, 164). Perhaps, as often observed, seen from the perspective of those in exile, such stories may have given them a glimmer of hope that one day they would return and reclaim "all the land" for themselves. This never happened, of course, unless one counts the modern state of Israel as the fulfillment of these hopes, as contemporary orthodox Jews are wont to do (Prior 1999). But the attempt to draw modern-day political boundaries on the literal reading of ancient texts has proven to be politically volatile, often resulting in violence and death. This is especially true in Israel and the Palestinian territories. One should also note the opening verse: "now Joshua was old and had come into the days." After such an introduction one expects a "farewell speech" as is seen in other parts of the biblical tradition (compare David, 1 Kgs 2:1-9; significantly, both stories use the exact same language to describe Joshua's and David's advanced age). Such a "farewell speech" by Joshua will be given in chapter 23 (see below), where he will again describe himself as being "old [and] coming into the days" v. 2b).

Summary of Tribal Allotments to the Reubenites and the Gadites (13:8-14)

> 8 With it (the other half-tribe of Manasseh) the Reubenite and the Gadite
> took their inheritance that Moses gave to them beyond the Jordan, toward
> the sunrise, as Moses the servant of Yahweh gave (it) to them. 9 From Aroer
> which is upon the edge (MT: "lip," "plateau"?) of the wadi Arnon, and the
> town that (is) in the middle of the wadi and *all* the level place (from)
> Medeba as far as Dibon; 10 also *all* the towns of Sihon, the king of the
> Amorite, who ruled in Heshbon as far as the boundary of the Ammonites
> (MT: "the sons of Ammon); 11 also Hagilead and the territory of the
> Geshurite and the Maacathite and *all* of the mountain of Hermon, and *all*
> of the Bashan as far Salecah; 12 *all* of the kingdom of Og in the Bashan
> who ruled in Ashtaroth and in Edrei. He was leftover from the remainder
> of the Rephaim, when Moses struck them down and dispossessed them.
> 13 But the Israelites did not take possession of the Geshurite and the
> Maacathite; so Geshur and Maacath live in the midst of Israel up to this
> day. 14 Only to the tribe of Levi did he (Moses) not give an inheritance;
> offerings of fire (to) Yahweh, the god of Israel, that (is) his (Levi's) inheri-
> tance even as he (Moses) had said to him (the Levi tribe).

In a reporting speech, the narrator introduces the theological rationale guiding his usage of all the allotment traditions: the land was distributed according to the command of Yahweh to Moses, his earthly chosen representative, and to Joshua, Moses' successor. The actual history of the tribes who lived east of the Jordan River is complicated. These Transjordanian tribes never played a major role in Israel's history, and the literary description given here is filled with difficulties (Soggin 1972, 147–59; Miller and Tucker, 104–13; Nelson 1997, 167–74).

Detailed Description of Allotments to the Tribes of Reuben and Gad (13:15-28)

> 15 But Moses gave (an inheritance) to the tribe of the sons of Reuben
> according to their clans. 16 And the territory was to them from Aroer,
> which is upon the edge (MT: "lip") of the wadi Arnon, the town that is in
> the middle of the wadi and *all* the level-place by Medeba (not in OG),
> 17 with Heshbon, and *all* her towns in the level-place, Dibon and Bamoth-
> baal and Beth-baal-meon; 18 and Jahaz and Kedemoth, and Mephaath;
> 19 also Kiriathaim, Sibah, and Zereth-hashahar on the hill of the valley;

20 and Beth-peor, and the slopes of the Pisgah, and Beth-jeshimoth; 21 and *all* the towns of the level-land and *all* the kingdom of Sihon, king of the Amorite, who was king in Heshbon, whom Moses struck down (along) with the chief princes of Midian, with Evi, and with Rekem and Zur, and with Hun and with Reba, princes of Sihon who (were) dwelling in the land; 22 and Balaam, son of Beor, the diviner, the Israelites killed with the sword (who was) among the slain. 23 And the border of the sons of Reuben (was) the Jordan, and its boundary (banks). This (was) the inheritance of the Reubenites (MT: "the sons of Reuben") according to their clans, the towns and their villages.

24 And Moses gave to the tribe of Gad, according to the sons of Gad, according to their clans. 25 And for them the territory was Jazer, and *all* the towns of Hagilead, and half of the land of the sons Ammon as far as Aroer which (is) east (MT: "upon the faces") of Rabbah. 26 And from Heshbon up to Ramath- hamispeh and Betonim, and from Mahanaim as far as the territory to Debir (MT: "Lidebir"); 27 and in the valley of Beth-haram, and Beth-nimrah, and Succoth, and Zaphon (north), the remainder (rest) of the kingdom of Sihon, king of Heshbon, the Jordan and border (banks) as far as the Sea of Kinneret (Galilee), beyond the Jordan toward the east (MT: "the place of sunrise"). 28 This (is) the inheritance of the sons of Gad according to their clans, the towns and their villages.

Allotment for the Half-tribe of Manasseh and the Tribe of Levi (13:29-33)

29 And Moses gave (an inheritance) to the half-tribe of Manasseh and it was for the half-tribe of the sons of Manasseh according to their clans. 30 And (their) territory from Mahanaim was *all* of the Bashan, *all* of the kingdom of Og, king of the Bashan and *all* the villages of Jair that are in the Bashan, sixty town(s); 31 and half of Hagilead, and Ashtaroth, and Edrei, the towns of the kingdom of Og in the Bashan, to the sons of Machir, the son of Manasseh, for half of the sons of Machir, according to their clans. 32 These (are the allotments) that Moses allotted in the plains of Moab from beyond the Jordan east of Jericho (MT: "Jericho place of the rising sun"). 33 But to the tribe of Levi Moses did not give an inheritance. Yahweh, the god of Israel, he, himself, (is) their inheritance even as he had spoken to them.

Only the tribe of Levi (v. 14) is excluded since from its ranks came priests who were scattered throughout Israel. The meaning of the phrase "offerings by fire to Yahweh" (v. 14), described as the inheritance of the tribe of Levi, is ambiguous. In contrast, v. 33 identifies the inheritance of this tribe as "Yahweh the god of Israel," not "offerings by fire to Yahweh the god of Israel." The expression may refer to the choice portions of the sacrifice, the breast and right thigh, which, according to Leviticus 7:28-36, belonged to Aaron and his sons. These portions were to be "a perpetual due from the Israelites" (Lev 7:34, 36; compare Deut 18:1-2, especially v. 2 which describes the inheritance of the tribe of Levi as only "Yahweh"). On the other hand, Leviticus 10:1-2, which recounts the deaths of two of Aaron's sons, Nadab and Abihu, for offering "strange fire" to Yahweh, may refer to ritual violations with regard to the altar fire used in sacrifices (Laughlin 1976). Whatever the case may be, the Levites received no territory of their own, but according to chapter 21 (see below), they were to be given towns to live in along with pasturelands (21:1-3; compare 18:7). The historical value of the description given here is questionable. In any event, what few sites on the list have been located and excavated (such as Heshbon and Dibon) do not seem to have been occupied before the tenth century BCE. After the sweeping summaries of total conquest in 10:40 and 11:16-20, we are rather abruptly informed that Joshua is "very old" and "much land" remains to be taken! Moreover, there are many other texts that contradict these claims of a total destruction of "Israel's" enemies:

> 15:63—But the Jebusites dwelling in Jerusalem, the sons of Judah were not able to dispossess them. Thus the Jebusites dwell with the sons of Judah in Jerusalem to this day.
>
> 16:10—But they did not take possession of the Canaanite who dwelled in Gezer; and the Canaanite has dwelled in the midst of Ephraim up to this day. But he is working as a forced laborer (slave).
>
> 17:12—But the sons of Manasseh were not able to take possession of these towns, and so the Canaanite is pleased to dwell in this land.
>
> 18:2—And there remain among the Israelites seven tribes who did not divide their property (inheritance).
>
> 19:47—When the territory of the sons of Dan went from them, the sons of Dan went up and fought against Leshem, and they captured it (MT: "her") and they put her to the edge of the sword and they possessed her and lived in her. And they named Leshem, Dan, according to Dan, their father (compare Judg 18:27-29, where the original name of the city is not Leshem, but Laish).

And then there are the opening verses in the book of Judges 1:1-2:

> And it happened that *after the death of Joshua*, the Israelites inquired of Yahweh saying (MT: "to say"): "*Who will go up* for us against the Canaanite in the beginning (first) to fight with him?" And Yahweh said: "*Judah will go up*. Behold I have given the land into his hand." (My emphasis; compare Judg 20:18, where the exact same formula is used again for Judah, though here "Judah goes up" to fight the Benjaminites, not Canaanites.)

Two things about this version of the "conquest" are noteworthy. First, Joshua is dead and the "Israelites" (MT: "the sons of Israel") have not yet even entered into the land (of Canaan). Second, These "Israelites" are told that Judah "*will go up*," not "*across the Jordan*" as claimed in Joshua (3:1-17, and so forth). The geographical context here is that the "Israelites" are going "up" from the Negeb into what would become "Judah" just as they are said to have "gone up" into the wilderness to spy out the land (Num 13:17, 21, 30, 31; 14:40). The discussion of this different story in Judges is beyond the scope of this commentary, but it raises serious historical issues concerning any attempt to interpret at face value the story in Joshua. Moreover, when these discordant literary traditions are added to the enormous archaeological data, it is difficult to provide credible arguments for assuming the historicity of the story of Joshua and the Israelites as described in these chapters (as elsewhere in Joshua).

Furthermore, the personage of Joshua may be a secondary addition to the story that begins to unfold in chapter 13. Not only is he introduced again as the "son of Nun," but this is done six times (14:1; 17:4; 19:49, 51; 21:1; 24:29)! Moreover, Joshua 14:5 maintains that the Israelites themselves "allotted the land," not Joshua. At what stage in the production of the book of Joshua this material was added is unclear, but all indicators point to a late date. Also, whatever theology is to be found here is almost certainly the work of the final redactor(s) (in addition to Polzin's comments, see Butler, 144–208). Once more the emphasis is on the all-inclusiveness of the tribes and the territories allotted (the word "*all*" occurs no less than seven times in this one chapter: vv. 2, 4, 6 [twice], 12, 30 [twice]). Moreover, it is geographically logical to begin with the Transjordanian tribes first since this is where they are located in this version of the "conquest." In addition, the tribes are not described with equal amounts of detail. While twelve towns are listed by name for Reuben (vv. 17-20), only four are named for Gad (v. 27a). Sixty towns are given to Manasseh, all unnamed (v. 30), and for the descendants of the son of Manasseh, three towns are listed (v. 31; compare Nelson 1997,

171). Of much greater importance is the artificiality of this entire list that reflects the narrator's ideology of land distribution that involved "*all*" Israel. Concerning the list for the Transjordanian tribes, Nelson concluded,

> This preoccupation [with the Transjordan tribes] was more ideological than practical. By the time of the DH, much of the territory described had been lost for generations. Reuben's allotment north of the Arnon had been Moabite since the mid-ninth century and Gilead was an Assyrian province after 732. Although one may suppose some sort of interest in the east bank region in the time of Josiah, these geographic notices remain utopian and idealistic. The notion of Reuben as an [sic] substantive reality would have long since been only a memory, and the territory assigned it here is as much the result of editorial schematic as genuine tradition. It is significant that Reuben is conspicuously missing from both David's census (2 Sam 24:5-6) and the Mesha Inscription. (1997, 170)

The Cisjordanian Tribes

Joshua 14:1–17:18

Introduction (14:1-5)

> 1 Now these (are the inheritances) that the Israelites inherited in the land of
> Canaan when Eleazar, the priest, Joshua, the son of Nun, and the fathers of
> the tribes allotted them to the Israelites. 2 By lot their inheritance was as
> Yahweh had commanded by the hand of Moses to the nine tribes and half
> of the tribe. 3 For Moses had given an inheritance to two of the tribes and
> half of the tribe beyond the Jordan. But to the Levites he (Moses) did not
> give an inheritance among them. 4 For the sons of Joseph were two tribes,
> Manasseh and Ephraim, and no portion was given to the Levites in the
> land, only towns to dwell in and common land for cattle and their crea-
> tures. 5 Even as Yahweh had commanded Moses, *the Israelites* (my
> emphasis) did, and they divided the land.

In order to bring the ancient traditions of tribal allotment on line with the "official" story, this general introduction claims that "Eleazar the priest and Joshua the son of Nun, and the fathers of the tribes" made the allotments (v. 1). However, the fact that Eleazar is listed before Joshua, the fact that Joshua is identified as the "son of Nun" again, and the fact that v. 5 claims that the people (MT: "the sons of Israel") themselves allotted the land all raise questions concerning the connection between Joshua and this tradition. But just as the Transjordanian allotments had fulfilled Yahweh's commands to Moses, the division of the land of Canaan also fulfilled divine intentions. Naming Eleazar the priest first may indicate priestly redaction here highlighting the importance of the priesthood following the exile. Furthermore, the fact that v. 5 says that "the sons of Israel" divided the land reflects once more the inclusiveness indicated by the word "*all*" so prominent throughout the book.

The Allotment to Caleb (14:6-15)

> 6 Then the sons of Judah drew near to Joshua at Hagilgal, and Caleb ("dog"), the son of Jephunneh, the Kenizzite, said to him (Joshua): "You know the word that Yahweh spoke to Moses, the man of god, about my cause and about your cause at Kadesh-barnea. 7 I (was) a son of forty years when Moses, the servant of Yahweh, sent me from Kadesh-barnea to spy out the land. And I brought back to him a true report (MT: "a word from my heart"). 8 But my brothers (kindred) who went up with me melted the heart of the people, but I continued to devote myself to Yahweh my god. 9 And Moses swore on that day saying: 'Will not the land (on) which your foot has trodden be for you an inheritance and for your descendants for a long duration, because you followed after Yahweh your god?'
>
> 10 So now, behold, Yahweh has preserved me even as he spoke there forty-five years from the time Yahweh spoke this word to Moses while Israel was walking in the wilderness. And now, behold, I am today eighty-five years old. 11 Still today I am strong even as (I was) on the day Moses sent me, and my strength now (is as) that day, for war, and for going out and for coming in. 12 Now give to me this hill country about which Yahweh spoke on that day, for you, even you, heard on that day, when the Anakim (were) there with great unassailable towns; perhaps Yahweh (is) with me and I will dispossess them even as Yahweh spoke."
>
> 13 Then Joshua blessed him and gave Hebron to Caleb, the son of Jephunneh, for an inheritance. 14 So it was that Hebron became for Caleb, the son of Jephunneh the Kenizzite, an inheritance to this day, because he (Caleb) followed after Yahweh, the god of Israel. 15 Now the name of Hebron before (was) Keriath-arba. He was the great man of the Anakim. And the land was quiet from war.

This story of Caleb receiving Hebron as a reward for faithfully following Yahweh during the wilderness experience (compare Num 13:30; 14:24) is extraordinary, given the role of Hebron during the history of Judah. Elsewhere (Judg 1:10), Judah is said to have taken Hebron. Moreover, Caleb is not even an Israelite, but a Kenizzite. This genealogy proved worrisome to the Chronicler (1 Chr 2:18-20, 42-50a), who claimed that Caleb was the grandson of Judah and the son of Hezron, not Jephunneh, thus making Caleb a true "Israelite" instead of a Kenizzite as he is in Joshua 14 (however, curiously, in 1 Chr 6:56 Caleb is once more identified as the "son of Jephunneh"). There is another curiosity in this story. Joshua 13:1 implies that a long time had passed since the people of Israel accomplished their initial "conquest" of the land, but 14:10 suggests it had been only five or seven years (compare Deut 2:14). Such discrepancies as these lead to the suspicion that the tradition of Caleb and Hebron was originally independent of the context in which it is now found. In any case, Judah, not Caleb, controlled Hebron throughout the history of the monarchy.

Furthermore, after the Babylonian destruction of Judah in 586 BCE, the "Israelites" lost control of Hebron and never regained it. Hebron played a significant role in both of the folktales about Abraham (Gen 23; 25:7-10) and David (2 Sam 2:1-11). Perhaps it was the purpose of the narrator to emphasize the role of Hebron during the "conquest" to instill once again hope in the hearts of the exiles that one day soon they would once more control this town and region. And once more it was a vain hope.

The Allotment to Judah (15:1-63)

1 And the lot fell out for the tribe of the sons of Judah according to their clans (or families); (it went) to the border of Edom, the wilderness of Zin, toward the Negeb, at the end of the southern (part), 2 and for them the south border was from the end of the Sea of Salt, from the tongue, the one turning toward the south, 3 and it goes out to the south country (Negeb) in regard to the ascent of Akrabbim, and passes on to Zin, and goes up toward the south of Kadesh-barnea, and passes by Hezron, and goes up to Addar and turns round to the Karka, 4 then passes on toward Azmon and comes out at the wadi of Egypt. And the extremity of the border comes to the sea (Mediterranean). This will be for *you* (my emphasis) the south border. 5 And the boundary on the east (is) the Sea of Salt (Dead Sea) as for as the mouth of the Jordan. And the boundary on the north side (is) from the bay ("tongue") of the sea at the end of the Jordan. 6 And the boundary goes up to Beth-hoglah and passes from the north of Beth-arabah; then the boundary goes up (to) the Stone of Bohan, the son of Reuben.

7 Then the boundary goes up to Debir from the valley of Achan, and northward turning toward Hagilgal, which is in front of the ascent of Adummin which (is) on the south with regard to the valley; and the boundary passes on toward the waters of En-shemesh and his (its) end is at En-rogel. 8 Then the boundary goes up to the valley of the son of Hinnom, to the side of the Jebusites, she is Jerusalem, from the south; then the boundary goes up to the top (MT: "head") of the mountain that is upon the surface of the valley of Hinnom toward the sea ("west"), which (is) on the northern end of the valley of Rephaim ("giants").

9 Then the boundary inclines from the top of the mountain to the spring of the Waters of Nephtoah, and goes out to the towns of Mount Ephron. Then the boundary turns toward Baalah, she is Kiriath-jearim. 10 Then the boundary goes around Baalah toward the sea (west) to Mount Seir, and passes on to the side of Mount Jearim, she (is) Chesalon, and descends to Beth-shemesh and passes on toward Timnah. 11 Then the

boundary goes out to the side of Ekron on the north, then the boundary
turns toward Shikkeron, and passes on to the mountain of the Baalah, and
goes out to Jabneel, and the boundary finishes at the sea (Mediterranean).
12 And the boundary of the sea, the Great Sea, (is) the boundary. This (is)
the circuit boundary of the sons of Judah according to their clans.

13 And to Caleb, the son of Jephunneh, he gave a portion among the
sons of Judah, according to the command (MT: "mouth") of Yahweh to
Joshua ("as Yahweh had told Joshua"), Kiriath-arba, the father of the Anak,
she is Hebron. 14 And Caleb dispossessed from there the three sons of the
Anak: Sheshai, Ahiman, and Talmai, born of the Anak. 15 Then he went up
from there to those living in Debir; now the name of Debir from before
this (was) Kiriath-sepher. 16 Then Caleb said: "Whoever strikes down
Kiriath-sepher and captures her, to him (I will give) Achsah, my daughter,
as wife (lit., "woman"). 17 Then Othniel, the son of Kenaz, the brother of
Caleb, seized her (Kiriath-sepher). And Caleb (MT: "he") gave to him
Achsah his daughter for a wife. 18 And it happened in her coming (to him)
that she prompted him (that is, Othniel) to ask her father (for) a field. And
as she got off her ass, Caleb said to her: "What do you want" (MT: "what
is it to you")? 19 And she said: "Give to me a blessing since to the land of
the Negeb (desert) you are putting me. And give to me basins of water."
And he gave to her upper basins and lower basins (or springs).

20 This (is) the inheritance of the tribe of the sons of Judah according
to their clans. 21 And the towns that were on the extremity in regard to the
tribe of the sons of Judah toward the boundary of Edom in the Negeb were
Edomʾ and Kabzeel and Jagur,
22 Kinah, Dimonah, Adadah,
23 and Kedesh and Hazor and Ithnan,
24 Ziph, Telem, and Bealoth, and
25 Hazor-hadattah, and Kerioth-hezron, she is Hazor,
26 Amam and Shema and Moladah,
27 and Hazor-gaddah, Heshmon and Beth-pelet,
28 Hazor-shual, and Beer-sheba and Biziothiah,
29 Baalah, Iim, and Ezem,
30 and Eltolad, Chesil, and Hormah,
31 Ziklag, and Madmannah, and Sansannah,
32 Lebaoth, and Shilhim, Haʿain and Rimmon: *all* (the) towns, twenty-
nine, and their villages.
33 And in the low-lands, Eshtaol, and Zorah, and Ashnah,
34 and Zanoah, and En-gannim, and Tappuah, and Enam,
35 and Jamuth, and Adullam, Socoh, and Azekah,
36 and Shaarim, and Adithaim, and Gederah, Gederothaim, fourteen
towns with their villages.
37 Zenan, and Hadashah, and Migdal-gad,

38 and Dilan, and the Mizpeh (watchtower), and Jokthe-el,
39 Lachish, and Bozkath, and Eglon,
40 and Cabbon, and Lahmas, and Chitlish,
41 and Gederoth, and Beth-dagon, and Naamah, and Makkedah, sixteen towns with their villages.
42 Libnah, and Ether, and Ashan,
43 and Iphtah, and Ashnan, and Nezib,
44 Keilah, and Achzib, and Mareshah; nine towns with their villages.
45 Ekron and her daughters and her villages,
46 from Ekron and toward the sea, *all* that (were) upon the hand ("near"), Ashdod and their villages.
47 Ashdod, with her daughters, and its villages, Gaza, her daughters and her villages as far as the wadi of Egypt, and the Great Sea and its boundary,
48 and in the hill-country, Shaimr, and Jattir, and Socoh,
49 and Dannah, and Kiriath-sannah (she was Debir),
50 and Anab, and Eshtemoh, and Anim,
51 and Goshen, and Holon, and Giloh: eleven towns and their villages.
52 Arab, and Dumah, and Eshan,
53 and Janim, and Beth-tappuah, and Aphekah,
54 and Humtah, and Kiriath-araba (she is Hebron), and Zior: nine towns and their villages.
55 Maon, Carmel, and Ziph, and Juttah,
56 and Jezreel, and Jokdeam, and Zanoah,
57 the Kain, Gibeah, and Timnah: ten towns and their villages.
58 Halhul, Beth-zur, and Gedor,
59 and Maarath, and Beth-anoth, and Eltekon: six towns and their villages.
60 Kiriath-baal (she was Kiriath-jearim), and the Rabbah: two towns and their villages.
61 In the wilderness, Beth-arabah, Middin, and Secacah,
62 and the Nibshan, and Ir Melah (the City of Salt), and En-gedi: six towns and their villages.
63 But the Jebusites living in Jerusalem, the sons of Judah were not able to dispossess them. So the Jebusites dwell with the sons of Judah in Jerusalem even to this day.

This long, detailed description of the borders of Judah, including the towns and villages, can be very confusing. Basically it claims that the southern boundary of Judah ran roughly from the southern end of the Dead Sea westward to the Mediterranean, the eastern border was the Dead Sea itself (v. 5a; the meaning of "tongue" in v. 2 is unclear), the northern border ran from the northern end of the Dead Sea to the Mediterranean (vv. 5b-11), and the western boundary was the Mediterranean (v. 12). An awkward use of the pronoun "you" (masculine plural) also occurs at the end of v. 4, since the entire chapter is otherwise given in third person, not second (compare v. 2 "for them"). This switch in pronouns is not expected, and while its referent can be assumed to be the Judahites, this is not clearly stated. In any case, only in the days of the monarchy did Judah ever come close to controlling the geographical limits described here, and even then the extreme desert regions and coastal plains were not a fundamental part of the tribe's territory. However, the most important tribe in the Bible for the Dtr was Judah. It was the home of David, Jerusalem, and the temple. Perhaps of even more importance, it was from the Judean perspective that the entire DH was most likely written (see Finkelstein's remarks above).

Another tradition about Caleb (15:13-19)

Once more we are told that Caleb was given Hebron (v. 13) and that it was Othniel, not Joshua (10:38-39), who took Debir. But perhaps the most interesting part of this tradition is the role of Caleb's daughter, Achsah (vv. 16-19). Few women figure prominently in the book of Joshua: Rahab (chs. 2, 6); the daughters of Zelophehad (17:3-6, see below); and Achsah (for an interesting perspective on these stories, see Fewell, 63–66). Here it is the woman and not her husband who seems to realize that in addition to land (the Negeb is basically a desert), they must have water in order to live. This story is repeated in Judges 1:12-15, although there it occurs after the death of Joshua (Judg 1:1).

Judah's Towns and Cities (15:20-63)

Some scholars believe that the list preserved here may have come from "official archives" kept in Jerusalem. This may explain why Judah is given more attention than any of the other tribes in this listing. The reminder (v. 63) that the people of Judah did not drive out the Jebusites who lived in Jerusalem is one of several scattered about in this part of the book that again indicates the "conquest" was not nearly as complete as the first twelve chapters imply (compare 13:13; 16:10; 17:12, 16). More to the point of the narrator, such a detailed description of Judah's inheritance would have reinforced Judah's preeminence among all the other tribes and given the exiles hope that one day they would return and once again occupy this territory. This longest of the tribal descriptions given in Joshua also reinforces the conclusion that this story is being told from a "southern" perspective.

The Allotments to Ephraim and Manasseh (16:1–17:18)

1 And the lot fell out for the sons of Joseph from the Jordan (by) Jericho by the waters of Jericho on the east toward the wilderness, going up from Jericho in the hill-country to Beth-el. 2 Then it goes out from Beth-el to Luz and passes on to the border of the Archites at Ataroth. 3 Then it goes down toward the sea to the border of the Japhletites as far as the territory of lower Beth-horon, and as far as Gezer; and its border is at the sea. 4 So the sons of Joseph—Manasseh and Ephraim—took their inheritance (MT: "they inherited"). 5 And the territory of the sons of Ephraim was according to their clans and the boundary of their inheritance eastward was Ataroth-addar as far as upper Beth-horon. 6 And the boundary goes out toward the sea, with the Michmethath on the north, then the boundary on the east turns toward Taanath-shiloh, and passes by it on the east to Janoah, 7 then it goes down from Janoah (to) Ataroth and to Naarah and meets at Jericho, then goes out to the Jordan. 8 From Tappuah the boundary goes west (MT: toward the sea) (to) the wadi Kanah, and its border is to the sea. This is the inheritance of the sons of Ephraim according to their clans, 9 and the towns, the ones in a separate place, for the sons of Ephraim in the midst of the inheritance of the sons of Manasseh, *all* the towns with their villages. 10 But they could not dispossess the Canaanites, the ones living at Gezer. So the Canaanite dwells among Ephraim even to this day, but he lives as a forced laborer.

The first thing to note about this list of borders/territories is that it is obscure, fragmented, and filled with translation difficulties (Miller and Tucker, 129–32; Nelson 1997, 195 and n. 1). Ephraim and Manasseh occupied the central-hill country north of the tribe of Benjamin. Actually, for all intents and purposes, Ephraim came to dominate the northern part of the country and would become synonymous with "Israel" during the period of the so-called Divided Monarchy (926–722 BCE; see Isa 7:2, 5, 8-9). The descriptions given here are sketchy, and there are no extensive lists of cities and towns as in the case of Judah. The note about the Canaanites still occupying Gezer (v. 10) may reflect some historical reality. According to biblical tradition, Gezer did not become an Israelite city until the time of Solomon (1 Kgs 9:15-17).

Introduction to the Allotment to Manasseh (17:1-2)

1 Then the lot fell out for the tribe of Manasseh because he (was) the first-born of Joseph. To Machir, first-born of Manasseh, the father of Gilead, for he (Machir) was a warrior (MT: "man of war"), and it was because of him (that the allotment went to) Hagilead and the Bashan. 2 Then it (the lot)

fell out to the sons of Manasseh, those who were left (still alive), to their clans, to the descendants of Abiezer, and to the descendants of Helek, and to the descendants of Asriel, and to the descendants of Shechem, and to the descendants of Hepher, and to the descendants of Shemida. These (were) the sons of Manasseh, the son of Joseph, the males, according to their clans.

The Daughters of Zelophehad (17:3-6)

3 But Zelophehad, son of Hepher, son of Gilead, son of Machir, son of Manasseh, had no sons (MT: "there was to him no sons"), only daughters. And these are the names of his daughters: Mahlah, and Noah, and Hoglah, Milcah, and Tirzah. 4 So they came before Eleazar, the priest, and before Joshua, the son of Nun, and before the chiefs, saying: "Yahweh commanded Moses to give to us an inheritance (see Num 27:1-11; 36:1-12) among our brothers." So he (Joshua?) gave to them according to what Yahweh had commanded (MT: "according to the mouth of Yahweh"), an inheritance among the brothers of their father. 5 Then there fell to the territory of Manasseh ten shares (portions) separate from the land of Hagilead and Ha-Bashan ("the bashan"), which is beyond the Jordan (In the Transjordan), 6 because the daughters of Manasseh inherited an inheritance among his sons. But the land of Hagilead was for the sons of Manasseh, those who were left.

The Description of Manasseh's Territory (17:7-13)

7 And the territory of Manasseh was (extended) from Asher to the Michmethath, which is in front of (east of) Shechem; then the boundary goes to the right, toward those living at En-tappuah. 8 The land of Tappuah fell out (by lot) to Manasseh, but Tappuah (itself) on the border of Manasseh (was) for the sons of Ephraim. 9 Then the boundary went down to the wadi Kanah. South of the wadi Kanah, these towns, in the midst of the towns of Manasseh, (belong) to Ephraim. Then the boundary of Manasseh (goes) north in relation to the wadi and comes to its border at the sea. 10 The south country belonged) to Ephraim, and the north to Manasseh, and the sea is its border. So they meet at Asher in the north and at Issachar in the east. 11 And it is to Manasseh, within Issachar and Asher, Beth-shean and her daughters (surrounding villages), and Ibleam and her daughters, and those living at Dor, and her daughters, and those living at En-gedi and her daughters, and those living at Taanach and her daughters, and those living at Megiddo and her daughters (three [is] Naphath: meaning uncertain). 12 But the sons of Manasseh were not able to possess these towns, so the Canaanite is willing to live in this land. 13 And it happened that when the Israelites became strong they put the Canaanites to forced labor, but they did not totally dispossess them.

The tradition concerning Manasseh is longer than the one about Ephraim due to two narratives that have been added to the material. The first is the story of the daughters of Zelophehad (vv. 3-6), which interrupts the description of the allotment to Manasseh. This story is based in part on the tradition in Numbers 27:1-11 that arose to deal with cases where the normal male heir did not exist. In the male-dominated society of ancient Israel, women did not usually inherit family property. However, in situations where this did occur, apparently they were expected to marry within their own tribe to ensure that the property would stay within tribal bounds (Num 36:1-12). This story serves to show once more not only how Joshua did all "according to the commandment of Yahweh" (v. 4) but also that women, usually not on equal footing with men, were included in Yahweh's commands to Moses as well as the men. The description here includes those cities in the Jezreel Valley such as Megiddo and Taanach, which the Canaanites controlled long after Israel settled on the land (v. 12). The claim that the Canaanites were made slaves (v. 13; compare 9:23; 16:10) may be more a literary creation than a reliable historical memory. In any case, the irony is once again noteworthy: Yahweh set the Hebrew slaves free so they could enslave others!

The territory of the sons of Joseph (17:14-18)

> [14] Then the sons of Joseph spoke to Joshua saying: "Why have you given to me one lot and one territory, yet I, especially I, (am) a numerous people, whom up to now Yahweh has blessed me?" [15] And Joshua said to them: "if you (are) a numerous people, go up for yourself to the forest and you can cut down for yourself there in the land of the Perizzites, and the Rephaim, since for you the hill-country of Ephraim is too narrow." [16] Then the sons of Joseph said: "The hill-country is not (enough) for us to find. And the chariot of iron is with every Canaanite who dwells in the land of the valley (plain), to those in Beth-shean and her daughters and to those in the valley of Jezreel." [17] And Joshua said to the sons of Joseph, to Ephraim and to Manasseh: "You (are) a numerous people and you (are) very strong, there will not be for you one lot, [18] for the hill-country (will be) for you, because (it is) a forest but you will cut it down and it will be for you its border, for you will possess the Canaanite though a chariot of iron (belongs) to him; though he is strong."

There seem to be two parallel traditions here (vv. 14-15; 16-18), both assuming the time when Joseph was one tribe, thus the editorial expansion in v. 17 ("to Ephraim and Manasseh"). The solution to this problem had already been given by the narrator with the previous allotments to these two tribes. This story also explains why Israel was unable to take the well-defended Canaanite cities located in the fertile valleys of Beth-shean and Jezreel. The reference to the Canaanites' "chariots of iron" is to the metal protective plates that were attached to the chariots. That this tradition remembers the "forest" of the hill country (vv. 15, 18) may be indicative of its age, since significant deforestation rapidly occurred there during the Iron Age. This story also presents Joseph as a complaining, unsatisfied tribe that is afraid of the Canaanites, reflecting once again the "southern" perspective of the Dtr. Just the opposite characterization is seen in the story of the Calebites (see above).

The Shiloh Tradition

Joshua 18:1–19:51

Sending Out the Surveyors (18:1-10)

1 Then *all* the congregation of the Israelites assembled (at) Shiloh, and they
set up there the tent of meeting, for the land was subdued before them.
2 And there remained among the Israelites seven tribes who had not
received their inheritance. 3 So Joshua said to the Israelites: "How long will
you be lazy to go in and to take possession of the land that Yahweh, the
god of your fathers, has given to you? 4 Provide yourselves three men from
each (MT: the) tribe, and I will send them out that they may arise and
walk back and forth in the land and write about it (MT: her) with regard
to their inheritance then they will come to me. 5 And they will divide the
land (MT: her) into seven portions; Judah will stand on his territory in the
Negeb (south), and the house of Joseph will stand in their territory in the
north. 6 Then you will describe in writing the land (in) seven portions, and
bring it to me here. Then I will cast (MT: throw) lots for you, here before
Yahweh your god. 7 But there is no portion for the Levite in your midst
because the priesthood of Yahweh is his inheritance. And Gad and Reuben,
and the half-tribe of Manasseh, have taken their inheritance from beyond
the Jordan to the east, which Moses, the servant of Yahweh, gave to them."

8 Then the men arose and departed; and Joshua commanded the ones departing to write (about) the land saying: "Go and walk *all* around the land (MT: to and fro), and describe (MT: write) her, then return to me and I will cast a lot for you before Yahweh in Shiloh."

9 Then the men departed and they passed through the land, and they
wrote in a book (about) the land (MT: her) in regard to the towns in the
seven portions. Then they returned to Joshua, to the camp at Shiloh.
10 Then Joshua cast lots for them at Shiloh before Yahweh; *and there Joshua
divided the land to the Israelites according to their divisions.* (My emphasis)

The location for the distribution of land to the remaining seven tribes takes place at Shiloh, not Hagilgal (compare 14:6). According to biblical traditions, Shiloh was an important cult center early in Israel's history. Samuel, along with the priest Eli and his sons, worked here (Judg 18; 1 Sam 1:1-28; 2:12-21; 3:21; 4:1-3, 12; 14:3; cf. 1 Kgs 2:27; 14:2, 4). Furthermore, during the reign of Jeroboam I (c. 930–910 BCE), Shiloh was the cultic home of Ahijah, the prophet (1 Kgs 11:29; 12:15; 15:29).

Chapters 18 and 19 form one story describing how the remaining seven tribes received their respective territories in the land of Canaan. That the two chapters are parts of one story can be seen clearly by comparing 18:1 with 19:51. The story begins and ends with the Israelites at Shiloh receiving their territories by the casting of lots "before Yahweh at the tent of meeting" (18:1; 19:51). Looking backwards from 19:51, a careful reader can see the overall literary intention of the narrator (whether the Dtr or not). First, in chapter 13, the two and a half Transjordanian tribes receive their inheritances from Moses. Notably, in this story nothing is decided by "lots"; only the description of the individual territories are recorded. Second, chapters 15 and 17 are concerned with the three most important tribes in the story. Chapter 15 is devoted exclusively to Judah, the most important tribe in the Bible (think again of David, Jerusalem, and the temple). This chapter, consisting of sixty-three verses, is also the longest chapter in Joshua. On the other hand, chapter 16 emphasizes the tribe of Ephraim, identified as one of the two sons of Joseph (the other being Manasseh). For all intents and purposes, Ephraim is "Israel" of the divided monarchy and was the most important tribe in the north. However, whereas Judah's inheritance took sixty-three verses to describe, Ephraim's takes only ten! Chapter 17 contains the description of the land given to the half-tribe of Manasseh that settled on the west side of the Jordan. But two other tales have been inserted into this story, making it a rather muddled chapter. The first intrusion is a story about the daughters of Zelophehad (vv. 3-6), and the second is a rather strange story involving both Ephraim and the half-tribe of Manasseh. They ask Joshua for more land and are told, rather sarcastically, that if they want more land, they can go and drive out the Canaanites who live in the city of Beth-shean and the Valley of Jezreel (17:16). Both tribes are portrayed in rather poor light as contentious and afraid. These stories provide an ironic contrast to the story of Caleb, who exhibits courage and no hesitation in confronting the mighty Anakim in the hill country of Judah (14:6-15). This portrayal of the two sons of Joseph suited well the bias of the narrator, which was to present the story of "Israel" from a southern perspective.

Some commentators have argued that the appearance of Shiloh in the Joshua story is an "interpolation" (so Soggin 1972, 189; on Shiloh in general see Frolov). The narrative told here seems logically to follow 14:2, especially since this latter passage states that the tribes were to receive their inheritance by lot (14:2). Here representatives from the remaining tribes are sent out to reconnoiter the land, dividing it into seven parts. There is also some grammatical confusion in vv. 8 and 9. After giving instructions as to what is to take place (vv. 3-7), v. 8 states that "the men *arose* (ויקמו) *and departed*" (וילכו ... = "and they went away," "walked away," thus "departed"; these verbal forms expressed *completed action*; another imperfect vav consecutive; see above). That is, from the standpoint of the narrator, the men got up and *left the camp* to perform their assigned task. But then we are informed that after they had "departed" the camp, Joshua gave to them further instructions in v. 8b. Following this "reported speech," we are again told that the men "*departed*," once more expressing completed action. The translation in NRSV is misleading: the phrase "so the men started on their way" does no justice to the verb forms involved. The men did not *start* to do anything. From the perspective of the narrator, they got up and they *departed* (completed action; for another clear biblical example of the same grammatical confusion read Exod 24:9-18, where we are informed that Moses "went up" [completed action] on Mount Sinai four times, but never came down even once!). Such confusion must be due to the textual and transmission history of this story. When the surveyors returned with their report, Joshua "cast lots" before Yahweh. Casting lots was supposedly an impartial way of determining a deity's will (compare 1 Sam 10:19-24; Cartledge). The actual process by which the tribes settled this part of Canaan was far more complex than this tradition indicates. Moreover, Nelson suggested that 18:1-10 is an "etiology" for a document justifying the seven portions allotted to the remaining seven tribes (1997, 207). No such document is claimed by the narrator for distribution of lands to the other tribes. Perhaps this story was a literary creation by the narrator to convince others "that this subsequent division was done in a completely proper manner, that is, by Joshua through the lot in the context of an assembly of the whole nation" (Nelson 1997, 208).

The Archaeology of Shiloh

The ruins of Shiloh lie about eighteen miles north of Jerusalem. Judges 21:19 locates the ancient town "north of Bethel, on the east of the highway that goes up from Bethel to Shechem, and south of Lebonah" (NRSV). Efforts were made to excavate the tel in the late 1920s by archaeologists from Denmark, but it was not until the 1980s that an excavation using modern scientific methods was carried out on the site. Directed by Israel Finkelstein, the excavators identified eight strata, the oldest of which dates to the Middle Bronze Age II (c. 1750–1650 BCE) and the latest to the Byzantine era (324–638 CE).

It is the discoveries in Finkelstein's Stratum V that are our interest here. The stratum was dated to the twelfth–eleventh century BCE, or Iron Age I. Remains from this period were ubiquitous on the site and included those of pillared buildings "sunk" into the tel's glacis that was built during the Middle Bronze Age III occupation (c. 1650–1550 BCE). From rooms in these buildings was found what the excavator described as "*the richest [ceramic assembly] ever discovered at an early Israelite site*" (Finkelstein, 1992a; my emphasis). Included in this assemblage are the (now) famous "collared-rim" storage jars, once believed to be "ethnic" markers for "Israelites." (Note already the somewhat circular argument used by Finkelstein when he called this phase of occupation "Israelite"; see below). Other significant finds from this period include fifteen silos interpreted as grain storage bins. Significantly, no domestic architectural remains were discovered. The pillared buildings were interpreted as storage facilities. Stratum V came to a violent end around 1050 BCE. There are good reasons to believe that the Philistines carried this destruction (1 Sam 4:10).

Shiloh is mentioned thirty-two times in the Hebrew Scriptures, twenty-three of which are found in the three books of Joshua, Judges, and 1 Samuel. According to the traditions preserved in these three biblical sources, Shiloh functioned as a cultic site where the "Tent of Meeting" was set up and from where the land was distributed among the seven tribes (Josh 18:1-10; 21:2; 22:12). We are also informed that it was at Shiloh where the Levites received their inheritance (21:1-42). In addition, Shiloh was where the Cisjordanian tribes gathered to prepare for war against the Transjordanian tribes of Gad, Gilead, and the half-tribe of Manasseh for constructing an "altar model" close to the River Jordan (Josh 22:12; see below).

However, caution is in order before assuming the historicity of these Shiloh traditions. Without assuming the biblical stories in advance, there is nothing in the material remains themselves that forces the conclusion that "Israelites" were here. Moreover, according to Judges 18:31, the "house of the god(s)" (בית האלהים, *bet-haelohim*) was located here. Even worse, Judges 21:15-25 describes an organized rape of (supposed) virgins at a yearly festival held at Shiloh by the men of Benjamin. A yearly festival also stands behind the story of the conception of Samuel told in 1 Samuel 1:1-20. Here, however, no raping is mentioned, only the worshiping of, and sacrificing to, "Yahweh of hosts" ("Yahweh of war"). While there is no archaeological evidence to support any of these stories, Samuel's association with this site

(1 Sam 1; 2:14; 3:21), as well as that of the "ark of the covenant" (1 Sam 4:1-4), may reflect old memories of such a connection. On the other hand, the claim that a temple was built here to Yahweh (1 Sam 1:9 specifically uses the word "temple" [היכל]; vv. 7, 24 use the word "house" [בית]) stands in direct contradiction to 2 Samuel 7:6-7, which states that no temple ("house") of Yahweh was built until the time of Solomon. The only other building in the Bible referred to as the "temple" (*hekal*) is the one said to have been constructed by Solomon in Jerusalem (2 Kgs 18:16; Jer 24:1; Ezek 8:16). Consequently, this tradition of a temple at Shiloh may have been an attempt by some to offer a counter-argument against the exclusive claims made by the Jerusalemite priesthood. In particular, there seems to have been a connection between the cult at Shiloh and the tribe of Dan. Judges 18:21 makes the cryptic claim that the Danites kept the idol of Micah (see chapter 18 for background) "as long as the house of the god(s) existed at Shiloh."

Shiloh may still have functioned as a cultic site at the end of the tenth century BCE when the prophet, Ahijah, according to biblical tradition, worked there (1 Kgs 11:29; 12:15; 15:29). This story is set in the context of Jeroboam I, whose reign is dated to the last years of the tenth century BCE. The only prophet in the Hebrew Bible who actually mentions Shiloh is the late seventh–early sixth century prophet, Jeremiah (Jer 7:12, 14; 26:6, 9; 41:5). As part of his "temple sermon," Jeremiah paints a negative image of the cultic activities still occurring at Shiloh in his time (7:12-14; compare Ps 78: 60).

The Allotments to Benjamin and Reuben (18:11-28)

> 11 And the lot for the sons of Benjamin came up according to their clans; and the territory of their lot fell out between the sons of Judah and between the sons of Joseph. 12 So it happened for them that the boundary (goes) to the north side of Jericho, then the boundary goes up the slope of Jericho on the north side then goes up into the hill-country toward the west, and its borders (end) in the wilderness of Beth-aven. 13 And from there the boundary passes on to Luz, toward the slope of Luz, she (is) Beth-el, toward the Negeb (south). Then the boundary descends to Ataroth-addar, on the hill (mountain) that (is) south of Lower Beth-horon. 14 Then the boundary inclines and goes around to the side of the sea (westward), southward from the mountain that (is) before Beth-horon toward the south; and its border is at Kiriath-baal; she (is now) Kiriath-jearim, a town belonging to the sons of Judah. This (is) the side toward the sea (western side). 15 The side on the south (is) the outskirts of Kiriath-jearim; then the border comes out toward the sea (westward) and goes to the spring of the Waters of Nephtoah.

[16] Then the border goes down to the end of the mountain that is before the Valley of the sons of Hinnom, which is in the valley of the Rephaim on the north; then it comes down the Valley of Hinnom to the slopes of the Jebusites on the south and goes down to En-rogel.

[17] Then it declines to the north and goes on to En-Shemesh, then goes on to Geliloth, which (is) in front of the ascent to Adummin; then it goes down to the Stone of Bohan, the son of Reuben. [18] Then it passes on toward the slope opposite the Arabah on the north, and then goes down to the Arabah. [19] Then the boundary passes on to the slope of Beth-hoglah on the north side (these) are the borders. The boundary (comes) to the tongue of the Sea of Salt on the north, at the end of the Jordan in the south. This (is the) southern border. [20] And the Jordan borders it on the east side. This (is) the inheritance of the sons of Reuben, according to her borders with regard to their clans round about.

[21] Now the towns belonging to the tribe of the sons of Reuben, according to their clans, were Jericho, and Beth-hoglah, and Emek-keziz, [22] and Beth of the Arabah, and Zemaraim, and Beth-el, [23] and Haavvim, and Haparah, and Haophrah, [24] and Chephar-ammoni, and Ophni, and Gebar-twelve towns with their villages; [25] Gibeon, and Haramah, and Beeroth, [26] and Hamizpeh, and Hachephirah, and Hamozah, [27] and Rekem, and Irpeel, and Taanach, and [28] Zelah-haeleph, and the Jebusite, she (is now) Jerusalem, Gibeah, Kiriath-(jearim)—fourteen towns with their villages. This (is) the inheritance of the sons of Benjamin according to their clans.

The first lot fell to Benjamin and included the territory squeezed in between Judah and Ephraim (Joseph). Benjamin's historical importance lies in the fact that it was the tribe from which Saul came. However, the description of its territory given here is thought to come from a much later period. It is not a little curiosity that v. 21 lists "Jericho" among the towns given to the Reubenites. Why a town that had supposedly been totally destroyed in an earlier tale (ch. 6) would be listed among the places given here to the tribe of Reuben is not clear. However, since it is claimed in 1 Kings 16:34 that a man named Hiel rebuilt Jericho during the time of Ahab (ninth century BCE), perhaps the inclusion of the town's name here is an anachronism reflecting the late date of the composition of this list.

The Allotments to the Remaining Six Tribes (19:1-51)

Simeon (19:1-9)

[1] Then the second lot came out for Simeon, for the tribe of the sons of Simeon, according to their clans. And their inheritance is in the midst

of the inheritance of the sons of Judah. [2] And there was for them in
their inheritance Beer-sheba, and Moladah, [3] and Hazor-shual, and
Balah, and Ezem, [4] and Eltolad, and Bethul, and Hormah, [5] and Ziklag,
and Beth-hammarcaboth, and Hazor-susah, [6] and Beth-lebaoth, and
Sharuhen—thirteen towns with their villages. [7] Ha'ain, Rimmon, and
'Ether, and 'Ashan—four towns with their villages. [8] And *all* their villages
that were around these towns as far as Baalath-beer, Ramah of the Negeb.
This (is) the inheritance of the tribe of the sons of Simeon according to
their clans. [9] Out of the territory of the sons of Judah, (was) the inheritance
of the sons of Simeon, because the portion (territory) for the sons of Judah
was too great for them; so the sons of Simeon inherited in the midst of
Judah's (MT: their) inheritance.

Simeon's portion is said to be within the tribe of Judah. There are few details in the Bible concerning this tribe, and apparently Judah quickly absorbed it. According to the tradition preserved in Genesis 49:5-7, the tribes of Simeon as well as Levi were scattered throughout Israel because of their violent nature. Notably, the descriptions for the remaining tribes are much shorter, indicating an almost perfunctory listing by the narrator.

Zebulun (19:10-16)

[10] Now the third lot came out for the sons of Zebulun according to their
clans. And the boundary of their inheritance goes as far as Sarid. [11] Then
their boundary goes up toward the west (MT: toward the sea), and
Maralah and meets at Debbesheth, then reaches to the wadi that is in front
of Jokneam. [12] Then it turns back from Sarid eastward toward the place of
the sunrise to the boundary of Chisloth-tabor. Then it goes out to
Hadaberath and goes up to Japhia. [13] And from there it passes on toward
the east toward the sunrise to Gath-hepher, Ittah-kazin, and goes on to
Rimmon, being turned toward Haneah. [14] Then the boundary (border)
goes around on the north to Hannathon, and they (the boundaries) came
to their end at the valley of Iphtah-el; [15] and Kattah and Nahalal, and
Simeron, and Idalah, and Beth-lehem—twelve towns with their villages.
[16] This (is) the inheritance of the sons of Zebulun, according to their
clans—these towns with their villages.

This short description of the inheritance of Zebulun is filled with textual difficulties as well as a complicated history of composition and transmission. Historically, the tribe occupied territory in central lower Galilee and is praised in the Song of Deborah (Judg 5:18a). The city of Beth-lehem (v. 15) is not, of course, the better-known Beth-lehem in Judah, but in Galilee.

Issachar (19:17-23)

> 17 For Issachar fell out the fourth lot, for the sons of Issachar and their clans. 18 And their territory is Jezreel, and Hachesulloth, and Shunem, 19 and Haparaim, and Shion, and Anaharoth, 20 and Harabbith, and Kishion, and Ebez, 21 and Remeth, and 'En-gannim, and 'En-haddah, and Beth-pazzez. 22 Then the boundary meets at Tabor, and at Shahazumah (*qere*: Shahazimah) and Beth-shemesh. Then the border of their territory comes to the Jordan—sixteen towns with their villages. 23 This (is) the inheritance of the tribe of the sons of Issachar according to their clans; the towns with their villages.

Zebulun's neighbor to the southeast was the territory of Issachar. Recent archaeological surveys have shown that after the Bronze Age, this area was not occupied before the time of the monarchy (Gal, 87, 90–91; for the most recent attempt to locate the boundaries of Zebulun, Issachar, Asher and Naphtali, see Gal, 98–106). Once more, the archaeological data indicate that the settlement process was long and complicated.

Asher (19:24-31)

> 24 Then the fifth lot fell out for the tribe of the sons of Asher to their clans. 25 And their territory is Helkath, and Hali, and Beten, and Achshaph, 26 and Allammelek, and 'Admad, and Mishal; and it meets at Carmel and Shihor-libnath toward the sea (in the west). 27 Then it turns back to the place of the sunrise (east) at Beth-dagon and meets at Zebulun and in the valley of Iphtah-el, then north to Beth-haemek, and Ne'iel, and goes on to Cabul in the north (MT: "from the left"), 28 and 'Ebron, and Rehob, and Kanah, as far as Great Sidon. 29 Then the boundary turns toward Haramah, and as far as the fortifications of Tyre. Then the boundary turns back (to) Hosah, and their boundary comes to the sea; Mahalab, Achzib, 30 and Ummah, and Aphek, and Rehob—twenty-two towns with their villages. 31 This is the inheritance of the tribe of the sons of Asher according to their clans—these towns with their villages.

Asher's territory is described as stretching along the Mediterranean coast from Mount Carmel in the south to the Phoenician city of Tyre in the north. According to the story preserved 1 Kings 9:10-14, Solomon gave some of this territory to Hiram, king of Tyre.

Naphtali (19:32-39)

> 32 For the sons of Naphtali the sixth lot came out; for the sons of Naphtali according to their clans. 33 And their boundary is from Heleph, from the oak in Zaanannim and Adami-(han)nekeb and Jabneel as far as Lakkum

> and its border is on the Jordan. [34] Then the border turns back toward the sea (west) to Aznoth-tabor and goes from there to Hukkoh, and meets at Zebulun on the south, and at Asher meets by the sea (in the west) and at Judah at the place of the rising sun, at the Jordan. [35] And the towns of fortification (are) the Ziddin, Zer, and Hammath, Rakkath, and Chinnereth, [36] and Adamah, and the Ramah, and Hazor, [37] and Kedesh, and Edrei, and 'Enhazor, [38] and Yiron, and Migdal-el, Horem, and Beth-anath, and Beth-shemesh—nineteen towns with their villages. [39] This is the boundary of the tribe of the sons of Naphtali according to their clans—the towns with their villages.

Most of the territory assigned to this tribe is in Upper Galilee, but its southern border reached as far south as Issachar. The meaning of the reference to "Judah on the east at the Jordan" is unclear (v. 34).

Dan (19:40-48)

> [40] To the tribe of the Danites (MT: "the sons of Dan"), in regard to their clans, the seventh lot came out, [41] and it fell out (that) the territory of their inheritance (was) Zorah and Eshtaol and Ir-shemesh (MT: "the city of the sun [god]"), [42] and Shaalabbin, and Aijalon and Ithlah; [43] and Elon and Timnah and Ekron, [44] and Eltekeh, and Gibbethon and Baalth; [45] and Jehud, and Bene-berek and Gath-rimmon, [46] and Me-jarkon, and Rakkon with the border in front of Joppa. [47] When the territory of the sons of Dan went from them, the sons of Dan went up and fought against Leshem, and they captured it (MT: "her") and they put her to the edge of the sword and they possessed her and lived in her. And they named *Leshem* (my emphasis) Dan, according to Dan, their father. [48] This (is) the inheritance of the tribe of the Danites, according to their clans—these towns and their villages.

This version of the conquest of the Danites needs to be compared with another version found in Judges 18:27-30:

> They (the Danites) took what Micah had made and the priest who belonged to him and came to Laish, to a people who were quiet and trusting. Then they (Danites) slew them with the edge (MT: "mouth") of a sword, and they burn the city with fire. There was no deliverer because she (Laish) (was) far from Sidon, and they had no contact (MT: "a word was not to them") with Aram. She (Aram) (was) in the valley that (is) near to Beth-rehab. Then the Danites rebuilt the city, and they lived in her. And they called the name of the city, Dan, because of the name, Dan, of their fathers, who was born to Israel. But *Laish* [was] the name of the city at first. The Danites set up for themselves the idol. And Jonathan, the son of

> Gershom, the son of Moses, he (Jonathan) and his sons (were) priests to the Danite tribe until the day the land was captured (MT: "uncovered"). (My emphasis)

Tel Dan: An Archaeological Profile

The biblical city of Dan was a major administrative, cultic, and military center during the time of the so-called "divided monarchy" (926–722 BCE; Laughlin 2009). The site is probably best known as one of two places where the Bible claims that Jeroboam I (c. 930–910 BCE) set up golden calves to be worshiped as the "gods (*'ᵉlohim*) . . . who brought you up out of the land of Egypt" (1 Kgs 12:28b). The archaeological ruins identified with biblical Dan lie about twenty-five miles north of the Sea of Galilee, close to both the Syrian and Lebanese borders. This makes Dan the farthest tribe from the perspective of the "southern" bias of the narrator. The tel's modern name is Tell el-Qadi (Arabic: "mound of the Judge"). Edward Robinson (d. 1863) was the first explorer who proposed this identification back in 1838. His identification has been confirmed by the systematic excavations that began on the site in 1966 under the direction of Avraham Biran (1909–2008). Prior to his death, Biran was the director of the Nelson Glueck School of Biblical Archaeology of Hebrew Union College-Jewish Institute of Religion, Jerusalem. The excavation continued under Biran's direction until 2000, making it the longest continuous archaeological project ever conducted in the state of Israel. The excavation at Dan was renewed in 2005 under the co-direction of David Ilan, who replaced Biran as head of the Nelson Glueck School.

This tel was occupied long before the first millennium BCE. In fact, before the time of biblical Dan, there were two periods of dense urbanization: the Early Bronze Age II–III (3000–2400 BCE) and the Middle Bronze Age (2000–1500 BCE). Altogether, sixteen strata have been identified dating from the Pottery Neolithic (Stratum XVI, late sixth-early fifth millennium BCE) through Iron Age II (Stratum I, end of eighth to early sixth century BCE). In addition, remains were recovered dating to the Persian (sixth to fourth century BCE), Hellenistic (fourth to first century BCE) and Roman (first century BCE to fourth century CE) periods. What made this site so attractive for millennia was no doubt the perennial water source located here (one of the three major sources of the River Jordan), the fertile valleys around it, which provided not only cultivable fields but also grazing grounds for livestock, and its location on major trade routes for caravans. According to the tradition recorded in Judges 18:29, the city was called "Laish" before its destruction and renaming by the Danites. Laish may be a very old name for the site since it is attested in the Egyptian Execration texts of the nineteenth–eighteenth centuries BCE and in Thutmose III's list of conquered territories (fifteenth century BCE; *ANET,* 329, 242).

While these older periods of occupation contain many important archaeological remains (including the now famous MBII mud-brick gate that has been described as "one of the most important architectural discoveries of the entire Near East," Biran 1994, 24), our concern here is the archaeological evidence for the transition between the end of the Late Bronze Age (thirteenth century BCE) and the beginning of Iron Age I (twelfth century BCE). The limited archaeological evidence for the end of the LBA (found only in two small sections and a badly disturbed sequence in another area) suggests a violent destruction of some kind. Based on the biblical stories, the excavator concluded that this destruction and subsequent Iron Age I occupation was the work of the tribe of Dan (Biran 1994, 132–35). When placed into the larger context of the demise of the Late Bronze Age culture in evidence throughout the Middle East, however, this conclusion appears to be premature. This is especially true in light of the weight that the excavator gave to the appearance of so-called "collared rim" pithoi discovered in Iron Age I contexts. Archaeologists once used this type of pottery as an ethnic marker for the presence of "Israelites." Indeed, the excavator used this ware to help corroborate the biblical story (Judg 17–18) of the migration of Dan from the tribe's supposedly original home in the coastal region in the south, west of the territory of Benjamin. But it is now known that this ceramic form appeared as early as the late thirteenth century BCE in Canaanite contexts at places such as Aphek and Beth-shean, and was even popular in Transjordan at such sites as Tall al-'Umeiri. Such wide distribution of this jar type is hard to explain in terms of ethnicity. Rather, the simplest explanation is that peoples living in different areas during this period found the jars useful for their lifestyles. The jars would have been especially practical for water transportation and storage for commodities such as oil and wine. These large vessels could hold up to eighty liters (over twenty-one gallons) of liquid. Thus, this ceramic type can no longer serve as a reliable guide to ethnicity (Ibrahim, 1978; Finkelstein 2007c, 77–78; Mazar 2077a, 89).

On the other hand, archaeologists generally recognize three ethnic markers today: burial practices, cultic rituals, and diets. The only one of these that applies to the Highlands settlements in Iron I Palestine is diet: in the Highlands there is a marked absence of pig bones. Pigs cannot be herded over long distances, and some scholars think the people who settled in this area during Iron I came from a pastoral background. Faunal remains include sheep, goat, and cattle bones. This diet was supplemented by wild game such as gazelle and deer. The nearby river also provided fish and mollusks. But no pig bones have been discovered dating to the period under discussion.

Little else is known about this period from the archaeological evidence, except that the metal industry established in the preceding LBA was continued. Rich discoveries in Area B at Dan confirmed the continuance of this industry. Many interesting pottery vessels were also discovered, including what was described as a "snake house," so-called because it is similar to objects discovered elsewhere such as Ugarit and Hazor (Biran 1994, 152–53). While the material remains indicate an extensive settlement at this time, not enough lateral exposure of the site has been completed to know the full extent of the size or population of the town.

Perhaps even more mysterious is that no burials dating to Iron I have been found here (nor from any other Iron I Highlands site; for one attempt to explain this curiosity see Faust, 2013). Perhaps the people who lived here buried their dead away from the city in the valleys close by. Dan (Laish), along with other sites such as Shiloh and Mizpah, may have been a fairly large town at this time. There is extensive evidence that the city met a violent end in the middle of the eleventh century BCE. Some evidence suggests the Philistines may be responsible for this destruction (Philistine pottery has been found in some areas). In any case, the site was rebuilt fairly quickly.

The tribal history of Dan is complex, and the place names listed in Joshua 19 do not form recognizable borders. The tradition preserved here remembers when the Danites occupied territory west of the tribe of Benjamin. This area is the geographical context of the stories of Samson, a Danite (Judg 13–15). But Dan was ultimately unable to hold this area and migrated north (v. 47; compare Judg 18:1-31). Elsewhere, the biblical evaluation of this tribe is not very positive (compare Gen 49:17; Deut 33:22; Judg 5:17b; Laughlin 2009, 350–55).

The Allotment to Joshua and Concluding Summary (19:49-51)

49 When they had finished dividing the land according to their borders, the
Israelites gave an inheritance to Joshua, the son of Nun, among themselves.
50 By the command (MT: "mouth") of Yahweh they gave to him the town
for which he had asked, Timnath-serah, in the hill-country of Ephraim. He
rebuilt the town and lived in her. 51 These (are) the inheritances that
Eleazar the priest, and Joshua, the son of Nun, and the heads of the fathers
according to the tribes of the Israelites, allotted by lot at Shiloh before

> Yahweh, at the entrance of the tent of meeting. And they finished in the dividing of the land.

Unlike the preceding allotments, all of which went to tribes, an allotment is now given to Joshua "by command of Yahweh." Thus, from the perspective of the narrator, individuals as well as nations could be blessed for faithful service. This tradition is also important because it connects Joshua with the "hill country of Ephraim" (v. 50). This chapter ends, as it began, with a reference to the door of the tent of meeting (18:1).

To all of the above, one might very well ask, "So what?" Of what possible use can such a totally confused and confusing list of ancient borders and towns be today in the twentieth-first century CE? This question becomes even more difficult when the apparent artificiality of these traditions is appreciated. An "Israelite" settlement process that took approximately two hundred years has been telescoped into what seems to be a short period and narrated centuries after the events supposedly took place. There may be a few ways to try to read these stories theologically (Butler 1983, inter alia; Creach, 2003, inter alia; Hess, 1996 inter alia; Earl, 2010a, inter alia), but to what end? Some would say that this material shows how Israel, when she obeyed Yahweh, was given the land, just as 2 Kings 17:7-23 explains theologically why Israel (and Judah) lost the land.

Perhaps the major point the Dtr was trying to stress to those who were in exile can be summarized as follows: Despite Israel's origins, which at best were obscure; and despite her own unworthiness (see Deut 9:1-24); and despite the ambiguity in applying the laws of Moses, Yahweh had triumphed over the gods of Canaan. In his victory over the other "gods" (*'^{e}lohim*), Yahweh had established his people on the land. Yet the implications of such a theology need to be squarely and critically confronted. Is there really a god who tries to solve human problems not only by condoning, but even worse, by commanding genocide? Whether such a claim has any meaning for people living in the twenty-first century CE is not for this author to decide, except for himself. These are theological issues that neither biblical historians nor archaeologists can prove or disprove. Consequently, if there are theological truths in these stories, they must be made on grounds other than those provided by historical/critical and archaeological analyses. As my own archaeology professor, Joseph Callaway, once told us fledging students, "Archaeology may take you to the threshold of faith, but it cannot take you across it."

Closing Stories

Joshua 20:1–24:33

A Miscellany

Joshua 20:1–22:34

Introduction

With 19:51, the second of the two major themes running through Joshua is brought to a close. The first is the "conquest" itself (chs. 1–12), and the second is the division and distribution of the land to the "twelve tribes" (chs. 13–19). Even though the traditions making up these themes were found to be complex and varied, the biblical narrators used them to express their own theological concerns. In the remaining five chapters, however, no such embracing theme is discernible. These stories appear to be independent of one another, and various approaches to understanding them have been suggested.

Cities of Refuge (20:1-9)

> [1] Then Yahweh spoke to Joshua saying: [2] "Speak to the Israelites: 'Set up
> for yourselves the towns of refuge (asylum) of which I spoke to you by the
> hand of Moses, [3] so that whoever kills by striking down a person by
> mistake (without intention) may flee there; and they will be for you an
> asylum from the avenger of blood. [4] And to one of these towns, the one
> who flees will stand at the entrance of the gate of the city and speak into
> the ears ("explain the situation") of the old ones ("elders") of that city; then
> they shall bring him into the city unto themselves, and they will give to
> him a place and he will dwell among them. [5] And if the avenger of blood
> chases after him, they will not give the slayer into his hand because without
> knowledge he struck down his friend (neighbor, friend); he did not hate
> him recently (MT: "from three days before"). [6] And he will remain in that
> city for his standing before the congregation for judgment until the death
> of the one who is at that time (MT: "in those days") the high priest. Then
> the slayer will return and go back to his town and to his house, to the town
> from which he fled.'"

> [7] So they set apart Kedesh in the Galilee, in the hill-country of Naphtali, and Shechem in the hill-country of Ephraim, and Kiriath-arba (she is Hebron) in the hill-country of Judah. [8] Then beyond the Jordan, east of Jericho, they set up Bezer, in the wilderness in the level country (or "tableland") from the tribe of Reuben, and Ramoth in the Gilead, from the tribe of Gad, and Golan in the Bashan from the tribe of Manasseh. [9] These (are) the towns, the ones appointed for *all* the Israelites, and for the sojourner living among them, *all* (those) who kill someone (MT: *nephesh* = "being," "person") because of error (without intending), so he will not be killed by the avenger of blood until they stand before the congregation.

To deal with the issue of accidental killings, cities of refuge were established—three in Cisjordan and three in the Transjordan (Hawk; Spencer; compare Num 35:1-15; Deut 4:41-43; 19:1-10). The idea presented here is to protect someone who accidentally killed another person from the "Avenger of Blood" (גאל הדם, *goel haddam*; Patrick). The "Avenger" was a close relative of the family member who had been killed, and it was his duty to find and execute the slayer (Num 35:16-27; Deut 19:1-13; Josh 20:3; 2 Sam 14:4-11). Joshua 20 lists six cities: three east of the Jordan (Transjordan) and three west of the Jordan (Cisjordan). All these cities are named, whereas the list in Deuteronomy (4:41-43) names only the cities in the Transjordan. The cities set aside in Cisjordan (west of the Jordan) in Deuteronomy 19:1-13 are not named. In contrast, none of the names of the cities of refuge in the Numbers account are listed (35:9-15). The locations of the cities seem to have been determined by selecting sites that the person who accidentally killed someone could reach relatively quickly. However, if the slayer left the city of refuge before the high priest died and was found by the avenger and killed, the avenger was not held liable (Num 35: 26-28). Why the slayer had to live in the city of refuge until the high priest died is never explained. Neither is it explained why the avenger is called the avenger of "*blood*." Perhaps it had something to do with the biblical examples of how someone could kill a person, all resulting, one should think, in a fair amount of bloodshed: an iron object, a stone, a weapon of wood, hurling an object at someone (Num 35:16-21).

While the idea of sanctuary was widespread in the ancient world, setting aside entire cities for this purpose appears to be unique to Israel (Butler, 209–18). However, the date of the tradition preserved here is uncertain, and there is no clear example in the Hebrew Bible of the practice described. Only hypothetical examples are given. Exodus 21:12-14 suggests that the place of asylum was a cultic site with an altar. The only story in the Bible illustrating such a scenario is 1 Kings 2:28-34. Joab, David's nephew and army commander, made a serious political mistake by supporting Adonijah's attempt to succeed David as king rather than Solomon's. Realizing his predicament, he went into the "tent of Yahweh" (v. 28) and grabbed the horns of the altar. When Solomon was informed of this, he simply had Joab killed, altar horns or no altar horns. Solomon, it turns out, was as ruthless as his father before him. Of course, in the case of Joab, he killed deliberately, not accidentally! However, nothing in the descriptions of the cities of refuge in the other traditions suggests they were cult sites. For the writers of the DH, Jerusalem was the place where Yahweh "caused his name to dwell" (2 Kgs 21:4). Furthermore, the reference to the high priest (v. 6) could only have come from the postexilic period. After summarizing various earlier scholarly opinions about Joshua 20, Butler (209–18) concluded that the institution of refuge was a very old, widespread tribal tradition adopted by Israel as she struggled to adapt to a more urban setting.

Cities of the Levites (21:1-42)

1 Then the heads of the families (MT: "fathers") of the Levites approached Eleazar the priest and Joshua, the son of Nun, and the heads of the fathers of the tribe of the Israelites. 2 And they said to them at Shiloh in the land of Canaan saying: "Yahweh commanded by the hand of Moses to give to us towns to dwell in with their pasture lands for our animals." 3 So the Israelites gave to the Levites from their inheritance according to the command (MT: "mouth") of Yahweh: these towns with their pasture lands.

4 Then the lot came out for the clans of the Kohathites. And it was by lot that thirteen towns for the sons of Aaron the priest, from the tribe of Judah, and from the tribe of Simeon, and from the tribe of Benjamin, (were) for the Levites. 5 And for the sons of Kohath, for those remaining clans, from the tribe of Ephraim, and from the tribe of Dan, and from the half-tribe of Manasseh, (there were) ten towns by lot. 6 And for the sons of Gershon, from the clans of the tribe of Issachar, and from the tribe of Asher, and from the tribe of Naphtali, and from the half-tribe of Manasseh in the Bashan, by the lot, (there are) thirteen towns. 7 To the sons of Merari according to their clans, from the tribe of Reuben, and from the tribe of Gad, and from the tribe of Zebulun, twelve towns. 8 So the Israelites gave to the Levites these towns with their pasture lands even as Yahweh commanded by the hand of Moses, by the lot.

9 And from the tribe of the sons of Judah, and from the tribe of the sons of Simeon, they gave these towns, these ones, called by name. 10 And it fell out for the sons of Aaron from the clans of Kohathites, from the sons of Levi that the first lot was for them. 11 And they gave to them

Kiriath-arba, the father of the Anak; she (is) Hebron, in the hill-country of Judah with her pasture lands around her. 12 But the fields of the towns with her villages they had given to Caleb, the son of Jephunneh, as his possession.

13 And to the sons of Aaron the priest, they gave the town of asylum for the slayer, Hebron with her pasture lands and Libnah with her pasture lands. 14 Also Jattir with her pasture lands and Eshtemona with her pasture lands. 15 And Holon with her pasture lands and Debir with her pasture lands. 16 And Ha'ain with her pasture lands, and Juttah with her pasture lands, and Beth-shemesh with her pasture lands—nine towns from these two tribes.

17 And from the tribe of Benjamin, Gibeon with her pasture lands, Geber with her pasture lands, 18 Anathoth with her pasture lands, and Almon with her pasture lands—four towns. 19 *All* the towns of the sons of Aaron the priest (totaled) thirteen towns with their pasture lands.

20 For the clans of the sons of Kohath of the Levites, the ones remaining from the sons of Kohath, towns were allotted from the tribe of Ephraim. 21 And they gave to them a town of asylum for the slayer, Shechem, with her pasture lands in the hill-country of Ephraim, and Gezer with her pasture lands, 22 Kibzain with her pasture lands, and Beth-horon with her pasture lands—four towns.

23 Then from the tribe of Dan, Eltekeh with her pasture lands, and Gibbethon with her pasture lands, 24 Ajalon with her pasture lands, Gat-rimmon with her pasture lands—four towns.

25 Then from the half-tribe of Manasseh; Ta'anach with her pasture lands, and Gat-rimmon with her pasture lands—two towns. 26 *All* the ten towns with their pasture lands according to the sons of Kohath, for those remaining.

27 Then to the sons of Gershon, from the clans of the Levites, from the half-tribe of Manasseh, (was given) a town of asylum for the slayer, Golan, in the Bashan with her pasture lands, and Beeshterah with her pasture lands—two towns.

28 And from the tribe of Issachar, Kishion with her pasture lands and Daberath with her pasture lands; 29 Jarmuth with her pasture lands, 'Ein-gannim with her pasture lands—four towns.

30 And from the tribe of Asher, Mishal with her pasture lands, and Abdan with her pasture lands, 31 Helkah with her pasture lands, and Rehob with her pasture lands—four towns.

32 And from the tribe of Naphtali, a town of Asylum for the slayer, Kedesh, in the Galilee with her pasture lands, and Hammoth-dor with her pasture lands, and Kartan with her pasture lands—three towns. 33 *All* the towns of the Gershonites according to their clans (are) thirteen towns, with their pasture lands.

34 Then to the clans of the sons of Merari of the Levites, to those remaining, from the tribe of Zebulun: Jokneam with her pasture lands, and Kerath with her pasture lands, 35 Dimnah with her pasture lands—four towns.

36 From the tribe of Reuben: Bezer with her pasture lands, and Jahaz with her pasture lands, 37 Kedemoth with her pasture lands, and Mephaath with her pasture lands—four towns.

38 Then from the tribe of Gad: a town of asylum for the Slayer, Ramoth, in Hagilead with her pasture lands; and Mahanaim with her pasture lands; 39 Hesbon with her pasture lands, Jazer with her pasture lands, *all* towns—four. 40 *All* the towns of the sons of Merari according to their clans, to those remaining of the clans of the Levites (were) allotted twelve towns. 41 *All* the towns of the Levites (are) in the midst of the possession of the Israelites; (there are) forty-eight towns with their pasture lands. 42 These towns are town for town with their pasture lands round about her; so (it was) for *all* these towns.

43 So Yahweh gave to Israel *all* the land that he had sworn to give to their fathers; and they possessed her and remained in her. 44 Then Yahweh gave rest to them *all* around according to *all* that he had sworn to their fathers; and not a man stood before them from *all* their hostile (foes), for Yahweh had given their enemies into their hand. 45 There did not fell a thing of *every* good thing that Yahweh had spoken to the house of Israel; *everything* came in.

The history of the Levitical priesthood cannot be traced here (a helpful discussion of this institution can be found in Kugler). They appear to have been country preachers scattered throughout the tribal territory of Israel. Not having any territory of their own (Josh 13:14, 33), they are given forty-eight cities thus fulfilling Yahweh's command to Moses (Num 35:1-8). Included in this list are the six cities of refuge listed in the previous chapter.

Agreement over the origin, date, and nature of the list given here among authorities has been in short supply. What does seem clear is that these cities would not have been in Israelite control at the same time prior to the eighth century BCE (Boling, 1982, 492–94). This chapter raises many textual problems, not only because of the differences between the LXX and the MT but also because there is a different version of this list in 1 Chronicles 6. Among the more notable differences is v. 42, which is much longer in LXX (see the textual notes in Butler, 221–23; Nelson 1997, 235–36). Form-critically speaking, this chapter might be classified simply as a "catalog" enumerating the cities and pasture lands given to the clans of the Levite priests who traced their genealogy back to Aaron, Moses' brother. However, this list, taken at face value, contradicts other texts that claim the Levites were to have no inheritance (Josh 13:14, 33; 18:7; Deut 10:8-9). Whatever the source of this chapter may be, its main purpose seems to be to make sure that the Levites were also part of "*all* Israel" to whom Yahweh gave the land. This rationale might also explain the ambiguity at the beginning of the chapter regarding who gave the "inheritance" to the Levites. Was it Eleazar, the priest, Joshua himself, and/or the fathers of the clans listed in v. 1 or the "Israelites" (MT: "the sons of Israel") in v. 3?

An Editorial Concluding "Speech" (21:43-45)

The dogmatic, absolutist claims made in these verses are incomprehensible in light of the actual process by which Israel came to occupy the land of Canaan. Not only have archaeological discoveries laid to rest any notion of such a complete "conquest" as idealized here, but other voices within the book of Joshua itself sing a different tune, recognizing that the process was neither quick nor total (13:13; 15:63; 16:10; 17:12-13). Polzin suggested that these verses should be interpreted as "irony" (1980, 130–34). But how many original readers/hearers of such claims would have thought of this conclusion as "irony" instead of "this is what really happened" is anyone's guess. Still, how it all turned out in the end is not a guess: the "Israel" of the exile never again established a monarchy with a scion of David on the throne. The simplistic answer of authoritative theological dogmatism only serves to cloud the issue, both then and now.

The "Show and Tell" Altar of the Transjordanian Tribes (22:1-34)

In an almost comical story about the Transjordanian tribes, we are told that an altar was built only for "show and tell," not sacrifice. As most commentaries point out, the story is made up of three different segments: vv. 1-6, which form the conclusion to the story begun in 1:12-18; vv. 7-8, an editorial transition to what follows; and vv. 9-34, the story of the altar. What actual episode lies behind this tale is unclear. Apparently, in its original version, it did not include Manasseh, who is absent from vv. 25, 32, 33 and 34. The story contains several "reporting speeches" and reflects pure Deuteronomistic theology:

> [1] Then Joshua called to the Reubenite, to the Gadite and to the half-tribe of Manasseh. [2] And he said to them: "You have kept *all* that Moses, the servant (slave) of Yahweh commanded you, and you listened to my voice regarding *all* that I have commanded you. [3] You have not forsaken your kindred (MT: "brothers") (these) many days until this day; and you have

kept charge of the commandment of Yahweh your god. 4 And now Yahweh
your god has given rest to your kindred (MT: brothers) even as he spoke to
them; so now turn and go for yourselves to your tents into the land of your
possession which Moses, the servant of Yahweh, has given to you beyond
the Jordan. 5 Only truly watch to do the commandments and the *torah*
(instruction) that Moses, the servant of Yahweh, commanded you, to love
Yahweh your god, to walk in *all* his ways, and to keep his commandments,
and to cling to him and to serve him with *all* your heart and *all* your
being." 6 Then Joshua blessed them and sent them away, *and they went to
their tents.*

7 Now to a half-tribe of Manasseh Moses had given in the Bashan and
Joshua gave to a half tribe along with their kindred beyond the Jordan
towards the sea (the Mediterranean). Then Joshua sent them to their tents
and blessed them 8 and said to them: "With many treasures return to your
tents and with very much cattle (livestock), with silver and gold, and with
bronze and iron, and with garments to make very many. Divide the spoil of
your enemies with your kindred."

9 Then the sons of Reuben and the sons of Gad and the half-tribe of
Manasseh turned back and walked (away) from the Israelites at Shiloh,
which is in the land of Canaan, to go to the land of Hagilead to the land of
their possession, which they took hold of by the mouth of Yahweh and by
the hand of Moses. 10 When they came into the territory of the Jordan,
that is, in the land of Canaan, then the sons of Reuben, and the sons of
Gad and the half-tribe of Manasseh built there an altar by the Jordan, an
altar great in appearance. 11 When the Israelites heard (of this) they said:
"Behold the sons of Reuben and the sons of Gad and the half-tribe of
Manasseh have built an altar opposite the land of Canaan towards the territory of the Jordan and across from the Israelites."

12 And when the Israelites heard (this), the whole assembly of the
Israelites gathered at Shiloh to go up against them for war. 13 The Israelites
sent Phinehas, the son of Eleazar, the Priest, to the sons of Reuben and to
the sons of Gad and to the half-tribe of Manasseh, to the land of Hagilead;
14 and the chiefs with him; one chief for the house of the father for *all* the
tribes of Israel; a man, the head of the house of their ancestors (MT:
"fathers"), these thousand of Israel. 15 And they came to the sons of
Reuben and to the sons of Gad and to the half-tribe of Manasseh, to the
land of the Gilead, and they said to them:

16 "Thus spoke *all* the congregation of Yahweh, 'what (is) this treach-
erous act that you have unfaithfully done against the god of Israel to turn
today from (going) after Yahweh by building for yourselves an altar in
regard to your rebelling today against Yahweh? 17 (Is) it a little (thing) for
us (that) the guilt of Peor that we have not purified ourselves from it even
to this day so that the blow fell upon the congregation of Yahweh, 18 that

you are turning away today from Yahweh, and you are rebelling against Yahweh, and tomorrow he will be angry against *all* the congregation of Israel? [19] And now if the land of your possession (is) unclean, cross over for yourselves to the land of the possession of Yahweh, where the tabernacle (sanctuary) of Yahweh dwells there and take from our midst, but you will not rebel against Yahweh or us in your building for yourselves an altar apart from the altar of Yahweh our god. [20] Did not Achan, the son of Zerah act unfaithfully concerning the herem (the ban) and wrath fell upon *all* the congregation of Israel ? And he, one man, did not perish in his guilt?"

[21] Then the sons of Reuben and the sons of Gad and the half-tribe of Manasseh answered and said to the thousand heads of Israel:

[22] "god of gods (’^{e}*lohim* of ’^{e}*lohim*) (is) Yahweh; god of gods (is) Yahweh! He knows, and Israel itself (MT: "himself") knows, if a rebellion or an unfaithful act (was) against Yahweh, do not spare us this day, [23] for building for ourselves an altar to turn away from Yahweh; and if bringing up upon it a whole burnt offering or grain offering or making sacrifices of peace-offerings upon it, let Yahweh exact a penalty. [24] But not so! (It was) from anxiety from this word (deed) that we did this to say in times to come that your son will say to our sons, 'what (is it) to you and to Yahweh, the god of Israel? [25] For Yahweh set a boundary between us and between you, the sons of Reuben and the sons of Gad, the Jordan. Is there not to you a portion in Yahweh'? And so your sons might cause our sons to cease from Yahweh. [26] Thus we said: 'let us now make for ourselves to build the altar not for whole burnt offering and not for sacrifice [27] but it (is) for a witness between you and between us and between our generations after us, to work to serve Yahweh in his presence (MT: "to his faces") with our whole burnt offerings and with our sacrifices and with our peace-offerings, so that your sons will not say to our sons in time to come: 'for you there is no portion in Yahweh.' [28] And we said so if it happened that they said in time to come, then we could say: 'see (look) this pattern (model) of the altar of Yahweh, which our ancestors (fathers) made, not for whole burnt offering and not for sacrifice, but for a witness between us and between you.' [29] Far be it from us, because of us, to rebel against Yahweh, to turn today from Yahweh, to build an altar for whole burnt offering or grain offering, or sacrifice, apart from the altar of Yahweh our god, that (is) before his dwelling place (tabernacle)!"

[30] And when Phinehas, the priest, and the chiefs of the congregation and the thousand heads of Israel heard, who were with him, heard the words that the sons of Reuben and the sons of Gad and the sons of Manasseh spoke, it was good before their eyes. [31] Then Phinehas, the son of Eleazar, the priest, said to the sons of Reuben, and to the sons of Gad,

> and to the sons of Manasseh: "today we know that Yahweh is in our midst because you have not acted treacherously against Yahweh this treacherous act. Now you have delivered the Israelites from the hand of Yahweh."
>
> 32 Then Phinehas, the son of Eleazar, the priest, and the chiefs returned from the sons of Reuben and the sons of Gad, from the land of the Gilead to the land of Canaan, to the Israelites, and they brought back
> word to them. 33 And the word was good in the eyes of the Israelites. And the Israelites blessed (their) god and they spoke not to go up against them for war to ruin the land (in which) the sons of Reuben and the sons of Gad
> were dwelling. 34 The sons of Reuben and the sons of Gad named the altar 'For a Witness:' "It is between us that Yahweh is the god."

Basic Deuteronomic theology allowed for the erection of an altar of sacrifice only where Yahweh's name dwelt (Deut 12:11, and so forth; 2 Kgs 21:4), always Jerusalem during the time of the Judean Monarchy. This may explain the emphasis here on the fact that the altar in this story was built only for show (vv. 23, 26, 28). It may also explain why the location of the "altar of Yahweh" in v. 19 is not specified (Shiloh? Hagilgal? Shechem?). Beyond this, the story deals with the larger question of who constitutes the people of Israel. The term "Israel" is used in this story to the exclusion of the Transjordanian tribes (vv. 11, 12, 13, and so forth). Can one be a part of "Israel" but live outside of "Yahweh's land" (v. 19)? This question of the connection between geographical space and religious correctness would have been of paramount concern to the exiles who were far from "Yahweh's land."

The "Farewell" Speeches of Joshua

Joshua 23:1–24:28

Joshua's First "Farewell" Address

Joshua 23:1-16

This chapter has evoked a lot of discussion among scholars with regard to its date, authorship, and relationship to the rest of the book, especially to chapter 24. It almost certainly comes late in Judah's history, if not from the exile itself (Soggin 1972, 218–19). At one time it may have formed the conclusion to the book, although it ends on an especially pessimistic note (vv. 15-16). Also, notably absent from this chapter is any indication of where this speech supposedly took place. Boling suggested (1985, 26) that by giving Joshua a "farewell speech," the narrator has placed him in a select group of people within the larger DH: Moses (Deut as a whole); Samuel (1 Sam 12:1-24); and David (1 Kgs 2:1-9).

> 1 Now it happened after many days (a long time), when Yahweh had given rest to Israel from *all* their (MT: "his") enemies round about, that Joshua was very old and had come into many days. 2 Then Joshua proclaimed to *all* Israel, to his elders, and to his heads, and to his judges, and to his officers, and he said to them: "I, even I, am very old (MT: "have come into the days") 3 and you have seen *all* that Yahweh your god has done to *all* the nations before you, for Yahweh your god, he himself is the one who fought (for you). 4 See, I caused to fall for you these nations who remain, with an inheritance for your tribes, from the Jordan and *all* the nations that I have cut off and the great sea (where) the sun enters, 5 for Yahweh your god, he will drive them before you, and he will cause you to possess them from before you, and you will inherit their land even as Yahweh your god spoke to you. 6 Now you will be very strong to keep and to do *all* that is written in the book of the *torah* (teaching, instruction) of Moses so as not to turn aside from it, right or left, 7 so (you will) not come into these nations, those (who are) left with you, and you will not remember by name their gods (*'elohim*), and you will not swear, serve or bow down to them. 8 For with Yahweh your god (*'elohim*) you will hold fast even as you have done until this day. 9 For Yahweh caused you to dispossess great and mighty

> nations from before you, so no man can stand before you even to this day.
> [10] One man from you pursues a thousand, for Yahweh your god ('^{e}*lohim*),
> he is the (one) who fights for you even as he has spoken to you. [11] Now be
> very on guard in regard to your lives to love Yahweh your god. [12] For if you
> turn back and you join together with the remainder of these nations, those
> who are left, and you make sons-in-laws with them and you go in among
> them and they among you, [13] you will surely know that Yahweh your god
> will not again dispossess these nations from before you but they will be for
> you as a bird trap (snare) and as bait and a scourge in your sides and as
> thorns in your eyes, until (you) perish from this good land Yahweh your
> god has given to you.
>
> [14] Now I am going today in the way of *all* the earth, and you know in
> *all* your hearts and in *all* your selves that not one thing has failed from *all*
> the good things that Yahweh your god spoke regarding you; *all* things have
> come to you, not one thing of them has failed. [15] And it has happened
> even as every good thing has come upon you that Yahweh your god has
> spoken to you. So Yahweh will bring upon you *all* the bad (evil) things
> until he destroys you from upon this good land that Yahweh your god has
> given you [16] if you pass over the covenant of Yahweh your god ('^{e}*lohim*)
> which he commanded you, and you walk (with) and serve other gods
> ('^{e}*lohim*), and you bow down to them. Then the anger (MT: "nostril") of
> Yahweh will burn against you and you will perish with haste from the good
> land that he has given you."

While "Joshua" admits that *all* the nations have not been subdued (v. 4), Israel will possess the land if she is "steadfast to keep and do *all* that is written in the book of the law of Moses" (v. 6). The warning against mixed marriages (compare Ezra 9:1-15) and the threat of loss of the land for transgressions against Yahweh's covenant demands stand in stark contrast to the utopian claim already encountered (21:43-45). For those in exile, this would have been another theological rationalization of why they were there. And its warning about marrying with the "Outsiders" fits well with the postexilic emphasis found in Ezra and Nehemiah on the evils of mixed marriages.

The Shechem Tradition: Joshua's Second "Farewell" Address

Joshua 24:1-28

1 Now Joshua gathered *all* the tribes of Israel to Shechem and he called to the elders of Israel, and to its (MT: "his") heads and its judges and its officers, and they stationed themselves before the god(s) (*ha'elohim*). 2 Then Joshua said to *all* the people: "Thus says Yahweh, the god of Israel: 'beyond the river (the Euphrates) dwelled your fathers ("ancestors") of old, Tera, the father of Abraham, and the father of Nahor—and they served other gods (*'ᵉlohim*). 3 But I took your father Abraham from beyond the river (Euphrates) and I led him through *all* the land of Canaan, and I made many his offspring and I gave him Isaac. 4 And I gave to Isaac Jacob and Esau. Then I gave to Esau the hill-country of Seir to possess it, but Jacob and his sons went down to Egypt. 5 Then I sent Moses and Aaron and I struck Egypt with what I did in its midst, and afterwards I brought (you) out. 6 I brought out your fathers from Egypt and you came to the sea, and the Egyptians chased after you with chariot and horsemen to the Reed Sea (MT: *yam suph*—"Sea of Reeds"; not "Red Sea"). 7 They cried out to Yahweh, and he put darkness between you and between the Egyptians and he brought upon him (the Egyptians) the sea, and covered him; and your eyes saw what I did in Egypt. Then you dwelled in the wilderness many days. 8 After that I brought you into the land of the Amorite who lived beyond the Jordan; and they fought with you and I gave them into your hand. You possessed their land and I destroyed them before you. 9 Then Balak, son of Zippor, the king of Moab, arose and fought against Israel. And he sent and called for Balaam, the son of Beor, to curse you. 10 But I was not willing to listen to Balaam so he actually blessed you and I delivered you from his hand. 11 Then you crossed over the Jordan and you came to Jericho. *And the inhabitants of Jericho fought against you* (my emphasis); also the Amorite and the Perizzite, the Canaanites and the Hittite; the Girgashite and the Hivite as well as the Jebusite. And I gave them into your hand.

12 Then I sent before you the hornet and he drove them out from before you, the two Amorite kings. It (was) not by your sword nor by your

hand (that this was done). 13 I gave you a land in which you did not toil and towns which you did not build, and you dwell in them. (From) vineyards and olive trees that you did not plant you are eating. 14 So now fear Yahweh and serve him in completeness and in faithfulness; take away (the) gods (’^{e}*lohim*) that your fathers served beyond the river and in Egypt and serve Yahweh. 15 Now if it (is) bad in your eyes to serve Yahweh, chose for yourselves today whom you will serve, whether gods (’^{e}*lohim*) that your fathers served that (are) beyond the river or the gods (’^{e}*lohim*) of the Amorite that you, in their land, are dwelling. But I, even I, and my house, we will serve Yahweh."

16 Then the people answered and said: "Surely (it is) not for us to abandon Yahweh to serve other gods (’^{e}*lohim*). 17 For Yahweh our god (’^{e}*lohim*), he brought us out, and our fathers, from the land of Egypt, from the house of slavery (servanthood), and (it is he) who did before our eyes those great things and he has kept us in *all* the way that we have walked in and in *all* the nations that we have passed through in their midst. 18 And Yahweh drove out *all* the peoples, the Amorite dwelling in the land, from before us. Moreover, we ourselves will serve Yahweh, for he is our god (’^{e}*lohim*)."

19 But Joshua said to the people: "You are not able to serve Yahweh, for a holy god (is) he, a jealous god (is) he; he will not take away your transgressions or your sins. 20 When you forsake Yahweh and serve foreign gods (’^{e}*lohim*) then he will turn back and do evil to you and be done with you after he was good to you." 21 And the people said to Joshua: "No, for we will serve Yahweh."

22 Then Joshua said to the people: "You (are) a witness to yourselves for you have chosen for yourselves, Yahweh, to serve him." And they said: "(we are) witnesses." 23 "Then now take away the foreign gods (’^{e}*lohim*)that (are) in your midst and turn your hearts to Yahweh, the god (’^{e}*lohim*) of Israel." 24 And the people said to Joshua: "Yahweh our god (’^{e}*lohim*), we will serve and to his voice we will listen (obey)."

25 Then Joshua made (MT: "cut") a covenant with regard to the people on that day, and he placed for him (the people) a statute and a judgment at Shechem. 26 Then Joshua wrote these words in the book of the *torah* of god(s) (’^{e}*lohim*) and he took a large stone and raised it (MT: her) there beneath the oak that (is) in the sacred place. 27 And Joshua said to *all* the people: "Behold, this stone will be for a witness for she has heard *all* the words of Yahweh that he spoke with us and she (the stone) will be for us a witness lest you deceive your god" (’^{e}*lohim*). 28 Then Joshua sent away the people (my emphasis), each to his inheritance.

The original setting of this chapter is not clear. While the MT reads "Shechem," the LXX reads "Shiloh" both in v. 1 and v. 25 (compare 18:1

and see comments by Butler, 533; Soggin 1972, 223). Both Shechem and Shiloh were important cultic centers in Israel's history. The tradition of the former was traced back to patriarchal times (Gen 12:6; 33:18-19; 35:4). Moreover, some scholars believe that there is some connection between this chapter and Joshua 8:30-35 (see above), but that may assume a basic historicity for these stories that seems most doubtful in light of the actual settlement process. More probable is the suggestion that some sort of cultic festival was carried out here, perhaps on an annual basis, a festival that was concerned with the theme of covenant renewal. Thus the contents of this chapter may have been independent of its present context.

The chapter begins much like the preceding one with the stereotyped formula of address. This is followed by a reported speech of Yahweh who recites a series of events, beginning with the patriarchs, performed on Israel's behalf. Notably absent from this recital is any mention of Moses at Sinai/Horeb and the stipulations of the Sinai covenant. According to this speech, the people of Israel were able to occupy the land of Canaan for one reason only: Yahweh's gracious acts (vv. 12-13). Also note the simple claim in v. 11 that "*the inhabitants of Jericho fought against you.*" Here there is none of the dramatic story told in chapter 6 (see above). Moreover, in the version in chapter 6, the inhabitants of Jericho are passive. There is no mentioning of their fighting against their attackers.

That Israel's existence as the people of Yahweh was not as automatic as the preceding speech by Yahweh implies becomes obvious when Joshua, not Yahweh, reminds them that they must choose whom they will serve (v. 15). When they respond that they will serve Yahweh because of his acts, Joshua, rather pompously, informs them that they cannot serve Yahweh because they are sinful (v. 19). This addition to Yahweh's words by Joshua illustrates again how, for the Dtr, the history of Israel was an exercise in the interpretation, modification, and application of what he (they) considered to be the divine will (so Polzin inter alia).

As has been emphasized throughout this commentary, the theological overlay of the book of Joshua by the Dtr is complex and easily distorted. But perhaps this much can be said: according to DH, Israel's existence was due exclusively to Yahweh's gracious acts on her behalf. What meaning, if any, such a claim may have for the modern world is dubious. But for the Dtr, the cost to Israel was understood to be her willingness to live in covenant fidelity to the will of Yahweh. That she had not done so was the testimony of both the prophets and the Dtr. The consequences of this failure, according to this theology, were disastrous: exile! But hope did not die with Israel's faithlessness. Perhaps now, confronted with this failure, Israel would once more face the challenge of Joshua of old and choose to serve Yahweh. The history of Judaism over the last twenty-five centuries offers abundant examples of heroic struggles by the Jewish people in their efforts to maintain and still (for some) practice the religion they have inherited from their ancestors.

There are other curiosities in this chapter. The masculine plural noun *'^{e}lohim*, used throughout Joshua to describe Yahweh, occurs no less than twelve times in this one chapter. In the seven cases where this word is in reference to "foreign gods," it is always translated correctly (literally) as "gods" (lowercase g and in the plural, vv. 2, 14, 15, 16, 20, 23). On the other hand, the five times the word is used to describe Yahweh, it is translated, in English, as "God" (uppercase G and in the singular, vv. 1, 2, 19, 23, 26). Verse 1 is particularly interesting because here Yahweh is described as "*the '^{e}lohim*" (האלהים) of Israel (a reader of the NRSV would never guess this). I cannot claim to know how the ears of the people who might have heard or read these "speeches" interpreted this word. But is it really likely that when they heard the word in reference to the "foreign" *'^{e}lohim* they accurately heard it as a plural noun, but when used in reference to Yahweh they heard it as a singular noun? The issue here is how translators, wittingly or not, can easily read their own theological assumptions into their translations (including this one!). The point is that Israelite religion did not emerge out of whole cloth. It was very polytheistic in the beginning and remained so for centuries. Monotheism was a product of the postexilic period, first seen in the biblical book of Second Isaiah (Isa 40–55; Smith 2001, 2002).

There is also another religious motif in this "farewell" speech that sounds strange to modern ears: stones that can "hear" (vv. 26-27). The use of stones in religious contexts is quite common in the Hebrew Bible (Laughlin 2001). For example, Jacob anointed the stone he used as a pillar to sleep on at Luz, changing the name of the place to *beit-el* ("the house of El [god]").

Burial Traditions

Joshua 24:29-33

29 And it happened after these speeches that Joshua, the son of Nun, the
servant of Yahweh, died. (The) son (was) a hundred and ten years (old).
30 And they buried him in the territory of his inheritance at Timnath-
serah, which is in the hill-country of Ephraim, north of Mount Gaash.
31 And Israel served Yahweh *all* the days of Joshua, and *all* the days of
the elders who prolonged (the) days after Joshua and who knew *all* the
work that Yahweh did for Israel. 32 Then the bones of Joseph that were
brought up by the Israelites from Egypt, were buried at Shechem, in a
portion of the field that Jacob had bought from the sons of Hamor, the
father of Shechem, for a hundred pieces (of what?). And it became an
inheritance for the sons of Joseph. 33 Then Eleazar, the son of Aaron, died,
and they buried him in Gibeah of Phinehas, his son, which had been given
him in the hill-country of Ephraim.

The book of Joshua closes with the three burial traditions of Joshua, Joseph, and Eleazar the priest. Originally the Dtr's work probably stopped with 24:28 because he continues his story in what is now Judges 2:6. In fact it is not until Judges 2:8 that he reports the death of Joshua (compare Judg 1:1). The note concerning Joshua's burial is cryptic. We are simply told that "they buried him in the territory of his inheritance at Timnath-serah, which is in the hill-country of Ephraim, north of Mount Gaash" (Josh 24:30; cf. Judg 2:9). Who buried him is a mystery, for, according to 24:28, Joshua had sent the people (*ha'am*) away before he died. But at some point in the final editing of these two books, the material in Judges 1:1–2:5 was added. Since the traditions recorded in Judges already assumed the death of Joshua, the announcement of his death was appended to the book bearing his name. Nothing, of course, is reported concerning any funeral eulogy or who would have given it had there been one. Nor is it likely that the "real" Joshua would have recognized himself had he been around to hear it. One wonders what the Joshua of history would have thought about the way he is described in the book bearing his name. An early riser (3:1; 6:12, 15; 7:16; 8:10), he is portrayed as the unwavering, devout servant of Yahweh, never hesitating to carry out this god's commands no matter how gruesome those commands were and no matter who got slaughtered in the process, including human infants and children.

But such violence and ruthlessness only serves to make his character harsh, cruel, and unyielding. One wonders if he ever smiled—much less laughed. He does not even have a wife to confide in about how he really felt concerning what was going on. Only in late rabbinical legends does Joshua have a wife—Rahab the prostitute. (What a nice touch! See Hirsch.) The reader of Joshua needs to remember that the book is not an "Authorized Biography" of a real man, but a violent and bloody caricature painted for us by elitist scribes living centuries after the time of the little-known figure through whom they voiced their own perverted theology. The god met in the book of Joshua is one of the most immoral gods you could ever hope to meet on the pages of a religious text (unless one subscribes to the Divine Command Theory as interpreted by such people as W. L. Craig; see above). One has to wonder, if there really was a Joshua of history, whether he would have recognized himself at all in the way he is portrayed in the DH. One also hopes he would not have. In the popular mind, whatever that is, Joshua is praised as the faithful, obedient servant of Yahweh, the heir to the legacy of the great Moses. He is the hero warrior of the "Conquest of Israel," unflinchingly following to the last detail all the commands of his god, Yahweh. It is one thing to "obey" a god when you are commanded to "love your neighbor as yourself," to "do unto others as you would have them to do unto you," or to "love your enemies." It is something entirely different when the divine command is to go out and utterly destroy everyone who breathed "as Yahweh the god of Israel commanded" (Josh 10:40). Since there is no recorded epitaph for Joshua, I will offer my own:

JOSHUA BEN NUN (B. JULY 14, 1200 BCE; D. October 5, 1090 BCE

Here lie the remains of Joshua ben Nun
He was the folk hero of the Deuteronomistic Historians' fictitious
Tale of the "Conquest of Israel"
The last words he supposedly mumbled before drawing his final breath
were: "Yahweh knows, this would have been a hell of a lot easier with no
one having to be slaughtered, if we *all* had just spent more time getting

> acquainted with one another while drinking good scotch and smoking good cigars."

To which I would add, "Amen and Amen"!

Conclusions

The year before his death (1988), Joseph Callaway published an article in a festschrift honoring the late D. Glenn Rose. In the article, Callaway, an ordained Southern Baptist minister, described how his work at Ha'ai (et-Tell) had forced him to change his mind about the entire story of the "conquest" as presented in the book of Joshua. What he wrote more than twenty-five years ago is still relevant today for anyone interested in a critical appraisal of the "conquest" story in Joshua:

> . . . one function of archaeological research is to redirect our thinking about the Bible. The research at Ai compels us, in my opinion, to review and evaluate the Deuteronomistic History's presentation of Israel's origins and to ascertain more realistically its relevance for today's world. Foremost among the items that should be reviewed is the "preaching" of holy war in Joshua 1–12 which, taken literally for centuries by conservative and fundamentalist Christians, has made the Bible-belt church members in particular the most militant segment of our population in every war we have fought. Who can conceive of the waste of resources and life as well as the damage to the social and religious fabric of our society, that wrong interpretation of the conquest of Ai, and of Canaan, have [*sic*] wrought! (1987, 97)

Callaway's ultimate assessment of the story of Ha'ai (et-Tell) specifically, and the entire "conquest" story in general, is echoed in a more recent assessment of the issues by John J. Collins:

> History is always ambiguous. But the ambiguities of history should not blind us to the fact that the unprovoked conquest of one people by another is an act of injustice, and that injustice *is often cloaked with legitimacy by claims of divine authorization. At the very least, we should by wary of any attempt to invoke the story of the conquest of Canaan as legitimation for anything in the modern world.* (2004, 195, my emphasis)

Much, if not all, in the book of Joshua should be repulsive to modern readers. In fact, most of the book seems to be ignored in contemporary Christian preaching. The Episcopal Lectionary for 2013 lists only two texts in Joshua: 5:9-12, dealing with Passover, and 24:1-3, 14-25, the covenant at Shechem. On this "cherry-picking" usage of Joshua, R. B. Coote observed,

> That the last pericope, with its lofty if paternalistic avowal "as for me and my household, we will serve the Lord," is assigned twice while most of the book is assigned not at all only corroborates the aversion and bowdlerizing selectivity with which people attuned to "family values" tend to hold Joshua at arm's length. (Coote 2005, 103–104)

To repeat once more the observation by David Clines (above), "At the very least, the critic in the postmodern age will need to be asking, What does this text do to me if I read it? *What ethical responsibility do I carry if I go on helping this text to stay alive"* (1998, 286, my emphasis)? The book of Joshua is a time-conditioned product of its human authors. It was for their age, not ours (see above on Collin's quote from Fish). The story of the conquest should also serve as a warning against accepting, without clear, empirical evidence, some human beings' claim to know the mind and will of a god, and thus to have divine authority to decide in our era who is on the "inside" and who is on the "outside," regardless of the title they go by: Pope, Imam, Priest, Bishop, Pastor, Professor, or whatever. The atrocities committed in the name of someone's religion are as old as written history and probably as old as religion itself. The paleontologists have shown that we humans, *Homo sapiens*, have been around for some two hundred thousand years. "Israelite religion" in its exilic/postexilic form has been around barely for 1.25% of that time. The implications of this scientific fact for the understanding of our place on this planet as well as in the universe at large is beyond the scope of this commentary. But at the very least, such knowledge should make us more humble and hopefully less tempted to use stories of the Bible, usually taken out of context, to serve our own purposes. Perhaps the late Carl Sagan said it best:

> It is properly said that the Devil can "quote Scripture to his purpose." The Bible is full of so many stories of contradictory moral purpose that every generation can find scriptural justification for nearly any action it proposes—from incest, slavery, and mass murder to the most refined love, courage, and self-sacrifice. And this moral multiple personality disorder is hardly restricted to Judaism and Christianity. You can find it deep within

> Islam, the Hindu tradition, indeed nearly all of the world's religions. (1996, 290–91)

Reading Joshua using all of the critical tools now available for serious analysis of the book may give us a lot of insight into the mindset of the authors who wrote it as we now know it. There is nothing wrong in trying to understand how humans who lived centuries ago understood their world, including their religious beliefs. Where the DH is concerned, it is a world-view created by a minute fraction of the sixth to fifth century BCE elitist Jews who wrote it. They too had as much right as anyone else to their own opinions. But they did not, even as we do not, have a right to their own "facts." We may never know fully what actually happened "on the ground" that resulted in the appearance of "biblical Israel" first documented historically during the mid-ninth century BCE. But what we do know, especially from recent archaeological excavations and surveys dealing specifically with the central-hill country of ancient Canaan, combined with a plethora of literary-critical studies of the book itself, should caution an informed reader from taking the "conquest" stories at face value. All indications point to the conclusion that the book of Joshua is primarily a work of fiction created by anonymous authors unceremoniously dubbed the "Deuteronomistic Historians." That these authors justified the violent destruction of other human beings, the "Outsiders," by appealing to a desert god who went by the name "Yahweh," should only make the fictitious nature of the story more apparent.

Moreover, taking the Joshua character as a role model for religious leaders, whether consciously or not, implies that such figures should be feared and obeyed (Josh 4:14). The NRSV translation of the verb "fear" used in this verse as "stood in awe" is misleading. For people who are threatened with death if they do not "obey" a self-proclaimed religious leader (Josh 1:18), fear is the appropriate emotional response, not "awe." Be afraid. Be very afraid.

This belief that "my god" has chosen "me" to think and decide for others what is right and wrong is part and parcel of the mentality of the authors of the book of Joshua.

Maybe it is time to put Joshua "on the shelf" and leave it there. There is no sensible way to redeem this book that justifies solving human problems by violence ordered and approved by some god. On page six of his book, *God and the Folly of Faith,* the astronomer Victor Stenger has this epigram: "science flies us to the moon; religion flies us into buildings" (do we really need to be reminded over and over again of the theology justifying

September 11, 2001?). Do we, in the twenty-first century CE, really need such a violent, morally repulsive story as found in Joshua to understand ourselves and our ethical responsibilities both towards one another and towards this planet we call home? I seriously doubt it.

Works Cited

Adam, A. K. M. 1999. "Post-modern Biblical Interpretation," *DBI* 2:305–309.

———. 2009. "Postmodern Biblical Interpretation," *NIDB* 4:572.

Aharoni, Yohanan. 1967. *The Land of the Bible A Historical Geography*, translated by A. E. Rainey. Philadelphia: Westminster.

Ahlström, Gösta W. 1991. "The Role of Archaeological and Literary Remains in Reconstructing Israel's History," in Edelman 1991, 116–41.

———. 1993. *The History of Ancient Palestine.* Minneapolis: Fortress.

Albright, W. F. 1957. *From The Stone Age to Christianity.* Garden City NY: Doubleday Anchor Books.

———. 1949. *The Archaeology of Palestine.* Harmondsworth Middlesex: Penguin Books.

Alt, Albrecht. 1967. *Essays in Old Testament History and Religion*, translated by R. A. Wilson. Garden City NY: Anchor Books Doubleday.

Altemeyer, Bob. 2006. *The Authoritarians.* http:/home.cc.umanitoba.ca/~altemeyl/ (free PDF Download).

Anderson, Bernhard W. 1986. *Understanding the Old Testament.* Fourth edition. Englewood Cliffs NJ: Prentice Hall.

Athas, George. 2005. *The Tel Dan Inscription: A Reappraisal and a New Interpretation.* London: T&T Clark.

Auld, A. Graeme. 1998. *Joshua Retold: Synoptic Perspectives.* Edinburgh: T&T Clark.

———. 1999. "Joshua" *DBI* 1:625–32.

Ayer, A. J. 1972. *Bertrand Russell.* Chicago: University of Chicago Press.

Banning, E. B. 2003. "Archaeological Survey in the Southern Levant." In *Near Eastern Archaeology. A Reader*, edited by Suzanne Richard. Winona Lake IN: Eisenbrauns, 164–67.

Barr, James. 1993. *Biblical Faith and Natural Theology.* Oxford: Clarendon.

Ben-Ami, Doron. 2013. "Hazor at the Beginning of the Iron Age," *NEA* 72:2, 101–104.

Ben-Gurion, David. 1954. *The Rebirth and Destiny of Israel.* New York: Philosophical Library.

Bietak, Manfred. 1990. "The Sea Peoples and the End of the Egyptian Administration of Canaan," *Biblical Archaeology Today*, edited by Avraham Biran and Joseph Aviram. Jerusalem: Israel Exploration Society. 292–306.

Biran, Avrham. 1994. *Biblical Dan.* Jerusalem: Israel Exploration Society/ Hebrew Union College-Jewish Institute of Religion.

Biran, Araham, and J. Naveh. 1993. "An Aramaic Stela Fragment from Tel Dan." *IEJ* 43:81–98.

Birch, Bruce C. 2006. "Ark of the Covenant." *NIDB* 1:263–69.

Bird, Phyllis. 1999. "The Harlot as Heroine," in *Women in the Hebrew Bible*, edited by Alice Back. New York: Routledge. 105–14.

Block-Smith, Elizabeth, and Beth Alpert Nakhai. 1999. "A Landscape Comes to Life: The Iron Age I," *NEA* 62/2:62–92, 101–27.

Bogan, Louise. 1981. *Journey Around My Room: The Autobiography of Louise Bogan.* New York: Penguin Books.

Boling, Robert G. 1982. *Joshua A New Translation With Notes and Commentary.* Garden City NY: Doubleday & Company, Inc.

———. 1985. "Levitical Cities Archaeology and Texts," in *Biblical and Related Studies Presented to Samuel Iwry*, edited by Ann Kort and Scott Morschauser. Winona Lake IN: Eisenbrauns. 23–32.

Brettler, Mark Zvi. 1995. *The Creation of History in Ancient Israel.* New York: Routledge.

Bronowski, Jacob. 1973. *The Ascent of Man.* Boston: Little, Brown and Company.

Bunimovitz, Shlomo, and Avraham Faust. 2010. "Re-Constructing Biblical Archaeology: Toward an Integration of Archaeology and the Bible," in Levy 2010, 43–54.

Butler, Trent C. 1983. *Joshua*, WBC 7. Waco TX: Word Books.

Callaway, Joseph A. 1972. *The Early Bronze Age Sanctuary at Ai (et-Tell) No. 1.* London: Bernard Quaritch LTD.

———. 1976. Excavations at Ai (Et-Tell), 1964–1972. *BA* 39/1:18–30.

———. 1980. *The Early Bronze Age Citadel and Lower City at Ai (Et-Tell) A Report of the Joint Archeological Expedition to Ai (Et-Tell): No. 2.* Cambridge MA: American Schools of Oriental Research.

———. 1985. "A New Perspective on the Hill Country Settlement of Canaan in Iron Age I," in *Palestine in the Bronze and Iron Ages Papers in Honour of Olga Tufnell*, edited by J. N. Tubb. London: London Institute of Archaeology. 31–49.

———. 1987. "Ai (Et-Tell): Problem Site For Biblical Archaeologists," in *Archaeology and Biblical Interpretation*, edited by Leo G. Perdue, Lawrence E. Toombs, and G. Lance Johnson. Atlanta: John Knox Press. 87–99.

———. 1988. "The Settlement in Canaan. The Period of the Judges," in *Ancient Israel: A Short History from Abraham to the Roman Destruction of the Temple*, edited by Hershel Shanks. Washington, DC: Biblical Archaeology Society. 53–85.

———. 1990. "Ai," *ABD* 1:125–30.

———. 1995. *Faces of the Old Testament.* Macon GA: Smyth & Helwys.

Carter, Tara, and Thomas E. Levy. "Texts in Exile: Towards an Anthropological Methodology for Incorporating Texts and Archaeology," in Levy 2010, 206–40.

Cartledge, Tony W. 2008. "Lots," *NIDB* 3:702.

Chavalas, Mark W., editor, 2006. *Historical Sources in Translation: The Ancient Near East.* Malden MA: Blackwell.

Clines, David J. A. 1995. *Interested Parties: The Ideology of Writers and Readers of the Hebrew Bible.* JSOTSup 205. Sheffield: Sheffield Academic.

———. 1998. "The Postmodern Adventure in Biblical Studies," in *Auguries: The Jubilee Volume of the Sheffield Department of Biblical Studies*, edited by David J. A. Clines and Stephen D. Moore. JSOTSup 269. Sheffield: Sheffield Academic. 276–91.

Collins, John J., 1990. "Is a Critical Biblical Theology Possible," in *The Hebrew Bible and Its Interpreters*, edited by William Henry-Propp, Baruch Halpern, and David Noel Freedman. Winona Lake IN: Eisenbrauns. 1–19.

———. 2004. *Introduction to the Hebrew Bible.* Minneapolis: Fortress.

———. 2005. *The Bible After Babel: Historical Criticism in a Postmodern Age.* Grand Rapids MI: Eerdmans.

Coogan, Michael D. 1987. "Of Cults and Cultures: Reflections on the Interpretation of Archaeological Information," *PEQ* 119:1–8.

———. 1990a. "Archaeology and Biblical Studies: the Book of Joshua," in *The Hebrew Bible and Its Interpreters*, edited by William Henry-Propp, Baruch Halpern, and David Noel Freedman. Winona Lake IN: Eisenbrauns. 19–32.

———. 1990b. "Joshua," *The New Jerome Biblical Commentary*, edited by R. E. Brown et al. Englewodd Cliffs NJ: Prentice Hall. 110–31.

———. 2014. *A Historical and Literary Introduction to the Hebrew Scriptures.* Third edition. New York: Oxford.

Coote, Robert B. 1990. *Early Israel: A New Horizon.* Minneapolis: Fortress.

———. 2005. "Joshua," *The Interpreter's Bible Old Testament Survey*, edited by Leander Keck. Nashville: Abingdon. 88–108.

Craig, William L. No date. "Slaughter of the Canaanites." http://www.reasonablefaith.org/site/News2? (accessed 1/9/2014).

Creach, Jerome F. D. 2003. *Joshua*, Interpretation: A Bible Commentary for Teaching and Preaching. Louisville: John Knox.

Crenshaw, James L. 1986. *Story and Faith: A Guide to the Old Testament.* New York: Macmillan.

Cross, Frank M. "אל 'el." *TDOT* 1:242–61.

Crossan, John Dominic. 1998. *The Birth of Christianity: Discovering What Happened in the Years Immediately after the Execution of Jesus.* San Francisco: HarperCollins.

Davies, W. D. 1991. *The Territorial Dimension of Judaism. With a Symposium and Further Reflections.* Minneapolis: Fortress.

Davies, Philip R. 2008. *Memories of Ancient Israel An Introduction to Biblical History—Ancient and Modern.* Louisville: Westminster John Knox Press.

Davis, Thomas W. 2004. *Shifting Sands. The Rise and Fall of Biblical Archaeology.* New York: Oxford University Press.

Dawkins, Richard. 2006a. "The Emptiness of Theology." *Free Inquiry* 18/2. http//old.richarddawkins.net/articles/88 (accessed 3/10/2014).

———. 2006b. *The god Delusion.* New York: Houghton Mifflin.

Dever, William G. 1985. "Syro-Palestinian and Biblical Archaeology," in *The Hebrew Bible and Its Modern Interpreters,* edited by D. A. Knight and G. M. Tucker. Chico CA: Scholars. 31–74.

———. 1990. *Recent Archaeological Discoveries and Biblical Research.* Seattle: University of Washington Press.

———. 1992. "How to Tell a Canaanite from an Israelite," in *The Rise of Ancient Israel.* Washington, DC: Biblical Archaeological Society. 27–56, 79–85.

———. 1993. "Archaeology, Material Culture and the Early Monarchical Period in Israel," in *The Fabric of History Text, Artifact and Israel's Past,* edited by Diana Vikander. JSOTSup 127. Edelman. Sheffield: Sheffield Academic Press. 103–15.

———. 2001a. *What Did The Biblical Writers Know & When Did They Know It: What Archaeology Can Tell Us About the Reality of Ancient Israel.* Grand Rapids MI: Eerdmans.

———. 2001b. "Excavating the Hebrew Bible, or Burying it Again?" *BASOR* 322.67–77.

———. 2003a. *Who Where the Early Israelites and Where Did They Come From?* Grand Rapids MI: Eerdmans.

———. 2003b. "Syro-Palestinian and Biblical Archaeology into the Next Millennium," in Dever and Gitin, 513–19.

———. 2005. *Did God Have a Wife? Archaeology and Folk Religion in Ancient Israel.* Grand Rapids MI: Eerdmans.

———. 2010. "Does 'Biblical Archaeology' Have a Future?" in Levy 2010, 349–60.

———. 2012. *The Lives of Ordinary People in Ancient Israel: Where Archaeology and the Bible Intersect.* Grand Rapids MI: Eerdmans.

——— and Seymour Gitin, editors. 2003. *Symbiosis, Symbolism, and the Power of the Past Canaan, Ancient Israel, and Their Neighbors from the Late Bronze Age through Roman Palestine: Proceedings of the Centennial Symposium W. F. Albright Institute of Archaeological Research and American Schools of Oriental Research, Jerusalem, May 29–31, 2000.* Winona Lake IN: Eisenbrauns.

Dorsey, David A. 1991. *The Roads and Highways of Ancient Israel.* Baltimore: Johns Hopkins.

Dothan, Trude, and Moshe Dothan. 2004. *People of the Sea: The Search for the Philistines.* New York: Macmillan.

Earl, Douglas S. 2010a. *Reading Joshua as Christian Scripture.* Winona Lake IN: Eisenbrauns.

———. 2010b. *The Joshua Delusion? Rethinking Genocide in the Bible.* Eugene OR: Cascade Books.

Edelman, Diana V., editor. 1991. *The Fabric of History Text Artifact and Israel's Past.* JSOTSup 127. Sheffield: Sheffield Academic.

Ely, Levine. 2007. "Gilgal," *NIDB* 2:572–73.

Exum, J. Cheryl, and David J. A. Clines, editors. 1993. *The New Literary Criticism and the Hebrew Bible.* Valley Forge PA: Trinity Press International.

Erlandsson, S. 1980. "זנה *zanah*; זנונים *zenunim*; זנות *zenut*; תזנות *taznut.*" *TDOT* 4:99–104.

Faust, Avraham. 2006. *Israel's Ethnogenesis: Settlement, Interaction, Expansion and Resistance.* London: Equinox.

———. 2007. "Rural Settlements, State Formation, and 'Bible Archeology,'" *NEA* 70/1: 4–9.

———. 2010. "Future Directions in the Study of Ethnicity in Ancient Israel," in Levy 2010, 55–68.

———. 2013. "Early Israel: An Egalitarian Society," *BAR* 4:45–49, 662–63.

Feinman, Peter. 2012. "Canaanites, Catholics and Chosen Peoples: William Foxwell Albright's Biblical Archaeology," *NEA* 75/3: 148–60.

Fewell, Dana N. 1992. "Joshua," in *The Women's Bible Commentary*, edited by Carol A. Newsom and Sharon H. Rindge. Louisville: Westminster John Knox.

Finkelstein, Israel. 1988a. *The Archaeology of the Israelite Settlement.* Jerusalem: Israel Exploration Society.

———. 1988b. "Searching for Israelite Origins," *BAR* 14/5: 34–35, 58.

———. 1991. "The Emergence of Israel in Canaan: Consensus, Mainstream and Dispute," *SJOT* 2:47–59.

———. 1992a. "Seilun, Khirbet," *ABD* 5:1069.

———. 1992b. "Responses," in Shanks et al. Washington, DC: Biblical Archaeology Society. 63–69.

———. 1994. "The Emergence of Israel: A Phase in the Cyclic History in the Third and Second Millennia BCE," in Finkelstein and Na'aman, 150–78.

———. 1995. "The Great Transformation: The 'Conquest' of the Highlands Frontiers and the Rise of Territorial States," in Levy, 349–65.

———. 1996. "Ethnicity and Origin of the Iron I Settlers in the Highlands of Canaan: Can the Real Israel Stand Up?" *BA* 59/1: 193–212.

———. 1999. "State Formation in Israel and Judah: A Contrast in Trajectory," *NEA* 62/1: 35–52.

———. 2007a. "Digging for the Truth: Archaeology and the Bible," in Finkelstein and Mazar, 9–20.

———. 2007b. "Patriarchs, Exodus, Conquest," in Finkelstein and Mazar, 41–55.

———. 2007c. "When and How Did the Israelites Emerge," in Finkelstein and Mazar, 73–83.

———. 2007d. "King Solomon's Golden Age: History or Myth?" in Finkelstein and Mazar, 107–17.

———. 2008. "The Bible's Buried Secrets." http://www.pbs.org/wgbh/nova/ancient/bibles-buried-secrets.html (accessed 10/3/2013).

———. 2010. "Archaeology as a High Court in Ancient Israelite History: A Reply to Nadav Na'aman." *JHebS* 10.

Finkelstein, Israel, Shlomo Bunimovitz, and Zvi Lederman. 1993. *Shiloh: The Archaeology of a Biblical Site.* Tel Aviv: Institute of Archaeology of Tel Aviv University.

Finkelstein, Israel, and Nadav Na'aman, editors. 1994. *From Nomadism to Monarchy: Archaeological and Historical Aspects of Early Israel.* Jerusalem: Israel Exploration Society.

Finkelstein, Israel, and Neil Asher Silberman. 2001. *The Bible Unearthed: Archaeology's New Vision of Ancient Israel and the Origin of the Sacred Texts.* New York: The Free Press.

———. 2006. *David and Solomon: In Search of the Bible's Sacred Kings and the Roots of Western Tradition.* New York: The Free Press.

Finkelstein, Israel, and Amiahi Mazar. 2007. *The Quest for the Historical Israel: Debating Archaeology and the History of Early Israel.* Edited by Brian B. Schmidt. Atlanta: SBL.

Frerichs, Ernest S., and Leonard H. Lesko, editors. 1997. *Exodus: The Egyptian Evidence.* Winona Lake IN: Eisenbrauns.

Fritz, Volkmar. 1987. "Conquest or Settlement? The Early Iron Age in Palestine," *BA* 50/2: 84–100.

Frolov, Serge. 2009. "Shiloh, Shilonite." *NIDB* 5:232–34.

Gal, Zvi. 1992. *Lower Galilee During the Iron Age.* Winona Lake IN: Eisenbrauns.

Gorman, Frank H., Jr. 2003. "Commenting on Commentary: Reflections on a Genre," in *Relating to the Text: Interdisciplinary and Form-Critical Insights on the Bible,* edited by Timothy J. Sandoval and Carleen Mandolfo. New York: T&T Clark. 100–19.

Gorman, J. Wenham. 2000. "The Deuteronomic Theology in the Book of Joshua," in Knoppers and McConville, 194–203.

Gottwald, Norman K. 1979. *The Tribes of Yahweh: A Sociology of the Religion of Liberated Israel 1250–1150 B.C.E.* Maryknoll NY: Orbis Books.

———. 1983. "Two Models for the Origins of Ancient Israel: Social Revolution and frontier Development," in Huffman, Spina, and Green, 5–24.

———. 1992. "Response to William G. Dever," in Shanks et al., 70–75.

Grabbe, Lester L. 2007. *Ancient Israel: What Do We Know and How Do We Know It?* New York: T&T Clark.

Greenspoon, Leonard J. 1983. *Textual Studies in the Book of Joshua.* HSM 28. Chico CA: Scholars Press.

Gunn, David. 1998. "Colonialism and the Vagaries of Scripture: Te Kooti in Canaan (a Story of Bible and Dispossession in Aotearona/New Zealand)," in *God in the Fray: A Tribute to Walter Brueggemann.* Edited by Tod Linafelt and Timothy K. Beal. Minneapolis: Fortress, 127–42.

Halpern, Baruch. 1983. *The Emergence of Israel in Canaan.* Chico CA: Scholars Press.

———. 1992a. "Shiloh (Place)." *ABD* 5:1213–15.

———. 1992b. "The Exodus from Egypt: Myth or Reality?" in Shanks et al., 88–113.

———. 2001. *David's Secret Demons: Messiah, Murderer, Traitor, King.* Grand Rapids MI: Eerdmans.

Harrelson, Walter. 1964. *Interpreting the Old Testament.* New York: Holt, Rinehart and Winston.

Hartmut, Rösel N. 2011. *Historical Commentary of the Old Testament: Joshua.* Leuven, Belgium: Peeters.

Hasel, Michael G. 1994. "'Israel' in the Merneptah Stela." *BASOR* 296:45–61.

———. 2008. "Merneptah's Reference to Israel: Critical Issues for the Origin of Israel," in Hess et al., 47–60.

Hawk, Daniel L. 2006. "City of Refuge," *NIDB* 1:678-679.

Hawkins, Ralph K. 2013. *How Israel Became a People.* Nashville: Abingdon.

Hayes, John H. 1979. *An Introduction to Old Testament Study*. Nashville: Abingdon.

———, editor. 1999. *Dictionary of Biblical Interpretation*. 2 volumes. Nashville: Abingdon.

Hayes, Stephen R., and Steven McKenzie, editors. 1993. *To Each His Own Meaning: An Introduction to Biblical Criticisms and Their Applications*. Louisville: Westminster John Knox.

Hendel, Ronald. 2010. "Culture, Memory, and History. Reflections on Method in Biblical Studies," in Thomas E. Levy, editor, 250–61.

Hess, Richard S. 1996a. *Joshua Tyndale Old Testament Commentaries*. Volume 6. Downers Grove IL: Inter-Varsity Press.

———. 1996b. "A Typology of West Semitic Place Name Lists with Special Reference to Joshua 13-21." *BA* 59/3: 1–10.

———. 2008. "The Jericho and Ai of the Book of Joshua," in Hess et al., 33–46.

———. Hess, Richard S., Herald A. Klingbeil, and Paul J. Ray, Jr. 2008. *Critical Issues in Early Israelite History*. Winona Lake IN: Eisenbrauns.

Hirsch, E. G. 1969. "Joshua (Jehoshua)." *JE* 7:281–88.

Hitchens, Christopher. 2007. *god is not GREAT: How Religion Poisons Everything*. New York: Twelve Hachette.

Hoerth, Alfred J. 1999. *Archaeology & the Old Testament*. Grand Rapids MI: Baker.

Holland, T. A., and Ehud Netzer. 1992. "Jericho," *ABD* 3:723–40.

Huffmon, H. B., F. A. Spina, and A. R. W. Green, editors. *The Quest for the Kingdom of God: Studies in Honor of George E. Mendenhall*. Winona Lake IN: Eisenbrauns.

Ibrahim, M. M. 1978. "The Collared Rim Jar of the Early Iron Age," in *Archaeology in the Levant: Essays for Kathleen Kenyon*, edited by R. Moorey and P. Paar. Warminster: Aris and Phillips. 116–26.

Isserlin, S. J. 2001. *The Israelites*. Minneapolis: Fortress.

Jones, G. H. 1975. "'Holy War' or 'Yahweh War.'" *VT* 25:642–58.

Kempinski, Aharon. 1986. "Joshua's Altar—An Iron Age I Watchtower." *BAR* 12/1: 42–49.

Kenyon, Kathleen M. 1957. *Digging up Jericho.* New York: Praeger.

Killebrew, Ann E. 2005. *Biblical Peoples and Ethnicity: An Archaeological Study of Egyptians, Canaanites, Philistines, and Early Israel 1300-1000 B.C.E.* SBLABS 9. Atlanta: SBL.

———. 2010. "The Philistines and Their Material Culture in Context: Future Directions of Historical Biblical Archaeology for the Study of Cultural Transmission," in Levy 2010, 156–67.

Kitchen, K. A. 2003. *On the Reliability of the Old Testament.* Grand Rapids MI: Eerdmans.

Knoppers, Gary N., and J. Gordon McConville, editors. 2000. *Reconsidering Israel and Judah: Recent Studies on the Deuteronomistic History.* Winona Lake IN: Eisenbrauns.

Kofoed, B. 2005. *Text and History: Historiography and the Study of the Biblical Text.* Winona Lake IN: Eisenbrauns. 113–63.

Kraus, H.-J. 1965. *Worship in Israel.* Richmond: John Knox.

Krauss, Lawrence. 2011. "Dealing with William Lane Craig." http://richarddawkins.net/articles/612104-dealing-with-william-lane-craig. (accessed 10/3/2013).

Kugler, Robert. 2009. "Priests and Levites." *NIDB* 4:596–613.

Laughlin, John C. H. 1976. "The 'Strange Fire' of Nadab and Abihu," *JBL* 95:559–65.

———. 1989. "Gilgal: Circle of Stones," *The Biblical Illustrator*, 49–51.

———. 1995. "Israel and the Liberation of Canaan," in Joseph A. Callaway, 85–98.

———. 2001. "Memorial Stones," *B I*: 32–34.

———. 2006. "Archaeology." *NIDB* 1:232–47.

———. 2009. "'To the God Who Is in Dan': the Archaeology and History of Biblical Dan." *Rev & Exp* 106:323–59.

Leach, Edmund. 1983. "Anthropological Approaches to the Study of the Bible During the Twentieth Century," in Edmund Leach and

D. Alan Adcock, editors, *Structuralist Interpretations of Biblical Myth.* Cambridge: Cambridge University Press. 7–32.

Leonard, Albert, Jr. 2003. "The Late Bronze Age," in Richard, 349–56.

Levine, Ely. 2007. "Gilgal." *NIDB* 2:572–73.

———. 2008. "Jericho." *NIDB* 3:236–40.

Levy, Thomas E., editor. 1995. *The Archaeology of the Society in the Holy Land.* New York: Facts on File.

———, editor. 2010. *Historical Biblical Archaeology: The New Pragmatism.* London: Equinox.

Lohfink, N. 1986. "חרם *haram.*" *TDOT* 5:180–99.

Margolis, M. 1931–1938; 1992. *The Book of Joshua in Greek.* Paris, Philadelphia.

Mayes, A. D. H. 1999. "Deuteronomistic History," *DBI* 1:269–73.

Mazar, Amihai. 1990. *Archaeology of the Land of the Bible 10,000–586 BCE.* New York: Doubleday.

———. 2003. "Remarks on Biblical Tradition and Archaeological Evidence Concerning Early Israel," in Dever and Gitin, 85–98.

———. 2007a. "The Israelite Settlement," in Finkelstein and Mazar, 85–98.

———. 2007b. "The Search for David and Solomon: An Archaeological Perspective," in Finkelstein and Mazar, 116–39.

McCarter, Kyle. 1992. "The Origins of Israelite Religion," in Shanks et al., 118–36.

McKenzie, Steven L. 1992. "Deuteronomistic History." *ABD* 2:160–68.

———. 2007. "Deuteronomistic History." *NIDB* 2:106–108.

McKenzie, Steven L., and S. R. Haynes, editors. 1999. *To Each Its Own Meaning: An Introduction to Biblical Criticisms and Their Applications.* Louisville: Westminster John Knox Press.

McNutt, Paula M. 1999. *Reconstructing the Society of Ancient Israel.* Louisville: Westminster John Knox.

Mediamatters. http://mediamatters./org/print/research/2005/09/13 /religious-conservatives.

Meeks, Theophile J. 1969. "The Code of Hammurabi." *ANET* 163–80.

Mendenhall, George E. 1962. "The Hebrew Conquest of Palestine." *BA* 25/3: 66–87.

Miller, J. Maxwell. 1977. "Archaeology and the Israelite Conquest of Canaan: Some Methodological Observations." *PEQ* 109:87–93.

———. 1990. "Gilgal." *Mercer Dictionary of the Bible*, edited by Watson Mills. Macon GA: Mercer, 332.

———. 1991. "Is it Possible to Write a History of Israel without Relying on the Hebrew Bible?" in Edelman 1991, 93–102.

———. 1992. "Early Monarchy in Moab?" in *Early Edom and Moab: The Beginning of the Iron Age in Southern Jordan*, edited by Piotr Bienkowski. Sheffield Archaeological Monograph 7. Sheffield: J. R. Collins. 77–91.

———. 1999. "Reading the Bible Historically: The Historian's Approach," in McKenzie and Haynes, 17–34.

———. 2003. "Text Sources for Levantine Archaeology: the Bible," in *Near Eastern Archaeology A Reader*, edited by Suzanna Richard. Winona Lake IN: Eisenbrauns, 60–62.

———. 2004. "History or Legend." *The Christian Century*, 24 February, 42–47.

Miller, J. Maxwell, and Gene M. Tucker. 1974. *The Book of Joshua*. The Cambridge Bible Commentary on the New English Bible. Cambridge: Cambridge University Press.

Miller, J. Maxwell, and John H. Hayes. 2006. *A History of Ancient Israel and Judah*. 2nd edition. Louisville: Westminster John Knox.

Miscall, Peter D. 2005. "Introduction to Narrative Literature," in *The New Interpreter's Bible: Old Testament Survey*. Nashville: Abingdon. 73–87.

Mitchell, Gordon. 1993. *Together in the Land: A Reading of the Book of Joshua*. JSOTSup 134. Sheffield Mitchell: Sheffield.

Muilenburg, James. 1955. "The Site of Ancient Gilgal." *BASOR* 140:11–27.

———. 1962. "Gilgal." *IDB* 2:398–99.

Na'aman, Nadav. 1994. "The 'Conquest of Canaan' in the Book of Joshua and in History," in Israel Finkelstein and Nadav Na'aman, editors. Jerusalem: Israel Exploration Society. 218–81.

———. 2006. *Ancient Israel's History and Historiography: The First Temple Period.* Winona Lake IN: Eisenbrauns.

Nelson, Richard D. 1981a. "Josiah in the Book of Joshua." *JBL* 100:531–40.

———. 1981b. *The Double Redaction of the Deuteronomistic History.* JSOTSup 18. Sheffield: Sheffield Academic.

———. 1997. *Joshua: A Commentary.* Louisville: Westminster John Knox.

———. 1998. *The Historical Books: Interpreting Biblical Texts.* Nashville: Abingdon.

———. 2007. "Holy War." *NIDB* 2:879–82.

Niditch, Susan. 1993. *War in the Hebrew Bible: A Study in the Ethics of Violence.* New York: Oxford.

Noth, Martin. 1981. *The Deuteronomistic History* (JSOTSup 15). Sheffield: JSOT Press (English translation of the 1957 German edition).

Ortiz, Stephen M. 2008. "Rewriting Palestinian History. Recent Trends in Philistine Archaeology and Biblical Studies." In Hess et al., editors, 191–204.

Patrick, Dale. 2006. "Avenger of Blood." *NIDB* 1:357.

Polhil, John B. 1990. "Circumcision." *MDB* 156–57.

Polzin, Robert. 1980. *Moses and the Deuteronomist: A Literary Study of the Deuteronomistic History.* New York: Seabury.

Porter, J. Roy. 1970. "The Succession of Joshua." In *Proclamation and Presence: Old Testament Essays in honour of Gwynne Henton Davies,* edited by John I. Durham and J. Roy Porter. Richmond VA: John Knox Press. 102–32.

Pressler, Carolyn. 2008. "Joshua, Book of." *NIDB* 3:406–13.

Prior, Michael. 1997. *The Bible and Colonialism: A Moral Critique.* Sheffield: Sheffield Academic.

———. 1999. *Zionism and the State of Israel: A Moral Inquiry.* London: Routledge.

Rad, Gerhard von. 1958. *Holy War in Ancient Israel*, translated and edited by Marva J. Dawn. Reprint, 1991. Grand Rapids MI: William B. Eerdmans Publishing Company.

Rainey, Anson F. 1986. “Zertal’s Altar—A Blatant Phony.” *BAR* 12/4: 66.

———. 2001. “Stones for Bread: Archaeology Versus History.” *NEA* 64:140–49.

———. 2008a. “Inside Outside. Where Did the Early Israelites Come From?” *BAR* 34/6: 45–58, 84.

———. 2008b. “Shasu.Who Were the Early Israelites?” *BAR* 34/6: 51–55.

Rainey, Anson F., and R. Steven Notley. 2006. *The Sacred Bridge: Carta’s Atlas of the Biblical World*. Jerusalem: Carta.

Ramsey, George W. 1992. “Joshua (Person).” *ABD* 2:999–1001.

Ray, Paul J., Jr. 2008. “Classical Models for the Appearance of Israel in Palestine,” in Hess et al., 79–93.

Rehm, Merlin D. 1992. “Levites and Priests.” *ABD* 4:297–309.

Redford, Donald B. 1992. *Egypt, Canaan, and Israel in Ancient Times*. Princeton NJ: Princeton University Press.

Richard, Suzanne, editor. 2003. *Near Eastern Archaeology: A Reader*. Winona Lake IN: Eisenbrauns.

Ringgren, Helmer. 1974. “אלהים, *’elohim*.” *TDOT* 1:267–84.

Römer, Thomas. 2000. “Deuteronomy in Search of Origins,” in Knoppers and McConville, 112–38.

Rösel, Harmut N. 2011. *Joshua*. Historical Commentary on the Old Testament. Walpole MA: Peeters.

Rowlett, Lori. 1996. *Joshua and the Rhetoric of Violence: A New Historicist Analysis*. Sheffield: Sheffield Academic.

Sagan, Carl. 1977. *The Demon-Haunted World: Science as a Candle in the Dark*. New York: Ballantine Books.

———. 1980. “A Scientist Looks at Velikovsky’s ‘Worlds in Collision’: Did a Near-Collision of a Comet with Earth Cause Manna to Fall in the Sinai and the Sun to Stand Still over Gibeon?” *BAR* 6/1: 40–51.

———. 2006. *The Varieties of Scientific Experience A Personal View of the Search for God*, edited by Ann Druyan. New York: Penguin Press.

Sandmel, Samuel. 1979. "Palestinian and Hellenistic Judaism and Christianity: The Question of Comfortable Theory." *HUCA* 50:137–48.

Schniedewind, William M. 1996. "Tel Dan Stela: New Light on Aramaic and Jehu's Revolt." *BASOR* 303:75–90.

Schmidt, Brian B. 2006. "Moabite Stone." In Chavalas, editor, 311–16.

Seow, C. L. 2007. "God, Names of." *NIDB* 2:588–95.

Shanks, Hershel, et al. 1992. *The Rise of Ancient Israel.* Washington, DC: Biblical Archaeology Society.

———. 2012 *BAR* 38/1: 60–62, 67.

Silberman, Neil Asher. 1992. "Who Were the Israelites?" *Archaeology* 45/2: 22–30.

Smith, Mark S. 2001. *The Origin of Biblical Monotheism.* New York: Oxford.

———. 2002. *The Early History of God: Yahweh and the Other Deities in Ancient Israel.* Second edition. Grand Rapids MI: Eerdmans.

Soards, Marion L. 2006. "Circumcision." *NIDB* 1:667–69.

Soggin, J. Alberto. 1972. *Joshua.* OTL. Philadelphia: Westminster.

———. 1989. *Introduction to the Old Testament: From Its Origin to the Closing of the Alexandrian Canon,* translated by John Bowden. Third edition. Louisville: Westminster John Knox.

Spencer, John R. 1992. "Refuge, Cities of." *ABD* 5:657.

Stager, Lawrence E. 1995. "The Impact of the Sea Peoples (1185–1050 BCE)." In Levy 1995, 332–48.

Stenger, Victor J. 2012. *God and the Folly of Faith. The Incompatibility of Science and Religion.* Amherst NY: Prometheus Books.

———. 1998. "Forging Identity: The Emergence of Ancient Israel," in *The Oxford History of the Bible*, edited by Michael D. Coogan. New York: Oxford. 90–131.

Thomas, D. Winton, editor. 1958. *Documents from Old Testament Times.* New York: Harper & Row.

Tov, Emanuel. 1992. *Textual Criticism of the Hebrew Bible.* Minneapolis: Fortress.

Trible, Phyllis. 1984. *Texts of Terror: Literary-Feminist Readings of Biblical Narratives.* Philadelphia: Fortress.

Vanderkam, James C. 2009. "Passover and Feast of Unleavened Bread." *NIDB* 4:383–92.

Van de Mieroop, Marc. 2007. *A History of the Ancient Near East ca. 3000-323 BC.* Second edition. Oxford: Blackwell.

Van der Steen, Eveline J. 1996. "The Central East Jordan Valley in the Late Bronze and Early Iron Ages." *BASOR* 302:51–74.

Van Seters, John. 1990. "Joshua's Campaign of Canaan and Near Eastern Historiography." *SJOT* 2:1–12.

de Vaux, Roland. 1978. *The Early History of Israel,* translated by David Smith. Philadelphia: Westminster.

Warrior, Robert Allen. 2006. "A Native American Perspective: Canaanites, Cowboys, and Indians." *Voices from the Margin: Interpreting the Bible in the Third Word,* edited by R. S. Sugirtharajah. Third edition. Maryknoll NY: Orbis. 235–41.

Weinfeld, Moshe. 1972. *Deuteronomy and the Deuteronomic School.* Oxford: Clarendon.

Whitelam, Keith. 1996. *The Invention of Ancient Israel: The Silencing of Palestinian History.* New York: Routledge.

Wood, Bryant. G. 2008. "The Search for Joshua's Ai," in Hess et al., 205–40.

Wright, G. Ernest. 1957. *Biblical Archaeology.* Philadelphia: Westminster.

———. No date. "The Conquest Theme in the Bible." bMS 667, Series V, Papers of Ernest G. Wright, Andover-Harvard Theological Library, Harvard Divinity School.

Yasur-Landau, Assaf. 2010. "Under the Shadow of the Four-Room House: Biblical Archaeology Meets Household Archaeology in Israel," in Levy 2010, 142–55.

Younker, Randall W. 2003. "The Iron Age in the Southern Levant," in Richard, 367–82.

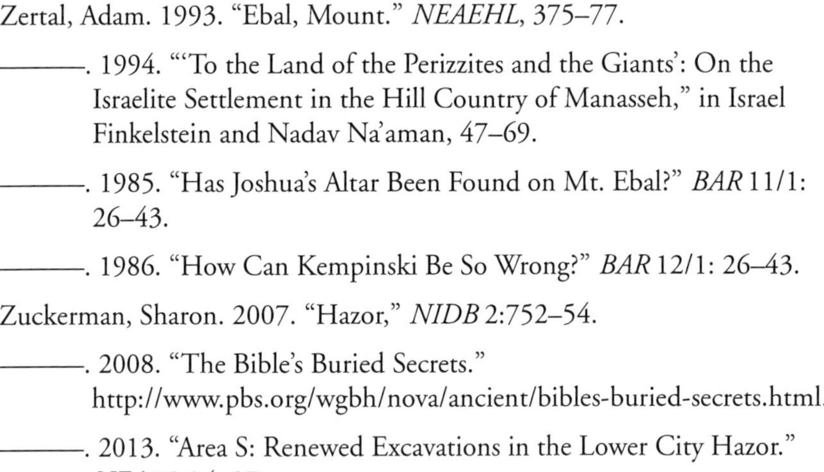

Zertal, Adam. 1993. “Ebal, Mount.” *NEAEHL*, 375–77.

———. 1994. “‘To the Land of the Perizzites and the Giants’: On the Israelite Settlement in the Hill Country of Manasseh,” in Israel Finkelstein and Nadav Na’aman, 47–69.

———. 1985. “Has Joshua’s Altar Been Found on Mt. Ebal?” *BAR* 11/1: 26–43.

———. 1986. “How Can Kempinski Be So Wrong?” *BAR* 12/1: 26–43.

Zuckerman, Sharon. 2007. “Hazor,” *NIDB* 2:752–54.

———. 2008. “The Bible’s Buried Secrets.” http://www.pbs.org/wgbh/nova/ancient/bibles-buried-secrets.html.

———. 2013. “Area S: Renewed Excavations in the Lower City Hazor.” *NEA* 78:94–97.

Crossroads in Christian Growth

W. Loyd Allen

Authentic Christian life presents spiritual crises and we struggle to find a hero walking with God at a crossroads. With wisdom and sincerity, W. Loyd Allen presents Jesus as our example and these crises as stages in the journey of growth we each take toward maturity in Christ. *978-1-57312-753-0 164 pages/pb* **$15.00**

A Divine Duet

Ministry and Motherhood

Alicia Davis Porterfield, ed.

Each essay in this inspiring collection is as different as the mother-minister who wrote it, from theologians to chaplains, inner-city ministers to rural-poverty ministers, youth pastors to preachers, mothers who have adopted, birthed, and done both. *978-1-57312-676-2 146 pages/pb* **$16.00**

The Exile and Beyond (All the Bible series)

Wayne Ballard

The Exile and Beyond brings to life the sacred literature of Israel and Judah that comprises the exilic and postexilic communities of faith. It covers Ezekiel, Isaiah, Haggai, Zechariah, Malachi, 1 & 2 Chronicles, Ezra, Nehemiah, Joel, Jonah, Song of Songs, Esther, and Daniel. *978-1-57312-759-2 196 pages/pb* **$16.00**

Ezekiel (Smyth & Helwys Annual Bible Study series)

God's Presence in Performance

William D. Shiell

Through a four-session Bible study for individuals and groups, Shiell interprets the book of Ezekiel as a four-act drama to be told to those living out their faith in a strange, new place. Shiell encourages congregations to listen to God's call, accept where God has planted them, surrender the shame of their past, receive a new heart from God, and allow God to breathe new life into them. *Teaching Guide 978-1-57312-755-4 192 pages/pb* **$14.00**

Study Guide 978-1-57312-756-1 126 pages/pb **$6.00**

Fierce Love

Desperate Measures for Desperate Times

Jeanie Miley

Fierce Love is about learning to see yourself and know yourself as a conduit of love, operating from a full heart instead of trying to find someone to whom you can hook up your emotional hose and fill up your empty heart. *978-1-57312-810-0 276 pages/pb* **$18.00**

To order call 1-800-747-3016 or visit www.helwys.com

Five Hundred Miles

Reflections on Calling and Pilgrimage

Lauren Brewer Bass

Spain's Camino de Santiago, the Way of St. James, has been a cherished pilgrimage path for centuries, visited by countless people searching for healing, solace, purpose, and hope. These stories from her five-hundred-mile-walk is Lauren Brewer Bass's honest look at the often winding, always surprising journey of a calling. *978-1-57312-812-4 142 pages/pb* ***$16.00***

Galatians (Smyth & Helwys Bible Commentary)

Marion L. Soards and Darrell J. Pursiful

In Galatians, Paul endeavored to prevent the Gentile converts from embracing a version of the gospel that insisted on their observance of a form of the Mosaic Law. He saw with a unique clarity that such a message reduced the crucified Christ to being a mere agent of the Law. For Paul, the gospel of Jesus Christ alone, and him crucified, had no place in it for the claim that Law-observance was necessary for believers to experience the power of God's grace. *978-1-57312-771-4 384 pages/hc* ***$55.00***

God's Servants the Prophets

Bryan Bibb

God's Servants, the Prophets covers the Israelite and Judean prophetic literature from the preexilic period. It includes Amos, Hosea, Isaiah, Micah, Zephaniah, Nahum, Habakkuk, Jeremiah, and Obadiah.

978-1-57312-758-5 208 pages/pb ***$16.00***

Hermeneutics of Hymnody

A Comprehensive and Integrated Approach to Understanding Hymns

Scotty Gray

Scotty Gray's *Hermeneutics of Hymnody* is a comprehensive and integrated approach to understanding hymns. It is unique in its holistic and interrelated exploration of seven of the broad facets of this most basic forms of Christian literature. A chapter is devoted to each and relates that facet to all of the others. *978-157312-767-7 432 pages/pb* ***$28.00***

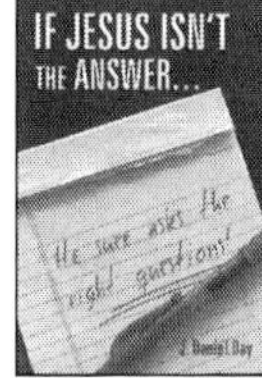

If Jesus Isn't the Answer . . . He Sure Asks the Right Questions!

J. Daniel Day

Taking eleven of Jesus' questions as its core, Day invites readers into their own conversation with Jesus. Equal parts testimony, theological instruction, pastoral counseling, and autobiography, the book is ultimately an invitation to honest Christian discipleship.

978-1-57312-797-4 148 pages/pb ***$16.00***

I'm Trying to Lead . . . Is Anybody Following?

The Challenge of Congregational Leadership in the Postmodern World

Charles B. Bugg

Bugg provides us with a view of leadership that has theological integrity, honors the diversity of church members, and reinforces the brave hearts of church leaders who offer vision and take risks in the service of Christ and the church. *978-1-57312-731-8 136 pages/pb* ***$13.00***

James M. Dunn and Soul Freedom

Aaron Douglas Weaver

James Milton Dunn, over the last fifty years, has been the most aggressive Baptist proponent for religious liberty in the US. Soul freedom—voluntary, uncoerced faith and an unfettered individual conscience before God—is the basis of his understanding of church-state separation and the historic Baptist basis of religious liberty.

978-1-57312-590-1 224 pages/pb ***$18.00***

The Jesus Tribe

Following Christ in the Land of the Empire

Ronnie McBrayer

The Jesus Tribe fleshes out the implications, possibilities, contradictions, and complexities of what it means to live within the Jesus Tribe and in the shadow of the American Empire.

978-1-57312-592-5 208 pages/pb ***$17.00***

Judaism

A Brief Guide to Faith and Practice

Sharon Pace

Sharon Pace's newest book is a sensitive and comprehensive introduction to Judaism. How does belief in the One God and a universal morality shape the way in which Jews see the world? How does one find meaning in life and the courage to endure suffering? How does one mark joy and forge community ties? *978-1-57312-644-1 144 pages/pb* ***$16.00***

Looking Around for God

The Strangely Reverent Observations of an Unconventional Christian

James A. Autry

Looking Around for God, Autry's tenth book, is in many ways his most personal. In it he considers his unique life of faith and belief in God. Autry is a former Fortune 500 executive, author, poet, and consultant whose work has had a significant influence on leadership thinking.

978-157312-484-3 144 pages/pb ***$16.00***

To order call 1-800-747-3016 or visit www.helwys.com

Marriage Ministry: A Guidebook

Bo Prosser and Charles Qualls

This book is equally helpful for ministers, for nearly/newlywed couples, and for thousands of couples across our land looking for fresh air in their marriages. *1-57312-432-X 160 pages/pb* **$16.00**

Meeting Jesus Today

For the Cautious, the Curious, and the Committed

Jeanie Miley

Meeting Jesus Today, ideal for both individual study and small groups, is intended to be used as a workbook. It is designed to move readers from studying the Scriptures and ideas within the chapters to recording their journey with the Living Christ.

978-1-57312-677-9 320 pages/pb **$19.00**

The Ministry Life

101 Tips for Ministers' Spouses

John and Anne Killinger

While no pastor does his or her work alone, roles for a spouse or partner are much more flexible and fluid now than they once were. Spouses who want to support their minister-mates' vocation may wonder where to begin. Whatever your talents may be, the Killingers have identified a way to put those gifts to work. *978-1-57312-769-1 252 pages/pb* **$19.00**

The Ministry Life

101 Tips for New Ministers

John Killinger

Sharing years of wisdom from more than fifty years in ministry and teaching, *The Ministry Life: 101 Tips for New Ministers* by John Killinger is filled with practical advice and wisdom for a minister's day-to-day tasks as well as advice on intellectual and spiritual habits to keep ministers of any age healthy and fulfilled. *978-1-57312-662-5 244 pages/pb* **$19.00**

Mount and Mountain

Vol. 2: A Reverend and a Rabbi Talk About the Sermon on the Mount

Rami Shapiro and Michael Smith

This book, focused on the Sermon on the Mount, represents the second half of Mike and Rami's dialogue. In it, Mike and Rami explore the text of Jesus' sermon cooperatively, contributing perspectives drawn from their lives and religious traditions and seeking moments of illumination. *978-1-57312-654-0 254 pages/pb* **$19.00**

Of Mice and Ministers

Musings and Conversations About Life, Death, Grace, and Everything

Bert Montgomery

With stories about pains, joys, and everyday life, *Of Mice and Ministers* finds Jesus in some unlikely places and challenges us to do the same. From tattooed women ministers to saying the "N"-word to the brotherly kiss, Bert Montgomery takes seriously the lesson from Psalm 139—where can one go that God is not already there? *978-1-57312-733-2 154 pages/pb* ***$14.00***

Place Value

The Journey to Where You Are

Katie Sciba

Does a place have value? Can a place change us? Is it possible for God to use the place you are in to form you? From Victoria, Texas to Indonesia, Belize, Australia, and beyond, Katie Sciba's wanderlust serves as a framework to understand your own places of deep emotion and how God may have been weaving redemption around you all along.

978-157312-829-2 138 pages/pb ***$15.00***

Preacher Breath

Sermon & Essays

Kyndall Rae Rothaus

"*Preacher Breath* is a worthy guide, leading the reader room by room with wisdom, depth, and a spiritual maturity far beyond her years, so that the preaching house becomes a holy, joyful home. . . . This book is soul kindle for a preacher's heart." —Danielle Shroyer

Pastor, Author of *The Boundary-Breaking God*

978-1-57312-734-9 208 pages/pb ***$16.00***

Quiet Faith

An Introvert's Guide to Spiritual Survival

Judson Edwards

In eight finely crafted chapters, Edwards looks at key issues like evangelism, interpreting the Bible, dealing with doubt, and surviving the church from the perspective of a confirmed, but sometimes reluctant, introvert. In the process, he offers some provocative insights that introverts will find helpful and reassuring. *978-1-57312-681-6 144 pages/pb* ***$15.00***

Reading Deuteronomy (Reading the Old Testament series)

A Literary and Theological Commentary

Stephen L. Cook

A lost treasure for large segments of today's world, the book of Deuteronomy stirs deep longing for God and moves readers to a place of intimacy with divine otherness, holism, and will for person-centered community. The consistently theological interpretation reveals the centrality of this book for faith. *978-1-57312-757-8 286 pages/pb* ***$22.00***

Reflective Faith

A Theological Toolbox for Women

Susan M. Shaw

In *Reflective Faith*, Susan Shaw offers a set of tools to explore difficult issues of biblical interpretation, theology, church history, and ethics—especially as they relate to women. Reflective faith invites intellectual struggle and embraces the unknown; it is a way of discipleship, a way to love God with your mind, as well as your heart, your soul, and your strength. *978-1-57312-719-6 292 pages/pb* ***$24.00***

Workbook *978-1-57312-754-7 164 pages/pb* ***$12.00***

Sessions with Psalms (Sessions Bible Studies series)

Prayers for All Seasons

Eric and Alicia D. Porterfield

Useful to seminar leaders during preparation and group discussion, as well as in individual Bible study, *Sessions with Psalms* is a ten-session study designed to explore what it looks like for the words of the psalms to become the words of our prayers. Each session is followed by a thought-provoking page of questions. *978-1-57312-768-4 136 pages/pb* ***$14.00***

Sessions with Revelation (Sessions Bible Studies series)

The Final Days of Evil

David Sapp

David Sapp's careful guide through Revelation demonstrates that it is a letter of hope for believers; it is less about the last days of history than it is about the last days of evil. Without eliminating its mystery, Sapp unlocks Revelation's central truths so that its relevance becomes clear.

978-1-57312-706-6 166 pages/pb ***$14.00***

Though the Darkness Gather Round

Devotions about Infertility, Miscarriage, and Infant Loss

Mary Elizabeth Hill Hanchey and Erin McClain, eds.

Much courage is required to weather the long grief of infertility and the sudden grief of miscarriage and infant loss. This collection of devotions by men and women, ministers, chaplains, and lay leaders who can speak of such sorrow, is a much-needed resource and precious gift for families on this journey and the faith communities that walk beside them.

978-1-57312-811-7 180 pages/pb **$19.00**

Time for Supper

Invitations to Christ's Table

Brett Younger

Some scholars suggest that every meal in literature is a communion scene. Could every meal in the Bible be a communion text? Could every passage be an invitation to God's grace? These meditations on the Lord's Supper help us listen to the myriad of ways God invites us to gratefully, reverently, and joyfully share the cup of Christ. *978-1-57312-720-2 246 pages/pb* **$18.00**

A Time to Laugh

Humor in the Bible

Mark E. Biddle

With characteristic liveliness, Mark E. Biddle explores the ways humor was intentionally incorporated into Scripture. Drawing on Biddle's command of Hebrew language and cultural subtleties, *A Time to Laugh* guides the reader through the stories of six biblical characters who did rather unexpected things. *978-1-57312-683-0 164 pages/pb* **$14.00**

A True Hope

Jedi Perils and the Way of Jesus

Joshua Hays

Star Wars offers an accessible starting point for considering substantive issues of faith, philosophy, and ethics. In *A True Hope*, Joshua Hays explores some of these challenging ideas through the sayings of the Jedi Masters, examining the ways the worldview of the Jedi is at odds with that of the Bible.

978-1-57312-770-7 186 pages/pb **$18.00**

Word of God Across the Ages

Using Christian History in Preaching

Bill J. Leonard

In this third, enlarged edition, Bill J. Leonard returns to the roots of the Christian story to find in the lives of our faithful forebears examples of the potent presence of the gospel. Through these stories, those who preach today will be challenged and inspired as they pursue the divine Word in human history through the ages. *978-1-57312-828-5 174 pages/pb* ***$19.00***

The World Is Waiting for You

Celebrating the 50th Ordination Anniversary of Addie Davis

Pamela R. Durso & LeAnn Gunter Johns, eds.

Hope for the church and the world is alive and well in the words of these gifted women. Keen insight, delightful observations, profound courage, and a gift for communicating the good news are woven throughout these sermons. The Spirit so evident in Addie's calling clearly continues in her legacy. *978-1-57312-732-5 224 pages/pb* ***$18.00***

William J. Reynolds

Church Musician

David W. Music

William J. Reynolds is renowned among Baptist musicians, music ministers, song leaders, and hymnody students. In eminently readable style, David W. Music's comprehensive biography describes Reynolds's family and educational background, his career as a minister of music, denominational leader, and seminary professor. *978-1-57312-690-8 358 pages/pb* ***$23.00***

With Us in the Wilderness

Finding God's Story in Our Lives

Laura A. Barclay

What stories compose your spiritual biography? In *With Us in the Wilderness*, Laura Barclay shares her own stories of the intersection of the divine and the everyday, guiding readers toward identifying and embracing God's presence in their own narratives.

978-1-57312-721-9 120 pages/pb ***$13.00***

Made in the USA
Middletown, DE
20 November 2015